Seeking God through Prayer and Meditation

David Howell

This book is a product of Prison Evangelism, Inc. (prisonevangelism.com).

A Christian evangelistic association that prints and distributes the books:

How to be a Child of God and

Seeking God through Prayer and Meditation

to the 2,000,000 incarcerated men and women in America's 2100 jails and prisons. Our mission is to:

"Change Hearts and Close Prisons"

You can assist us in bringing the knowledge of Jesus Christ to those who are considered to be the least and the lost by sending a check to:

Prison Evangelism, Inc.

P O Box 571977

Houston, Texas 77257

We are a 501(c)(3) corporation and contributions are tax deductible.

Seeking God Through Prayer and Meditation

This title may be purchased in bulk for educational and evangelical purposes. Please contact the publisher for more information.

David Howell
PO Box 571977
Houston, Texas 77257

davidhowell@prisonevangelism.com
info@HowtobeaChildofGod.com
www.HowtobeaChildofGod.com
www.prisonevangelism.com

ISBN: 978-0-578-14069-8

Art direction by John Magee, Houston, Texas
JohnMageeDesign.com

All illustrations by Randy Rogers, The Woodlands, Texas
artistguy@att.net

Table of Contents

Talking to Your Father

An Introduction to Prayer..1
Beginning to Pray..4
The ACTS Model of Prayer...5
A – Adoration...6
C – Confession..10
T– Thanksgiving...16
S – Seeking or Asking...19
Closing a Prayer..24
Prayer as Worship...25
Group Prayer..26
Writing your Prayers..26
Praying without Ceasing.. 27
Praying for One Hour... 28

Christian Meditation

The Meaning of Christian Mediation..................................30
"Chewing the Cud" Instruction.......................................30
Personal Meditation Guide...32
Conversational Meditation...36
Listening to Lectures and Sermons...................................37
Meditation through Journaling.......................................40
Meditation in Song..41
Fasting with Prayer and Meditation.................................. 43
Guard Your Heart..47
Benefits of Meditation 49
Summary...51
Bible References..53
Resources 58
Thirty-One Day Devotional 59
Perspectives 91
Prayer of Salvation..94

Foreword

(We) Sought through prayer and meditation to improve our conscious contact with God as we understood Him, praying only for knowledge of His will for us and the ability to carry that out. *THE ELEVENTH STEP OF ALCOHOLICS ANONYMOUS*

Introduction

This book is designed to give a believer a basis for prayer and meditation, the principle means of communicating and spending time with God. Prayer and meditation on the word of God, or the Bible, are two habits Christians are encouraged to learn and practice. Just as we spend time with our friends and family, we must communicate and spend time with our heavenly Father if we are to have a successful and meaningful relationship with Him. We can do this by learning the practice of prayer and meditation. It might be best to treat the two as separate disciplines, taking them one at a time. In that way, you can use this single book as two smaller books: one on prayer, the other on meditation. Each can be read in a single sitting, but the concepts will take more time to develop. The simple approach outlined in these pages will start you on the path of talking and listening to your heavenly Father. No man can teach us to pray, but if you are willing, God's Spirit will help you as you learn about conversation with your Father. Try and imagine the person of Jesus sitting with you as you pray or conversing with you while giving you the words to say.

The emphasis of this study is on Scripture, which comes from the Bible and is the Word of God. The Bible is God's way of giving us life instruction. He is the author and our guide, and we are to leave the instruction up to Him. The Bible or Word of God is the greatest design for living that we as humans have ever known. The illustrations that are shown in this book are inspired by God and are designed to add clarity and emphasis to the concepts presented.

Christ in You
Colossians 1:27

The theme of this book is Christ in you. If you understand that Jesus Christ lives in you, it becomes easier to talk to Him in prayer, meditate on His Word and let Him live His life through you and in you. He seeks to be in every part of your life and participate in everything you do. This is your identity in Christ. Christ is your life.

It is most important to remember that Jesus Christ lives in you. He is your God, your Lord, your Savior and if you are to know and understand the meaning of the blessing and abundance of living the Christian life, then Jesus must literally be your life and you must understand that He lives in you and you in Him.

"My old self has been crucified with Christ. It is no longer I who live, but Christ lives in me. So I live in this earthly body by trusting in the Son of God, who loved me and gave himself for me." Galatians 2:20

* * *

"Or have you forgotten that when we were joined with Christ Jesus in baptism, we joined him in his death? For we died and were buried with Christ by baptism. And just as Christ was raised from the dead by the glorious power of the Father, now we also may live new lives. Since we have been united with him in his death, we will also be raised to life as he was. We know that our old sinful selves were crucified with Christ so that sin might lose its power in our lives. We are no longer slaves to sin." Romans 6:3-6.

"**Since** you have been raised to new life with Christ, set your sights on the realities of heaven, where Christ sits at the place of honor at God's right hand. Think about the things of heaven, not the things of earth. For you died to this life and your real life is hidden with Christ in God." Colossians 3:1-3

"**For** he raised us from the dead along with Christ and seated us with him in the heavenly realms because we are united with Christ Jesus." Ephesians 2:6

* * *

Just imagine having this kind of intimacy with the living God whom we can call Father!

Talking to Your Father
An Introduction to Prayer

Talking directly to the God of the Universe is difficult to imagine. Yet, that is what we are called to do, and God invites us to talk to Him if we are to have a relationship with Him. At first, we don't really know how, but the Bible says we can call on the Holy Spirit of God to speak to us and through us by giving us the words to say and the way to say them.

"And the Holy Spirit helps us in our weakness. For example, we don't know what God wants us to pray for. But the Holy Spirit prays for us in groanings that cannot be expressed in words. And the Father who knows all hearts knows what the Spirit is saying, for the Spirit pleads for us believers in harmony with God's own will." Romans 8:26-27

The Trinity of God

God exists as three persons. He is God the Father, God the Son (Jesus), and God the Holy Spirit. He is three persons that are one, but in different dimensions. Think in terms of water, ice and steam as an example of three forms of the same thing (liquid, solid, and gas). They are all the same substance (H20) in different forms. As humans and children of God, we also have three forms or dimensions: we are spirit, we live in bodies, and we have a soul, which includes our mind, will and emotions and is our personality. *"For in Christ lives all the fullness of God in a human body. So you also are complete through your union with Christ who is the head over every ruler and authority." Colossians 2:9-10*

We don't know much about God the Father on a personal basis, nor God the Holy Spirit. We are able to identify more readily with Jesus the Son because He is the principal person and focus throughout the Bible. We are able to understand Him more because He (God) became a man (Jesus) and walked on this earth. He is our example because He was both man and God. God made it easier for us to form a relationship with Him by having Jesus born of a woman as we were. He grew up as we did having feelings, emotions, and experiences in life as a human that help us to identify with Him. Had Jesus come to earth as a hundred-foot-tall light with angels all around, we would easily *WORSHIP* a mighty God like that, but we would probably not attempt a *RELATIONSHIP* with Him.

Looking at God

A major key to having a more intimate and satisfying prayer life is to focus on Jesus, whom we can visualize and understand as God. When you have seen or imagined Jesus, you have seen God the Father because they are one.

The Bible says that no one has seen the Father God, yet we know Jesus is God, and He says that when we have seen Him (Jesus) we have seen the Father. We are instructed to form our relationship with God through Jesus the Son with the understanding that Jesus is God.

"The Father and I are one." John 10:30

* * *

Jesus replied, "Anyone who has seen me has seen the Father!" John 14:9b

* * *

"I pray that they will all be one, just as you and I are one--as you are in me, Father, and I am in you. And may they be in us so that the world will believe you sent me." John 17:21

2

God Answers Prayer

God often answers prayer even when we do not know Him. Even if we have not yet believed and trusted Him, He will listen to us and answer us as long as our prayers are sincere. He knows our heart and is waiting for us to ac-knowledge Him as Savior. Many who have experienced problems with addiction, bad habits, and other controlling desires have learned to ask God to remove the desires for these destructive habits, and He has done it. When we call on Him, God answers prayer! He takes care of us and protects us as a way of helping us get to know Him and to show the great love He has for us. Perhaps He knows that at a certain time, you will know Him and He is saving you in some ways before you even know you need a Savior.

"The eyes of the Lord search the whole earth in order to strengthen those whose hearts are fully committed to Him." 2 Chronicles 16:9a

* * *

"And I will give them a singleness of heart and put a new spirit within them. I will take away their stony, stubborn heart and give them a tender, responsive heart, so they will obey my decrees and regulations. Then they will truly be my people, and I will be their God." Ezekiel 11:19-20

Over and over, the Bible reminds us we are "in Christ." Imagine sitting on the lap of the Living God.

"For God, who said, " Let there be light in the darkness," has made this light shine in our hearts so we could know the glory of God that is seen in the face of Jesus Christ." 2 Corinthians 4:6

* * *

"But if you remain in me and my words remain in you, you may ask any-thing you want and it will be granted." John 15:7

* * *

"Take delight in the Lord, and he will give you your heart's desires." Psalm 37:4

3

Beginning to Pray

"I tell you, you can pray for anything, and if you believe that you've received it, it will be yours. But when you are praying, first forgive anyone you are holding a grudge against, so that your Father in heaven will forgive your sins too." Mark 11:24-35

* * *

We are instructed to open each prayer by addressing that prayer to our Heavenly Father. This instruction is given to us in the model prayer that Jesus gave us when He answered the disciples request to teach them to pray in Matthew 6:9-13:

Jesus said, "Pray like this:
Our Father in Heaven,
May Your name be kept holy,
May Your Kingdom come soon.
May Your will be done on earth,
as it is in heaven.
Give us today the food we need,
And forgive us our sins,
As we have forgiven those who sin against us.
And don't let us yield to temptation,
But rescue us from the evil one.
For Yours is the kingdom and the power and the glory forever.
Amen."

* * *

God is our Heavenly Father, and we are to talk to Him in much the same way as children might talk to their earthly father. In addition, we are instructed to mention the name of Jesus when we pray to our heavenly Father. We begin or end our prayers in the name of Jesus, Jesus Christ, Lord Jesus, or other variations of His name. We do this in obedience to our heavenly Father, and this gives authority to the prayer through Jesus the Son.

Jesus promised:

"You can ask for anything in my name, and I will do it, so that the Son can bring glory to the Father. Yes, ask me for anything in my name, and I will do it!"
John 14:13-14

* * *

Understand that as children of God, we are spiritual beings and as we mature in Christ, our desires will be more and more of a spiritual nature. Our material needs will be met by our heavenly Father.

Christ in You
Colossians 1:27

4

The ACTS Model of Prayer

ACTS in Prayer by E. W. Price, Jr., contains a useful formula for prayer that is portable enough to carry around in your memory. The first edition of this simple booklet was published in 1974, and it's still being printed. It is a wonderful guide to prayer. The formula for using ACTS in prayer is as follows:

A: Adoration and Praise

C: Confession

T: Thanksgiving

S: Seeking Prayer: Asking for needs of others and yourself.

We can simplify conversations with our heavenly Father and find ways to have intimate talks with Him. When you pray, imagine sitting, relaxed and comfortable, talking to Jesus as God. In this way, you can identify with and relate to Him more easily. Imagine Jesus as your good friend or brother, and someone you can talk with and pour out your greatest joys and deepest sorrows.

Jesus, the Living God, is our companion and confidante. We trust Him not only as God, but also as our best friend or brother.

Jesus even speaks of being our friend when we choose to be obedient to him:

"There is no greater love than to lay down one's life for one's friends. You are my friends if you do what I command'. ...'This is my command: love one another.'" John 15:13-14, 17

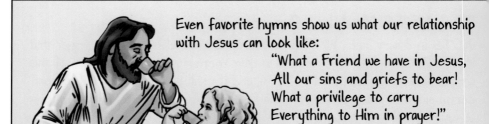

Even favorite hymns show us what our relationship with Jesus can look like:

"What a Friend we have in Jesus,
All our sins and griefs to bear!
What a privilege to carry
Everything to Him in prayer!"
("What a Friend We Have in Jesus" by Joseph Scriven)

"Finally, all of you should be of one mind. Sympathize with each other. Love each other as brothers and sisters. Be tenderhearted and keep a humble attitude." 1 Peter 3:8

A - Adoration and Praise

Show love to our heavenly Father by telling Him you love Him. Give Him praise and ADORATION. Many of us have difficulty in expressing love, praise, and adoration for another person and even for God. This is another reason we talk to Jesus the Son. When we understand salvation and what God did for us through Jesus on the cross, it becomes easier to be grateful to Him. Praise is simply our response to who God is and what He has done for us, both on the cross and everyday in our lives. Imagine God dying for you to pave your way to eternal life. Imagine the great wonder of all of your sins and wrongdoings being eliminated through the death of Jesus. Imagine the humiliation and the torture our God in human form experienced so we would not have to go through that brutality ourselves. Hallelujah! What a Savior! What a God! What a Father! It is important that we learn the discipline and practice of love, adoration and praise for our heavenly Father. We must do this until loving Him and telling Him we love Him becomes habit and a natural thing for us to do.

One aid to praise and adoration is the use of hymns or worship songs that express that love to our heavenly Father. As your quiet time with God develops, you might include the use of a hymnal. Hymnals have songs with truths often based on scripture. Many of these church songbooks are divided into subjects such as Salvation, Confession, Worship, and Adoration and Praise. Some libraries have hymnals, or you can buy a personal copy at Christian bookstores and Amazon.com or other online bookstores. Search online for "Christian Hymns" as the subject, or use the Baptist Hymnal (or any other church songbook) available in Lifeway and other bookstores. Don't worry about how well you sing. The words in hymns are wonderful just to speak or even think about as you focus on the goodness of God.

Another way you can focus your attention on giving God adoration and praise is by reading the Book of Psalms in the Bible. Psalms is known as the Bible's hymnbook and is filled with songs and prayers of praise and adoration. Imagine the verses below as words to a song you are singing to God your Father:

"O God, you are my God.
    I earnestly search for you.
My soul thirsts for you,
    my whole body longs for you
in this parched and weary land
    where there is no water.
I have seen you in the sanctuary
    and gazed upon your power and glory
Your unfailing love is better than
life itself;
    how I praise you!
I will praise you as long as I live,
    lifting up my hands to you in prayer.
You satisfy me more than my richest feast.
    I will praise you with songs of joy

I lie awake thinking of you,
    meditating on you through the night.
Because you are my helper,
    I sing for joy in the shadow of your wings.
I cling to you;
    your strong right hand holds me securely"
Psalm 63:1-8

"Let all that I am praise the Lord:
  with my whole heart, I will praise his holy name.
Let all that I am praise the Lord:
  may I never forget the good things he does for me.
He forgives all my sins
  and heals all my diseases
He redeems me from death
  and crowns me with love and tender mercies.
He fills my life with good things.
  My youth is renewed like the eagle's!
The Lord gives righteousness
  and justice to all who are treated unfairly."
Psalm 103:1-6

* * *

Other passages in the Bible are intentionally focused on praising God.

"Therefore, let us offer through Jesus a continual sacrifice of praise to God, proclaiming our allegiance to his name." Hebrews 13:15

* * *

"You are worthy, O Lord our God,
to receive glory and honor and power.
For you created all things,
and they exist because you created what you pleased." Revelation 4:11

We have access to the Father through Jesus who died for us.
"Jesus paid it all; all to Him I owe. Sin had left a crimson stain; he washed it white as snow."
(Chorus from the hymn "Jesus Paid it All" by Elvina M. Hall)

"When we were utterly helpless, Christ came at just the right time and died for us sinners." Romans 5:6

* * *

As Christians, we are set apart when we trust Jesus Christ and become children of God. We now have a new family lineage and a heavenly Father.

As Christians, we are set apart when we trust Jesus Christ and become children of God. We now have a new family lineage and a heavenly Father.

"And remember that the heavenly Father to whom you pray has no favorites. He will judge or reward you according to what you do. So you must live in reverent fear of him during your time as "foreigners in the land." For you know that God paid a ransom to save you from the empty life you inherited from your ancestors. And the ransom he paid was not merely gold or silver. It was the precious blood of Christ, the sinless, spotless Lamb of God. God chose him as your ransom long before the world began, but he has now revealed him to you in these last days."
1 Peter 1:17-20

* * *

As you start your prayer time, try reading one of these passages aloud, imagining that you are talking directly to God. Picture Jesus sitting across from you at a table, and express your feelings of praise and adoration directly to Him. You can even change the words and personalize the thoughts as a way of making your prayer more personal and intimate.

Adoration and praise can be a difficult concept for many of us to master. This facet of prayer does not come naturally. We tend to be much too self-absorbed and self-centered to openly show our heartfelt love to another. It takes time and practice, and you just might have to "fake it 'til you make it," as the saying goes. So think about what Jesus did for you, even though you may not feel His presence close to you when you start to pray. He loves us so very much. The death He died was for YOU.

"Come close to God and God will come close to you." James 4:8a

* * *

When we begin to practice the discipline of prayer, God knows our hearts and is cheering us on to a greater and closer fellowship with Him.

Additional verses for knowing praise and adoration: Psalm 113, Psalm 115, Psalm 145: 1-13, 17-21

C — Confession of Wrongdoings

Personal housekeeping is an important part of keeping our lines of communication open with God, and we begin personal housekeeping by confessing our wrongdoings, or sins, to our Father. CONFESSION is agreeing with Him regarding all the ways in which both you and God know you've been disobedient and confessing them as a way to clear the air between yourself and God. We all sin, and these wrongdoings separate us from the close fellowship we could be experiencing with our heavenly Father.

God always loves us, and that love never changes. This is true no matter what we do or how we stray. However, just like a wayward son strays outside of his father's house and rejects the blessings that were part of living in his father's presence and care, our sins separate us from the ability to experience God's love and care. We have to turn around, recognize we have wandered out of His will, and return to Him. (Luke 15:11-32)

It becomes necessary to refresh our relationship with God through the confession part of prayer. When we do this, we renew and resume fellowship with Him. The death of Jesus on the cross was the forgiving act once and for all time—past, present, and future. He still wants us to talk to Him and confess what He already knows. It cleans up our side of the street. Confession can include talking to a friend and admitting to that person the wrong things you've done to him or others, even though our sins in reality are always against God. This activity might be a means of building a rela-

Christ in You
Colossians 1:27

tionship with another believer that can grow into a valuable friendship. That friend could even become an accountability partner. An accountability partner is someone you can totally trust and rely on to listen to and counsel you when you confess and are absolutely honest. It is important that you practice having an attitude of being honest, open, and willing to listen and respond to someone's spiritual guidance. We sometimes call this trait *TRANSPARENCY*.

Transparency is clear sight with no obstructions. It is the practice of rigorous or total honesty. You often know when a spouse, friend, child, or relative has wronged you or possibly deceived or lied to you. You already know it, but you would like to hear that person acknowledge the deception or wrongdoing. It makes things right and directs all parties toward a more trusting relationship. God sees confession in this same way.

We accumulate a lot of junk. God knows it all and is waiting for us to acknowledge our short-comings. He wants total honesty from His children. He wants us to surrender our old ways and follow Him.

"**But** if we confess our sins to him, he is faithful and just to forgive us our sins and to cleanse us from all wickedness (unrighteousness)." 1 John 1:9

* * *

Confession, surrender, and submission are all terms that describe coming to a place where we know that our own plans and our own strength are not enough. We make up our minds to return to God's plan and totally trust Jesus and rely on Him for everything. He literally becomes Lord, God, and Savior to us. Confessing our faults and shortcomings is the first step of acceptance and surrender and coming to the end of self.

Be Specific

It is easiest to say, "I am sorry for all of my sins," in a general way, but God wants you to be personal and specific. The object of Christian growth and development is to have a personal relationship with Jesus Christ and to speak to Him on an intimate and personal basis. Being vague isn't intimate or personal. Confession should be specific and it needs to be definite and aimed at a specific event, person or act. An example might be, "I confess and I am sorry, Father, for cursing and yelling in the traffic as I drove to work this morning." We confess and move on, believing, knowing and accepting love and forgiveness from our heavenly Father.

Sin is Harmful

"Sin" is not a mystical church term. It is about not doing right by God and doing harmful things to yourself and others. God wants us to avoid sin because it takes us further from Him and it is damaging to every part of our lives. It can destroy or seriously wound us in deep and lasting ways: physically, mentally, emotionally, and spiritually. Solution: give it to God.

Our best efforts got most of us in a world of trouble. Jesus wants us to surrender all to Him: all we are and all we have, good and bad. We are only as sick as our darkest secrets and we humbly ask Him to take it all. As born again believers, and new creatures in Christ, we have no use for the things from our old life. We give it all to Him as we finish the work we need to do to begin our new life.

"Yes," Jesus replied, "and I assure you that everyone who has given up house or wife or brothers or parents or children, for the sake of the Kingdom of God, will be repaid many times over in this life, and will have eternal life in the world to come." Luke 18:29-30

* * *

"Come and listen, all you who fear God,
   and I will tell you what he did for me.
For I cried out to him for help,
   praising him as I spoke.
If I had not confessed the sin in my heart,
   the Lord would not have listened.
But God did listen!
   He paid attention to my prayer.
Praise God, who did not ignore my prayer
   or withdraw his unfailing love from me."
Psalm 66:16-20

All to Jesus I surrender,
   All to Him I freely give.
   I will ever love and trust Him,
   In His daily presence live.
"I Surrender All"
Hymn by Judson Van DeVenter

God's Wonderful Promises About Confessing Our Sins

God gives us wonderful promises related to confessing and turning away from our sins. Some of His greatest blessings occur when we specifically confess our sins and understand that God cleanses us and these sins are forgiven and forgotten. Then we are free, and we can learn to obey what God says in His Word. Obedience brings blessings, and God promised blessings and abundant living when Jesus said:

"My purpose is to give them a rich and satisfying life." John 10:10b

* * *

Restoration occurs as we acknowledge forgiveness from our Father, God's restoration happens on many different levels:
- Our relationship with Him is restored as if the sin had never been committed.
- The guilt of our sin is lifted, and we are renewed.
- We learn that God values us personally because He listened to our prayers and responded to our cries for help and forgiveness.
- When we know forgiveness, we become willing to forgive others.

Forgiveness of others helps put us in closer fellowship with God.

And forgive us our sins, as we forgive those who sin against us. Matthew 6:12

* * *

"But even greater is God's wonderful grace and his gift of forgiveness to many through this other man, Jesus Christ." Romans 5:15b

After we spend time confessing our sins to our heavenly Father, our own willingness to forgive others and make amends increases. As we experience this forgiveness from our heavenly Father, we have a desire to offer this same experience to others.

We will have a need to deal with our anger, resentments, and hard feelings we might hold toward others. At the start of this book, Scripture showed us how God sends the Holy Spirit to help us as we pray. The realization that we need to forgive others also comes from the Holy Spirit. Prayers of confession will naturally lead us to the desire to restore relationships we have damaged.

"My dear brothers and sisters, if someone among you wanders away from the truth and is brought back, you can be sure that whoever brings the sinner back, will save that person from death and bring about the forgiveness of sins." James 5:19-20.

How to be Righteous and Clean

In the eyes of God, you are righteous if you are a child of God. It is hard to imagine that God our Father counts us as righteous even though we do wrong most of the time. We confess our sins, nevertheless, and get a clear conscience.

"Confess your sins to each other and pray for each other so that you may be healed. The earnest prayer of a righteous person has great power and produces wonderful results." James 5:15-16

* * *

Don't be intimidated by the word "righteous". Review 1 John 1:9 which says:

"But if we confess our sins to Him, He is faithful and just to forgive us our sins and to cleanse us from all wickedness (unrighteousness)." 1 John 1:9

* * *

The two verses above tell us that, through heartfelt confession and prayer, you become righteous in the eyes of God as you are cleansed of wickedness or unrighteousness.

Sin Life Inventory

Confession is the greatest tool for cleansing our souls. To get deeper into this discipline, you might look more into writing a sin inventory (or moral inventory) of wrongs you have done to yourself and others. Go back as far and as early as you can remember and record the hurt, sorrow, resentment and anger from specific events in your childhood.

In the process of confession, your attitude is important. You come to your Father in humility, confess obvious sins and then ask the Holy Spirit to search your heart and remind you of sins that have not come to mind. At times, you may need to write a sin life inventory. This process might include identifying different types of behavior and ways of thinking:

- Wrongs against God or against a fellow man. You generally don't have to think too hard about this. Write it down.
- Character defects like pride, fear, angry outbursts and worry.
- Sins of neglect, such as not making amends or apologizing to someone you have harmed.
- Not taking care of your own spiritual needs in Bible study, quiet time or prayer and worship.
- Not using the spiritual gifts God has given you: teaching, prayer, hospitality, and mercy.
- Harboring resentment and bad feelings toward someone you might perceive has wronged you at some time in your life. Oftentimes, this person is someone in your family, like a parent, sibling or cousin. Get on with making amends. Often this means taking responsibility for not communicating properly.

Christ in You
Colossians 1:27

Once you write a list of your sins, hurts and resentments toward others you're carrying, as well as wrongs and wounds that others may have committed against you, acknowledge these to your Father. Confess them to Him as if you were talking to a close friend. Then believe you received His forgiveness and move on, trusting that He has forgiven you and will allow you to move on with a clear conscience. Holding on to past problems is a recipe for disaster in life.

Helpful Hint: Confession of sins can become meaningless if not accompanied by a change of heart and mind and a desire to not commit that sin again. This process is called repentance. In Christian life, confession and repentance should be linked.

Other verses about confession:
Psalm 51:1, Psalm 51:10-12, Psalm 103:12, Psalm 139:23-24, Isaiah 44:22, Isaiah 59:2, Jeremiah 31:34, Matthew 6:12, Philippians 3:13-14

T – Thanksgiving for All Things

If you are continually giving thanks or acknowledging someone or something greater and more powerful than yourself, then you are beginning to learn that you are ultimately powerless to live a good life on your own. The practice of thankfulness requires humility and surrendering to God. The Bible teaches us to be grateful to God all the time. If we follow that command, we are showing God we are learning to rely and surrender our lives to Him. If we are obedient and continue to give thanks to God for everything, we are not giving ourselves credit for the good that happens to us, but acknowledging that we are responsible to God, who is providing for our needs.

It has been said, "There is a God, and it is not you." Don't give yourself credit for the good that happens to you, nor blame God for the bad events. Acknowledge the true God and give Him thanks constantly. Being gracious and thanking God is an act of humility. Learning and practicing humility is the pathway to leading a powerful Christian life.

"God blesses those who are humble for they will inherit the whole earth." Matthew 5:5

Our heavenly Father provides for everything we have or will have. He is the Creator of the world we live in. By showing thankfulness to Him for everyday things, like your home, your toothpaste, the clothes you are wearing and the transportation you have, you learn to be more aware of God's care and provision in your life. Thank Him for your spouse, your friends, your job and even the food you eat. Learn to thank Him in advance for what He is going to do for you. Mealtimes are a great occasion to thank God for providing our needs in the meals we enjoy and for all other things He brings to your life. Thankfulness at the beginning of a meal gets you in the habit of thanking Him at specific times and praying and giving thanks at every meal can get you in the habit of regular prayers of gratitude.

Like your prayers of adoration and confession, be specific when you give thanks. These verses can help guide your thoughts:

"Always be joyful. Never stop praying, be thankful in all circumstances, for this is God's will for you who belong to Christ Jesus." I Thessalonians 5:16-18

* * *

"And give thanks for everything to God the Father in the name of our Lord Jesus Christ." Ephesians 5:20.

* * *

"At that time, Jesus prayed this prayer: 'O Father, Lord of heaven and earth, thank you for hiding these things from those who think themselves wise and clever, and for revealing them to the childlike. Yes, Father, it pleased you to do it this way!' " Matthew 11: 25-26

Everything we have comes from God. Thank Him for every single blessing you have. Every blessing. In all things, give thanks. Being thankful is one of the basic elements of prayer. If you are constantly thanking God for all that you have, you are in a constant state of prayer and that is exactly what God has told us to do when we are told to pray constantly and unceasingly. If you are constantly thanking God for all you have, you don't give thanks and credit to yourself as readily.

"Don't worry about anything; instead, pray about everything. Tell God what you need and thank him for all he has done. Then you will experience God's peace, which exceeds anything we can understand. His peace will guard your hearts and minds as you live in Christ Jesus. And now, dear brothers and sisters, one final thing: Fix your thoughts on what is true, and honorable, and right, and pure, and lovely and admirable. Think about the things that are excellent and worthy of praise. Keep putting into practice all you learned and received from me—everything you heard from me and saw me doing. Then the God of Peace will be with you." Philippians 4:6-9

Fix your thoughts on what is true, and honorable, and right, and pure, and lovely, and admirable. Think about things that are excellent and worthy of praise. Phillippians 4:8

"And now, just as you have accepted Christ Jesus as your Lord, you must continue to follow Him. Let your roots grow down into Him, and let your lives be built on Him. Then your faith will grow strong in the truth you were taught, and you will overflow with thankfulness." Colossians 2:6-7

* * *

"Every time I think of you, I give thanks to my God. Whenever I pray, I make my requests for all of you with joy, for you have been my partners in spreading the Good News about Christ from the time you first heard it until now. And I am certain that God, who began the good work within you, will continue his work until it is finally finished on the day when Christ Jesus returns." Philippians 1:3-6

* * *

Additional Bible verses for giving thanks: John 11:41-42, 2 Corinthians 9:14-15

S - Seeking: God's Help for Yourself and Asking for the Needs of Others

If you've followed this prayer pattern, after telling our Father of our love for Him, confessing our sins to Him and thanking Him for all things, you are prepared to both ask for His provision and to surrender yourself to His ultimate will in your life. This final step of our praying process is called **Seeking**, which means asking or seeking through prayer. We are asking God to provide for our needs. We pray for the needs in the lives of our friends and people that are close to us. More importantly, we ask our Heavenly Father to take care of us and make Himself known in our lives. We are acknowledging and surrendering to His promise to take care of His children.

There are two words we consider when using the term seeking, asking or supplication. The first is petition. To petition means to request something from a superior authority. When we are seeking or asking God for something for ourselves, we use the term *PETITION*.

On the subject of effective prayer, Jesus said:

"**K**eep on asking, and you will receive what you ask for. Keep on seeking, and you will find. Keep on knocking, and the door will be opened to you. For everyone who asks receives. Everyone who seeks finds. And to everyone who knocks the door will be opened." Matthew 7:7-8.

* * *

"**O**nly ask, and I will give you the nations as your inheritance, the whole world as your possession." Psalm 2:8

God wants to take care of you and meet all of your needs and the desires of your heart. He is our great provider. He is waiting for you to ask for His help and for you to acknowledge that He is your life. He has many followers, but He wants to be your life. Jesus desires to live His life through you and use your body, personality and sphere of influence to expand the Kingdom bringing others to Him. He is waiting for you to come home. He is waiting for you to surrender.

In times of need, we are taught:

"So let us come boldly to the throne of our gracious God. There we will receive His mercy, and we will find grace to help us when we need it most." Hebrews 4:16

* * *

When we are seeking or asking for the needs of others, we use the term *INTERCESSION.* To intercede means to act or ask for something on someone else's behalf. The Bible gives these examples:

"When He (Jesus) saw the crowds, He had compassion on them because they were confused and helpless, like sheep without a shepherd. He said to His disciples, 'The harvest is great, but the workers are few. So pray to the Lord who is in charge of the harvest; ask Him to send more workers into His fields.' " Matthew 9:36-38

* * *

"I pray that your hearts will be flooded with light so that you can under-stand the confident hope He has given to those He called His holy people who are His rich and glorious inheritance." Ephesians 1:18

The least, the last and the lost. Remember those who have come to the end of self and are humbly seeking the truth.

"Remember those in prison, as if you were there yourself. Remember also those being mistreated, as if you felt their pain in your own bodies." Hebrews 13:3

"You will open the eyes of the blind. You will free the captives from prison, releasing those who sit in dark dungeons." Isaiah 42:7

* * *

"For I was hungry, and you fed me. I was thirsty, and you gave me a drink. I was a stranger, and you invited me into your home. I was naked and you gave me clothing. I was sick, and you cared for me. I was in prison and you visited me." Matthew 25:35-36

"I urge you, first of all, to pray for all people. Ask God to help them; intercede on their behalf, and give thanks for them. Pray this way for kings and all who are in authority so that we can live peaceful and quiet lives marked by godliness and dignity." 1 Timothy 2:1-2

"I thank God for you—the God I serve with a clear conscience, just as my ancestors did. Night and day I constantly remember you in my prayers. I long to see you again, for I remember your tears as we parted. And I will be filled with joy when we are together again." 2 Timothy 1:3-4

* * *

"I always thank God when I pray for you." Philemon 4

* * *

"And we are confident that he hears us whenever we ask for anything that pleases Him. And since we know he hears us when we make our requests, we also know that he will give us what we ask for." 1 John 5:14-15

"I also tell you this: if two of you agree on earth concerning anything you ask, my Father in heaven will do it for you. For where two or three gather together as my followers, I am there among them." Matthew 18:19-20

* * *

Helpful Hint: When you tell a person you will pray for them don't put it off, but pray right away, even if it's brief. One minute of prayer using these principles accomplishes your purpose and allows you to keep your word to pray for that person. Your heavenly Father just wants to hear from you on behalf of others.

Know that Jesus, the living God, is with you everywhere you go, cheering you on, giving you assurance, confidence and always the words to say.

Stay in the Spiritual Arena

Keep your prayer requests for yourself and others spiritually centered rather than in the material world. It is better to pray for a person's salvation, prayer life, brokenness, forgiveness and spiritual healing rather than a new car, house or money. Pray for God to open the way for that person to understand Him and receive His unconditional love and grace. He is the source for all good things that will happen in our lives.

"Whatever is good and perfect comes down to us from God our Father, who created all the lights in the heavens. He never changes or casts a shifting shadow. He chose to give birth to us by giving us his true word. And we, out of all creation, became his prized possession." James 1:17-18

* * *

"But the wisdom from above is first of all pure. It is also peace loving, gentle at all times, and willing to yield to others. It is full of mercy and good deeds. It shows no favoritism and is always sincere. And those who are peacemakers will plant seeds of peace and reap a harvest of righteousness." James 3:17-18

* * *

Look at addictions such as food, drugs, sex or alcohol as a form of spiritual disease. A person can receive healing from these addictions and the symptoms can be eliminated if he asks God to remove the compulsion. This is true for any habit or obsession that causes harm in a person's life. An addiction is always an obstacle that separates a person from fellowship and a relationship with his heavenly Father.

Christ in You
Colossians 1:27

When you humbly ask God to remove your character defects and spiritual shortcomings, He gives you a clear path to a deeper relationship with Him, and it is always a great prayer to pray. He is faithful to cleanse you in this way and make you whole. Our heavenly Father wants fellowship with His children and will draw you closer to Him as you make prayer a regular part of your life; your goal is to turn prayer from being a good idea into being a regular spiritual discipline.

Remember, be specific when asking for any needs, and always keep in mind that our Father knows what is best for us. To pray, "Your will be done, God, not mine," is always appropriate to consider when asking Him for favor.

Closing a Prayer and Amen

We close our prayer by mentioning the name of Jesus. Even if you spoke of Jesus in the opening, close it in the same manner, "in Jesus' name," as this is what He told us to do in John 14:13-14.

The final word on ending a prayer is "Amen." The word Amen means, "So be it," and it is a word of submission or surrender. Abandon yourself to Him, give up the fight, and choose to surrender to the Living God completely. Surrender is another word for acceptance of whatever God's will is for you. And probably His will for you is *TO DO THE NEXT RIGHT THING.*

Helpful information: By saying "Amen" we have expressed agreement to what we have just heard. Amen means affirmation of what is said and the statement is certain, reliable and can be trusted. Not only what was said, but what will be said. Amen is sometimes used before and after a statement. (Revelation 7:12) It means: I agree. So be it! The word Amen is used at least 126 times in the New Testament with 100 of those from the mouth of Jesus! It is a word of assurance saying, "Truthfully". Spoken out loud in a worship service or a teaching environment, it is a word of affirmation from the listener to the speaker that the truth has been spoken. Amen is a spoken testimony that, "I am in a accord with the truth of God's word."

Using ACTS

The example using ACTS as a guide to prayer as discussed might go like this:

Heavenly Father, (**Opening of prayer**)

I love, praise, and adore you more that I can express (**Adoration**)

I confess to you, Father, my sins. In particular, I confess today that I was cruel and harsh to my daughter. (**Confession**)

I thank you Father for my life and all the provisions you have given me. You have taken care of all my needs. (**Thankfulness**)

I need your help, Father. I am asking you to take away my desire to smoke. I must have Your help as I cannot do this on my own. (**Seeking, Asking, Petition**)

I pray this in the name of Jesus Christ. (**Praying in Jesus' name**)

Amen (**So be it**)

Pray Anytime & Anyplace

When you have learned the use of ACTS (A=Adoration, C= Confession, T= Thanksgiving, S=Seeking) then you are prepared to use it anywhere. You will be able to recall and use this simple method of prayer anytime and anyplace. These basic facets of your prayer life will help you talk to your heavenly Father easily and consistently. It allows you to build a structure that will improve your prayer life, and you can use it while walking, driving, exercising, or doing most any other activity. It will become entirely natural for you.

You are never alone when you trust Jesus. He is with you every step of the way in work or play. Whether you remember the ACTS acronym or not, Jesus is always there when you invite Him into the conversation.

Prayer as Worship

We pray continually because it is a joy and pleasure to pray and talk to our heavenly Father. Prayer can be as natural as breathing. Christ is in us! We are His children! We are children of the Living God! We are free to hang out and visit lovingly with our Dad. Relax, drop the formalities, and think of being with your Father who loves you unconditionally. He loves you more than you can imagine and can't do enough for you. He keeps asking what else He can do for you, and you absolutely adore Him. Love Him with all your heart and soul. This is worship.

> "But the time is coming, indeed it is here now, when true worshipers will worship the Father in spirit and in truth. The Father is looking for those who will worship Him that way. For God is Spirit, so those who worship Him must worship in spirit and in truth." John 4: 23-24

Group Prayer

The ACTS model for prayer is also an excellent and easy way to add depth to the concept of group prayer. When two or more are gathered in Christian fellowship and for the purpose of praying and counseling one another, try sharing this model with your friends and see how much richer and fulfilling your prayer time becomes.

Writing your Prayers

A wonderful means of keeping up with your prayer life is through the practice of journaling or writing your prayers. For example, you might be praying for the salvation of a spouse, child or friend. You could simply write "Prayed today that Ron, Sylvia and Samantha would open their hearts and minds and trust and love Jesus Christ." 9/21/13.

It is important to write down the date so you can keep track of how long you have been praying for that person or that event as well as the date when you started. If you are writing with pen and paper, leave room to record the answers. (skip a line after the prayer record) God always answers prayer. Try Him out.

If you have the time and inclination, you might decide to actually write down the entire prayer you are praying for a person. You might want to write the prayer and send it to that person. It is good for you and it is good for the person you are praying for. You simply write out the prayer as you would say it and send it in what ever way you correspond; by letter and regular mail or email. If you send it by mail, make sure you make a copy for your own prayer record.

Praying without Ceasing

The Bible instructs each of us to pray continuously and without ceasing. The Apostle Paul writes,

"Never stop praying." 1 Thessalonians 5:17

* * *

How can this be? Are we to walk around on our knees, head bowed and eyes closed? Probably not, but we can always be in a prayer mode if we are practicing one of these facets of prayer at all times. One way or another, we are called to always be praising or expressing our adoration to our Savior, confessing our sins, wrongdoings, and character defects to Him, thanking Him for everything or seeking for others and ourselves. Never stop praying!

Helpful Hint: Practice praying aloud. Listen to yourself talking to your Father. Relieve yourself of what might be inhibitions about talking to God. Practice praying as you drive to an appointment, but keep your eyes open!

27

HOW TO SPEND ONE HOUR EACH DAY IN PRAYER AND MEDIATION

Jesus said, "Couldn't you watch with me even one hour? Keep watch and pray.." Matthew 26: 40-41. NLT

Allow five minutes in each of these twelve steps of prayer, praise and mediation to form a deeper relationship with God. This is an organized and disciplined way to spend time with your heavenly Father. Visualize Jesus as you pray and mediate.

THE HOUR THAT CHANGES ME AND COULD CHANGE THE WORLD

12. PRAISE — Matthew 6:13
1. PRAISE — Matthew 6:9, Psalm 63:3, Hebrews 13:15
2. WAITING — Psalm 37:7, Isaiah 40:31, Lamentations 3:25
3. CONFESSION — Psalm 139:23, Psalm 139:23, 1 John 1:9
4. THE WORD — Psalm 19:7-9, 10
5. INTERCESSION — 1 Timothy 2:1-2, Matthew 9:36-38, Psalm 2:8
6. PETITION — Matthew 6:11, Matthew 7:7, James 4:2
7. THE WORD — Numbers 23:19
8. THANKSGIVING — Philippians 4:6, 1 Thessalonians 4:18
9. SINGING — Ephesians 5:19, Psalm 100:1-2, Psalm 144:9
10. MEDITATION — Joshua 1:8
11. LISTENING — Ecclesiastes 5:2, 1 Kings 19:11-12

The 12 Step Wheel of Prayer

1.) PRAISE: Let your Father know you love Him. 2.) WAITING: Understand patience. Find comfort in waiting. 3.) CONFESSION: Confess your sins to your heavenly Father. 4.) PRAY THE WORD: Use scripture to inspire your prayer. 5.) WATCHING: Observe and see what God is doing for you through those around you. 6.) INTERCESSION: Pray for the needs of others. 7.) PETITION: Pray for yourself and better spiritual insights. 8.) THANKSGIVING: Give your heavenly Father thanks for everything.
9.) SINGING: Sing a song to Jesus. Use hymns to praise God and tell Him you love Him. 10.) MEDITATION: Focus your thinking on a bible verse or passage. 11.) LISTENING: Listen for the voice of God. Imagine Jesus whispering in your ear. 12.) PRAISE: Know that the Jesus is God. Express adoration through Him to your heavenly Father.

28

Christian Meditation

Christ in You
Colossians 1:27

The Meaning of Christian Meditation

Christian Meditation in the Christian context is focusing on, thinking about, and reviewing God's Word, the Holy Bible.

By meditating on God's Word, the Bible, we start a process of eliminating wrong thoughts, habits, and attitudes, and replace those thoughts with Godly thinking and biblical teachings. The purpose of meditating on God's Word is to fill our mind with the truth of God's Word and to purge our mind of wrongful thinking.

"Study this Book of Instruction continually; meditate on it day and night, so you will be sure to obey everything written in it. Only then will you prosper and succeed in all that you do." Joshua 1:8

* * *

"But they delight in the law of the Lord,
    meditating on it day and night.
They are like trees planted along the riverbank,
    bearing fruit each season.
Their leaves never wither,
    and they prosper in all they do." Psalm 1:2-3

* * *

Jesus is the way, the truth and the life.

Meditation is concentrated focus, devoted thinking and reflection on a single topic, verse or Bible passage. It might include visualization, dreaming or imagining. God can use meditation to reveal Himself through your concentration and deep thought. An example of this might be a dream, vision, or mental picture that comes after deep study and concentration on a subject, that might give you an answer to a question or a solution to a problem.

Meditation requires sustained attention to a subject. In **The Purpose Driven Life** *, Rick Warren describes Christian and biblical meditation in this way:

"Meditation is focused thinking. It takes serious effort. You select a verse and reflect on it over and over in your mind...if you know how to worry, you already know how to meditate." *

Chewing the Cud

Cows and other split-hoofed animals chew their cud. These types of animals that both chew their cud and have split hooves were considered clean in Old Testament times and suitable as food for humans (Leviticus 11: 2-6). They have compartments in their stomachs that allow them to chew, swallow and regurgitate (throw up into their mouths) so they can chew the same food or "cud" over again. They chew and chew and swallow and re-digest and mash and chew every possible bit of nourishment out of the food they are eating. It is a concentrated, continuous, and thorough process, but effective in

 *Rick Warren, The Purpose Driven Life: What on Earth Am I Here For (Zondervan, 2013) Pg. 92

getting everything that matters nutritionally out of those morsels of food. The process of chewing cud is an example for how we should approach meditating on Scripture. We are to mull over, ponder, consider and chew on the Word of God, rolling it over and over in our mind as we digest everything He has for us. Then His word becomes part of our being and we become more Christ-like. We are transformed!

"May the words of my mouth
and the meditation of my heart
be pleasing to you,
O Lord, my rock and my redeemer."
Psalm 19:14

* * *

Imagine thinking about one of your favorite experiences. Remember the setting, the smells, the people who were involved, what kind of day it was and all the other small details. Meditation is like this, only you are focused on all the details of a specific Bible passage. You can dwell on a subject, a Bible verse, or a question and as you concentrate on it, looking at it from all angles, you are meditating.

Once we trust Jesus as our Lord and Savior, we become children of God. We are bodies in these earth suits, but spiritually we are with our heavenly Father. We have to learn to think that way. Visualize yourself with your Father in heaven. You are safe and secure, with no tears, regrets or sorrows. You are free of worries and anxieties. You know you are being taken care of.

"Think about the things of heaven, not the things of earth. For you died to this life, and your real life is hidden with Christ in God." Colossians 3:2-3

"So we don't look at the troubles we can see now; rather, we fix our gaze on things that cannot be seen. For the things we see now will soon be gone, but the things we cannot see will last forever." 2 Corinthians 4:18

Personal Meditation Guide

Here are some steps you can take to start the process of meditating and learning to make that practice a habit. Most of us live by habits, and this practice of meditation is a great one to develop. You can create a wonderful habit of meditation by practicing the process outlined below every day for 21 days. Experts say it takes 21 days to form a habit, so follow these guidelines for three weeks and see what God teaches you:

1.) Read a Bible verse or passage like the one below, but read it with the deliberate intent of understanding of what is being said.

"Take delight in the Lord,
and He will give you your heart's desires.

Commit everything you do to the Lord,
Trust him, and he will help you.

He will make your innocence radiate like the dawn,
and the justice of your cause will shine like the noonday sun.

Be still in the presence of the Lord,
and wait patiently for him to act."
Psalm 37: 4-7a

* * *

2.) Read it again and ponder the verse or passage carefully. Do a word study, looking at each word, one by one understanding and digesting the meaning of each. You can use a dictionary or thesaurus to help you, if you like. Think of these words as spiritual food that we must chew thoroughly, swallow, and digest to reap the full benefit and obtain the maximum nourishment. Think of how much you care for Him, and let that give you the greatest pleasure. Focus on the feeling that you care so much for Jesus that every-thing you do, you want to do for Him. Certainly, you have had those thoughts about a worldly or physical person, so take a minute to think of Jesus as the great love of your life.

3.) Prayer with Meditation: By now, the verse is becoming familiar, and you will be better able to understand the words in these verses. This is how the actual meditation process begins to take hold. Now, prayerfully read the verse a third time (or more) and ask God to reveal the truth to you. Accomplish this by asking your Father to show you the truth He wants you to see. Simply ask Him what He is saying to you per-sonally through each verse. Always ask Him in the name of Jesus.

4.) Contemplative Meditation: The contemplative stage of meditation comes by allowing the words you have read and prayed through to penetrate your mind and heart while waiting for God to reveal to you what He wants you to learn and absorb. You will achieve this by resting and concentrating as if you are sitting with your heavenly Father, you have asked a question, and you are waiting for Him to respond.

Take delight in the Lord, and He will give you your heart's desires.

Imagine the thrill of taking lessons from the living God who is yearning to provide to you the desires of your heart. He just wants to share His love with you and show you how to live life successfully.

"**W**ait patiently for the Lord. Be brave and courageous. Yes, wait patiently for the Lord." Psalm 27:14

✝

"**B**e still in the presence of the Lord, and wait patiently for him to act." Psalm 37:7a

5.) Meditation on Illustrations: The illustrations throughout this book and the companion book, **How to be a Child of God** *, add a valuable dimension to meditation. By following the same tips listed above, you can study a picture in a more meaningful way. Read, ponder, and focus on the Scripture connected to that particular illustration. After a few minutes of contemplation, pray and ask your heavenly Father to reveal what you are to know and understand. You can check the verses in the reference section of this book or in your own Bible to expand your point of view. See how the verse reads in another version of the Bible in order to gain additional perspective. It's impossible to read the Bible or reread verses too much.

In this way, you can use this book during a morning or evening quiet time. By meditating on the images and some of the Scripture passages, you will bring an added dimension to this text. The practice of meditating on illustrations has been around for ages and is an effective means of revealing and embedding truth in the mind of the viewer.

I am in my Father, and you are in Me, and I am in you. John 14:20

Use the illustrations of this book and those in the companion book, How to be a Child of God (see publisher's page in front of this book), to learn to meditate on Scripture while looking at a picture that explains the verse. Imagine, visualize and take ownership of the fact that you are in Christ and that He is in you. If you can let it register that Jesus Christ actually lives in you, your insecurities and inadequacies will slip away and the truth of who you are in Christ will set you free. The abundant life will be yours!

"Since I live, you also will live. When I am raised to life again, you will know that I am in my Father, and you are in me, and I am in you." John 14:19b-20

* * *

"I have given them the glory you gave me, so they may be one as we are one. I am in them and you are in me. May they experience such perfect unity that the world will know that you sent me and that you love them as much as you love me." John 17:22-23

* * *

The early church commissioned popular artists of their day to paint scenes that depicted important Bible messages and passages. Painters were hired by the church, and they created many timeless and wonderful works of art. The purpose was to provide picture stories and art forms for those who were unable to read the bible. Visual meditation on these masterful paintings and art works provided spiritual and biblical truth to all.

During their work, these artists may have also meditated on Scriptures or Bible passages. As a result, the Holy Spirit's teaching was involved in many of these great paintings. God is the source of all creation, and when artists create good works, they are applying the truth of Scripture and passing along the Word of God through paintings. Artists read or heard the Word of God, and the images that came to their minds were used to produce their inspired works.

A picture can take the place of many words, and careful meditation can reveal otherwise difficult to understand biblical truths, like the Trinity depicted in this painting. 1.) God the Father is speaking in the verse, 2.) the dove is the Spirit of God, and 3.) Jesus the Son is being baptized by John the Baptist. This is the Trinity, God in three persons. For an explanation of the Trinity see the bottom of page 1.

Let God the Holy Spirit influence your soul to give you His inspired revelation. Each of us is capable of interpreting and receiving the things God wants us to learn through the power of Jesus Christ, the living God within us.

Christ in You
Colossians 1:27

"This messenger was John the Baptist. He was in the wilderness and preached that people should be baptized to show they had repented of their sins and turned to God to be forgiven." Mark 1:4

* * *

"After his baptism, as Jesus came up out of the water, the heavens were opened and he saw the Spirit of God descending like a dove settling on him. And a voice from heaven said, 'This is my dearly loved Son, who brings me great joy.' " Matthew 3:16-17

* * *

"Then John testified, 'I saw the Holy Spirit descending like a dove from heaven and resting upon Him. I didn't know he was the one, but when God sent me to baptize with water, he told me, The one on whom you see the Spirit descend and rest is the one whom you will baptize with the Holy Spirit.' I saw this happen to Jesus, so I testify that he is the Chosen One of God." John 1:32-34

Conversational Meditation

Group or conversational meditation can occur when two or more are gathered and they discuss a subject or Bible verse as a group. A leader might read a verse and express his or her thoughts or give an explanation as a way of starting a conversational meditation. Others might follow in the same way. For example, a group leader could start with this verse:

"Confess your sins to each other and pray for each other so that you may be healed. The earnest prayer of a righteous person has great power and produces wonderful results." James 5:16

* * *

A group discussion on a verse such as this can produce interesting results as the Spirit of God inspires and speaks through each individual. Each person is invited to contribute to the conversation. The thoughts might be random, but participants can share a spiritual word as they are given that word or thought to speak or share. Not all words spoken are necessarily from God, but when two or more are gathered and begin to include the living God and His ways in the conversation, His presence can be felt, and it can enlighten those who are present. Our Savior is there when we invite Him in.

When using a topic as the conversation starter, the leader can use words like surrender, humility, submission, love, selflessness, forgiveness and others of a spiritual nature. You will be fascinated by the way the Spirit of God will inspire each person and give new insights to many in the group. Remember to open and close these group sessions in prayer. Ask the Lord Jesus to participate with you in the discussion, and to teach you about Himself and His plans and purposes for you. At the end of the session, be sure to thank the Lord Jesus Christ for the insights or information he has given you or the group.

The Spirit of God can be present anytime and anywhere. Surrender is the topic of conversation in this group discussion. This discussion can be called a group sharing or conversational meditation. God's power and creativity is revealed when He can use our diverse personalities to speak through and have His say. (Group prayer can be accomplished in the same manner.)

"For where two or three gather together as my followers, I am there among them." Matthew 18:20

Listening to Lectures and Sermons

We can also meditate when we attentively listen to a speaker. The theme or subject of a sermon delivered by a preacher or teacher can open our minds.

37

The speaker gives examples, illustrations, and stories to prove or bring to light a point, and he or she teaches the application we are to take to heart. When we meditate on a particular subject that is being taught or discussed through God's Word, we can implement His truth into our lives.

Listen carefully as God gives you life instructions through the spoken word as well as the written word. The Sermon on the Mount in Chapters 5-8 of the Book of Matthew is a wonderful design for living.

Jesus teaches on salt and life:

"You are the salt of the earth. But what good is salt if it has lost its flavor? Can you make it salty again? It will be thrown out and trampled underfoot as worthless. You are the light of the world—like a city on a hilltop that cannot be hidden. No one lights a lamp and then puts it under a basket. Instead, a lamp is placed on a stand, where it gives light to everyone in the house. In the same way, let your good deeds shine out for all to see, so that everyone will praise your heavenly Father." Matthew 5:13–16

"But the gateway to life is very narrow and the road is difficult, and only a few ever find it."

Jesus teaches on the narrow gate:

"You can enter God's kingdom only through the narrow gate. The highway to hell is broad and its gate is wide for the many who choose that way. But the gateway to life is very narrow and the road is difficult, and only a few ever find it." Matthew 7:13-14

* * *

Jesus teaches us to build on a strong foundation:

"Anyone who listens to my teaching and follows it is wise, like a person who builds his house on solid rock. Though the rain comes in torrents and the floodwaters rise and the winds beat against that house, it won't collapse because it is built on bedrock. But anyone who hears my teaching and doesn't obey it is foolish, like a person who builds his house on sand. When the rains and floods come and the winds beat against that house, it will collapse with a mighty crash." Matthew 7:24-27

* * *

Meditating on the points of a sermon or lecture is more powerful and effective when you have spent time reading, studying, and focusing on God's word as it relates to that teaching. A Bible study or sermon lesson is best understood when the passage has been examined ahead of time or reviewed after the lesson. When you study or meditate on Scriptures, you become familiar with them, and God gives you personal insights and instruction on how to apply the message in your own life. Then, when you are sitting in a church service and hear someone preaching on a passage that is familiar, you are

God has gifted preachers and teachers to deliver the Word of God in a way that will influence each one of us as He has prepared our hearts. Listen and concentrate closely on the words and message of a sermon, lecture or Bible study. God will often use these to speak into your life.

exposed to his or her inspirations and experiences with God through that passage. Your understanding is broadened, and you see God in a new light.

When you were a child, you might have heard that you get out of something what you put into it. For example, you wouldn't expect to be good at basketball or baseball if you didn't practice and learn the skills required to play the sport. If you want to be a better player, you go further, learn specific plays, and condition your body so you can compete at a level equal to the others on the court.

Intimacy with God through prayer, finding practical life lessons through Bible study, and learning about God through mediation are also skills to learn. God wants to speak to you, and transform your heart and life through these spiritual disciplines. The more you engage and seek a close personal relationship with Him, the more you will find His presence, purpose and power in your life. More important, you will begin to understand He is your life.

Meditate Anytime

Like prayer, you can meditate on God's Word anyplace and anytime. Prayer and meditation are most effective when you build them into daily habits. Personal discipline is the key to learning these skills, and meditation is best done in a quiet place, at a prescribed time, and with the least amount of interruption. Still, you can meditate in any place and at any time. Consistency in this practice establishes a habit, and you will receive the most from your time in meditation and prayer when you make these practices your daily habits.

It is important to find a body position that will keep you awake and alert when you start your time of meditation. Pick a place where you are comfortable and relaxed, as well.

Helpful Hint: Don't lie down in bed to meditate (or pray) as you will fall asleep! It is good to be comfortable, but not too comfortable. Turn off your phone or other items that might distract your thinking.

Meditation through Journaling—Write it down.

An underused means of meditation is talking to your heavenly Father through journaling or writing Him a letter. Sometimes we are more precise and exacting when we write something or write to someone. We think through each word and how we might phrase and construct each sentence. What could be a more fitting method for talking to our God and chief problem solver? If you are comfortable talking to God in writing or journaling,

40

you can set aside time to do it on a regular basis, three to five times a week could yield greater rewards than you can imagine. You are talking to God in a unique, but intimate way and you have a record of the conversations to go back to and review. Be sure to date each one. Write to God in a personal style as if you were sitting beside him talking and telling Him of your dreams, visions, personal feelings. Let Him know about your angers, fears, concerns and anxieties. Thank Him for the joys and good things in your life.

As you are processing through a problem, you might want to utilize the method of writing down the problem in the form of questions. Why am I attempting this project? What is its purpose? How will I accomplish it? When you have a particular problem that you want to resolve with God make sure you are prepared physically, spiritually, and mentally. Be sure of what you are attempting to do. Make a list of people and circumstances God is urging you to take some action on regarding meditative prayer.

Helpful Hint: In any meditation, keep in mind the cornerstones of Christian life being: faith in God, the unconditional love God has for us, His total forgiveness and the hope in the coming of Jesus Christ.

Meditation in Song

God seeks unity with all those who believe in Him. He wants all of his children to be like-minded and united in thought. Singing praises to God that are based on scripture and biblical principles promotes this unity and is a form of meditation. In fact, singing with others assumes unity and concert as we attempt to harmonize and stay on key.

Meditation through singing hymns and praise songs is a fulfillment of God's requirement to pray and sing with His Spirit. Meditation through song is an indicator of a spirit filled believer and shows adoration for God. Singing to God cultivates an attitude of praise and worship. It is a lyrical or musical form of prayer and meditation as we sing to and focus our attention on the Living God.

"Be filled with the Holy Spirit, singing psalms and hymns and spiritual songs among yourselves, and making music to the Lord in your hearts. And give thanks for everything to God the Father in the name of our Lord Jesus Christ." Ephesians 5:18-20

41

O victory in Jesus,
My Savior, forever.
He sought me and bought me
With His redeeming blood;
He loved me ere I knew Him,
And all my love is due Him,
He plunged me to victory,
Beneath the cleansing flood
(Chorus from Victory in Jesus,
Hymn by E.M Bartlett, Sr.)

"Let the message about Christ in all its richness fill your lives. Teach and counsel each other with all the wisdom he gives. Sing psalms and hymns and spiritual songs to God with thankful hearts. And whatever you do or say, do it as a representative of the Lord Jesus, giving thanks through him to God the Father." Colossians 3:16-17

* * *

"Well then, what shall I do? I will pray in the spirit, and I will also pray in words I understand. I will sing in the spirit, and I will also sing in words I understand." 1 Corinthians 14:15

* * *

"I will sing to the Lord because he is good to me." Psalm 13:6

* * *

"I will sing of the Lord's unfailing love forever! Young and old will hear of your faithfulness. Your unfailing love will last forever. Your faithfulness is as enduring as the heavens." Psalm 89:1-2

* * *

"I will sing of your love and justice, Lord. I will praise you with songs." Psalm 101:1

* * *

"My heart is confident in you, O God, no wonder I can sing your praises with all my heart! Wake up, lyre and harp! I will wake the dawn with my song. I will thank you Lord, among all the people. I will sing your praises among the nations. For your unfailing love is higher than the heavens. Your faithfulness reaches to the clouds. Be exalted, O God, above the highest heavens. May your glory shine over all the earth." Psalm 108:1-5

* * *

Singing praise songs, psalms and hymns based on scripture builds faith, as faith comes by hearing the word of God. (Romans 10:17) As we sing scriptures, we are focusing and meditating and building our faith by hearing, listening and concentrating on the word of God.

Most libraries have hymnbooks or denominational songbooks that are available to look at, copy from or check out. They can also be found for purchase online at Amazon.com or at Christian bookstores like Lifeway. Many large churches have bookstores with songbooks or hymnals available for purchase. If all else fails, just sing or let the Spirit of God sing through you the words of almost any chapter from the Old Testament Book of Psalms. There are 150 of them and you can write your own music.

Christ in You
Colossians 1:27

Fasting with Prayer and Meditation

Fasting: 1) to abstain from food, either entirely or partly 2) an act of abstinence from food. (Webster's Dictionary of the English Language)

"In fact, for days I mourned, fasted and prayed to the God of heaven." Nehemiah 1:4

* * *

Fasting is mentioned many times throughout the Bible and it is an important tool and aid to meditation.

A period of fasting combined with meditation and prayer can be useful in resolving important issues of work, relationships, and many other life decisions. When we fast, we totally focus our heart, mind and body all in the same direction, which can almost always lead to spiritual breakthroughs. These breakthroughs can be in the form of inspiration, specific guidance and directions for you to follow, or boldness and courage you might need to move forward in some area of your living.

When you begin a fast, there will be a strong initial appetite that will soon go away. It is a result of habit not hunger as we generally eat more than we need. But even these initial stages of the fast can signal the thought processes and help you go into a deeper and more concentrated mode of thinking. Fasting is a spiritual act. By depriving yourself of material things like food in the case of fasting, you are practicing the opposite of the material.

Fasting brings about a much deeper level of spiritual focus and concentration. Fasting is a way of saying, "no," to our mental and physical desires and cravings. As a result, this practice draws us closer to God especially while meditating and reading His Word.

There are many types and durations of fasts. The three types found in Scripture are the total fast, the normal fast, and the partial fast.

Total Fast. You take in nothing. No food, no water, nothing. This is extreme and you must absolutely know what you are doing. We can only live a short time without water. You must be totally under the guidance of God and preferably some worldly medical supervision, as well. (Esther 4:16)

Normal Fast. The normal fast is water only and preferably pure distilled water. Most fasting is of this type. Jesus fasted forty days and He was hungry. Scripture did not mention thirst and we can assume He drank water during this time. (Matthew 4:1-4, Ezra 8:21)

Partial Fast. This type of fast means missing a meal (or two or three) or fasting using only clear broth or juices. There are many of these types of fasts where a certain type of fruit or vegetable might be used. The beginning faster might want to try these methods as a way of conditioning prior to trying a short or longer normal fast with water only. (Daniel 1:12-14)

Initially, you might consider either a one, three, five or seven-day fast. During this period, decide ahead of time what kind of fast you will do or how many meals during a day you will skip. Fasting in this way doesn't mean giving up your entire food intake for a long period. Many people find that they have to start out slowly, and learn the habit of fasting before they can successfully fast for long periods.

For example, you could fast by giving up:

- One meal a day for a specific length of time
- Two meals a day for a specific length of time
- Certain foods for a specific length of time
- Drinking only liquids
- Drinking only water

Pray for others while fasting

When you fast, the purpose is to listen to God while praying and meditating on God's Word. It takes time to eat or prepare to eat, and this is the extra time you will have to spend with your heavenly Father.

While you are fasting, you can focus on resolving a particular life issue or interceding (praying on behalf of someone else).

Major life choices will arise where you might suddenly be offered a job in another city, offered a change in vocation or in relationships, or many other life issues that require the right answer the first time. This is the perfect occasion to fast as a way of seeking God for His guidance. A brief fast can be ideal for this application.

There are many guides to fasting, and some are listed in the reference section located on page 58 of this book.

Jesus Fasted

A wonderful example of the power of fasting comes when Satan tempts Jesus in the wilderness soon after His baptism by John the Baptist.

"Then Jesus was led by the Spirit into the wilderness to be tempted there by the devil. For forty days and nights He fasted and then became very hungry. During that time the devil came and said to Him, 'If you are the Son of God, tell these stones to become loaves of bread.' But Jesus told him, "No, the Scriptures say, 'People do not live by bread alone, but by every word that comes from the mouth of God.'" Matthew 4:1-4

Jesus was entirely focused as He fasted in the wilderness for forty days. He spoke Scripture from Deuteronomy 8:3 written below. He could have memorized this Scripture or even taken a scroll with Him into the desert, but His strength came from meditating on the Word of God. That is His instruction to us.

"Yes, he humbled you by letting you go hungry and then feeding you with manna, a food previously unknown to you and your ancestors. He did it to teach you that people do not live by bread alone; rather, we live by every word that comes from the mouth of the Lord." Deuteronomy 8:3

* * *

"And when you fast, don't make it obvious as the hypocrites do, for they try to look miserable and disheveled so people will admire them for their fasting. I tell you the truth: that is the only reward they will ever get. But when you fast, comb your hair and wash your face. Then no one will notice that you are fasting except your Father, who knows what you do in private. And your Father, who sees everything, will reward you." Matthew 6:16-18

* * *

The verses above indicated that Jesus practiced fasting and assumed that, as His followers, we would fast also. Moses also fasted often, as shown in Exodus 34:28. Fasting requires discipline and the ability to deny yourself of short-term pleasures in order to gain long-term breakthroughs. It also helps build self-discipline, which develops as we grow in spiritual maturity. One way to grow spiritually is by denying yourself pleasures of the flesh. Many of us have excesses in our life, such as food, sex, drugs, alcohol, work, sports, hunting and fishing. Fasting from food is a means of beginning the practice of self-denial in one area of your life so you can learn the skills you need to deny yourself in other areas. God desires that we live a life of balance and moderation and reject or moderate our self-indulgences.

Spiritual Beings

We are spirit beings in a physical body, and we need to learn we have victory through Christ over the power of self-indulgence in the material things of the world. We have the power to reject the desires of our old sinful self and live a life that reveals our spiritual being, Christ in us. Fasting is a practice toward that end. It is most effective when done in a spirit of prayer and meditation on God's Word.

Scriptures related to fasting:

Exodus 34:28, Deuteronomy 9:9 & 18, 1 Samuel 7:6, 2 Samuel 12:16, Ezra 8:21, Nehemiah 9:1-2, Esther 4:16, Psalm 35:13, Psalm 109:24,

46

Isaiah 58:6-9, Jeremiah 36:9, Daniel 6:18, Daniel 9:3, Joel 2:12, Jonah 3:5, Matthew 9:15, Matthew 17:21, Luke 4:1-2, Acts 13:3, 2 Corinthians 6:5, 2 Corinthians 11:27

Guard Your Heart

Meditation on God's word is a means of guarding your heart against the forces of evil that seek to steal the heart you have for God. Jesus Christ is your protector. Call on His name and He will guard your hearts against those who are children of Satan.

"Guard your heart above all else, for it determines the course of your life." Proverbs 4:23

* * *

"People judge by outward appearance, but the Lord looks at the heart." 1 Samuel 16:7

"God blesses those whose hearts are pure, for they will see God." Matthew 5:8

* * *

"A good person produces good things from a treasury of a good heart, and an evil person produces evil things from the treasury of an evil heart. What you say flows from what is in your heart." Luke 6:45

* * *

"For if you confess with your mouth that Jesus is Lord and believe in your heart that God raised him from the dead, you will be saved." Romans 10:9

* * *

"His peace will guard your hearts and minds as you live in Christ Jesus." Philippians 4:7

* * *

"And let the peace that comes from Christ rule in your hearts. For as members of one body, you are called to live in peace. And always be thankful." Colossians 3:15

"You were cleansed from your sins when you obeyed the truth, so now you must show sincere love to each other as brothers and sisters. Love each other deeply with all your heart." 1 Peter 1:22

* * *

"Take delight in the Lord, and he will give you your heart's desires." Psalm 37:4

* * *

"If we had forgotten the name of our God or spread our hands in prayer to foreign gods, God would certainly have known it, for he knows the secrets of every heart." Psalm 44:20-21

Christ in You
Colossians 1:27

* * *

"Create in me a clean heart, O God. Renew a loyal spark within me." Psalm 51:10

* * *

"My child, pay attention to what I say. Listen carefully to my words. Don't lose sight of them. Let them penetrate deep into your heart, for they bring life to those who find them, and healing to their whole body. Guard your heart above all else, for it determines the course of your life." Proverbs 4:20-23

* * *

"The Lord detests people with crooked hearts, but he delights in those with integrity." Proverbs 12:20

* * *

"The heart of the godly thinks carefully before speaking, the mouth of the wicked overflows with evil words." Proverbs 15:28

* * *

"As a face is reflected in water, so the heart reflects the real person." Proverbs 27:19

* * *

"That is why the Lord says, 'Turn to me now, while there is still time. Give me your hearts. Come with fasting, weeping, and mourning. Don't tear your clothing in your grief, but tear your hearts instead.' Return to the Lord your God, for he is merciful and compassionate." Joel 2: 12-13

* * *

"I will give them hearts that recognize me as the Lord. They will be my people, and I will be their God, for they will return to me wholeheartedly." Jeremiah 24:7

* * *

"And I will give them a singleness of heart and put a new spirit within them. I will take away their stony, stubborn heart and give them a tender, responsive heart, so they will obey my decrees and regulations. Then they will truly be my people and I will be their God." Ezekiel 11:19-20

"So my people come pretending and sit before you. They listen to your words, but they have no intention of doing what you say. Their mouths are full of lustful words, and their hearts seek only after money." Ezekiel 33:31

Benefits of Meditation

As we meditate on Bible verses and carefully think about and listen to what God is saying to us, we begin to understand more of the things God has for us and that we are in Christ. We learn we are:

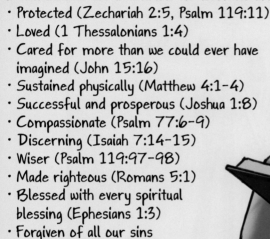

- Protected (Zechariah 2:5, Psalm 119:11)
- Loved (1 Thessalonians 1:4)
- Cared for more than we could ever have imagined (John 15:16)
- Sustained physically (Matthew 4:1-4)
- Successful and prosperous (Joshua 1:8)
- Compassionate (Psalm 77:6-9)
- Discerning (Isaiah 7:14-15)
- Wiser (Psalm 119:97-98)
- Made righteous (Romans 5:1)
- Blessed with every spiritual blessing (Ephesians 1:3)
- Forgiven of all our sins (Colossians 1:13-14)
- Freed from the power of sin (Romans 6:1-6)
- Filled with the Spirit of God (1 Corinthians 2:12)
- Children of God and co-heirs with Christ (Romans 8:17)

A quieting of our mind, heart and spirit happens when we absorb and ponder the words of the Living God. By deep and concentrated thinking over the Word of God, we gain greater understanding of Jesus and how He is sharing with us His inheritance as children of God. Our ability to understand the truth about people, ideas and relationships will be sharpened and our personal discernment will increase when we regularly read God's Word, pray about it, meditate on it and fast. We will grow in our awareness of the very presence of God. By quieting the mind, heart and spirit, we calm our bodies and allow greater rest, relaxation and release of tension. God gives us wisdom and calmness that is important for us in making better decisions for every aspect of our lives.

When you meditate, you are also conditioning yourself to be aware of what you are thinking. As you train yourself to think pure thoughts (Philippians 4:8) you will also be training your mind to think before you act and speak. When you discipline your mind, your tongue will begin to change its behavior as well.

"And now dear brothers and sisters, one final thing. Fix your thoughts on what is true, and honorable, and right, and pure, and lovely and admirable. Think about things that are excellent and worthy of praise." Philippians 4:8

As you meditate on the word of God and study His ways, you will have a greater desire to walk with Him, be with Him and go where He goes. We learn to do the right thing as we learn to think like Christ and seek to be imitators of God. We start to realize that we have the mind of Christ and we want to go where He goes and do what He does.

"Look! I am creating new heavens and a new earth, and no one will
Even think about the old ones anymore.
Be glad, rejoice forever in my creation!
And look! I will create Jerusalem as a place of happiness.
Her people will be a source of joy
I will rejoice over Jerusalem and delight in my people.
And the sound of weeping and crying will be heard in it no more."
Isaiah 65:17-19

* * *

The purpose and principle benefit to meditation is to bring you into intimacy and close communion with God and to learn the truth that will set you free (John 8:31-32). That is the essential mission of all Christian meditation.

"But they delight in the law of the Lord,
    meditating on it day and night.

They are like trees planted along the riverbank,
  bearing fruit each season.
Their leaves never wither,
  and they prosper in all they do."
Psalms 1:2-3

Eleventh Step Prayer

This book began with the Eleventh Step of Alcoholic
Anonymous regarding prayer and meditation. I would
like to conclude with what is called the Eleventh Step Prayer

Christ in You
Colossians 1:27

of Alcoholics Anonymous that was found in France in 1912 and distributed
widely since that time. It is attributed to St. Frances of Assisi and is used
by those in AA and other twelve step programs who get this far in the program.

"Lord, make me a channel of your peace—that where there is hatred, I
may bring love—that where there is wrong, I may bring the spirit of
forgiveness—that where there is discord, I may bring harmony—that
where there is error, I may bring truth—that where there is doubt, I
may bring faith—that where there is despair, I may bring hope—that
where there are shadows, I may bring light—that where there is sadness, I may bring joy. Lord, grant that I may seek rather to comfort
than to be comforted—to understand, than to be understood—to
love than to be loved. For it is by self-forgetting that one finds. It is
by forgiving that one is forgiven. It is by dying that one awakens to
Eternal Life." Amen. Anonymous

Summary

These simple instructions are
an introduction for Christians
who want to learn more about

prayer, meditation, and meditative prayer and are beginning to practice these
disciplines. The lines between the three are not clear. Some have said that
prayer is talking to God and meditation is listening to Him. This is true, but
there is more as explained and illustrated in these pages.

First, we must have a heart for God. If our hearts are right and in tune with
the will of God and we are seeking fellowship with Him, His Spirit will always
show us the way and give us the words to say. When you are seeking a close
relationship with your heavenly Father, He knows you are pursuing Him and,
in fact, He is pursuing you more than you are pursuing Him. He will open the
door for you and reveal Himself to you in deeper ways. Prayer and meditation
sharpen the senses and increase the desire for a greater and more intimate
fellowship with our God.

Ultimately no one can teach us to pray. The Spirit of God intercedes for us to our heavenly Father. So it is not us, but the living Christ within who speaks to the Father for us and through us. Let go and let God!

"My old self has been crucified with Christ. It is no longer I who live, but Christ lives in me. So I live in this earthly body by trusting in the Son of God, who loved me and gave Himself for me."
Galatians, 2:20

PRAY THE WORD: Numbers 23:19, Psalm 119:38–46, John 15:7, Ephesians 3:14–19, Colossians 1:9–12

LISTENING TO GOD: 1 Samuel 3:9–10, Ecclesiastes 5:2, Jeremiah 29:12–13, 1 Kings 19:11–12

WAITING FOR GOD: Isaiah 40:31, Lamentations 3:25, Psalm 37:4–7

READ THE WORD: Psalm 19:7–10, Psalm 105:1–5, Psalm 119:11, Jeremiah 1:12, John 8:31–32, 2 Timothy 3:16

Full Text of Bible Verses in Alphabetical Order

Acts 13:3 So after more fasting and prayer, the men laid their hands on them and sent them on their way. Page 47

Colossians 1:9-12 So we have not stopped praying for you since we first heard about you. We ask God to give you complete knowledge of his will and to give you spiritual wisdom and understanding. 10 Then the way you live will always honor and please the Lord, and your lives will produce every kind of good fruit. All the while, you will grow as you learn to know God better and better. 11 We also pray that you will be strengthened with all his glorious power so you will have all the endurance and patience you need. May you be filled with joy, 12 always thanking the Father. He has enabled you to share in the inheritance that belongs to his people, who live in the light. Page 52

Colossians 1:13-14 For he has rescued us from the kingdom of darkness and transferred us into the Kingdom of his dear Son, 14 who purchased our freedom and forgave our sins. Page 49

Colossians 1:27 For God wanted them to know that the riches and glory of Christ are for you Gentiles, too. And this is the secret: Christ lives in you. This gives you assurance of sharing in his glory. Pages I, 4, 7, 10, 16, 24, 36, 43, 48, 51

1 Corinthians 2:12 And we have received God's Spirit (not the world's spirit), so we can know the wonderful things God has freely given us. Page 49

1 Corinthians 7:5 Do not deprive each other of sexual relations, unless you both agree to refrain from sexual intimacy for a limited time so you can give yourselves more completely to prayer. Afterward, you should come together again so that Satan won't be able to tempt you because of your lack of self-control. Page 47

2 Corinthians 6:5 We have been beaten, been put in prison, faced angry mobs, worked to exhaustion, endured sleepless nights, and gone without food. Page 47

2 Corinthians 9:14-15 And they will pray for you with deep affection because of the overflowing grace God has given to you. 15 Thank God for this gift too wonderful for words! Page 19

2 Corinthians 11:27 I have worked hard and long, enduring many sleepless nights. I have been hungry and thirsty and have often gone without food. I have shivered in the cold, without enough clothing to keep me warm. Page 47

Daniel 1:12-14 "Please test us for ten days on a diet of vegetables and water," Daniel said. 13 "At the end of the ten days, see how we look compared to the other young men who are eating the king's food. Then make your decision in light of what you see." 14 The attendant agreed and to Daniel's suggestion and tested them for ten days. Page 46

Daniel 6:18 Then the king returned to his palace and spent the night fasting. He refused his usual entertainment and couldn't sleep that night. Page 46

Daniel 9:3 So I turned to the Lord God and pleaded with him in prayer and fasting. Page 46

Deuteronomy 9:9 This happened when I was on the mountain receiving the tablets of stone inscribed with the words of the covenant that the LORD had made with you. I was there for forty days and forty nights, and all that time I ate no food and drank no water. Page 46

Deuteronomy 9:18 "Then, as before, I threw myself down before the LORD for forty days and nights. I ate no bread and drank no water because of the great sin you had committed by doing what the LORD hated, provoking him to anger. Page 46

Ecclesiastes 5:2 Don't make rash promises, and don't be hasty in bringing matters before God. After all, God is in heaven, and you are here on earth. So let your words be few. Page 52

Ephesians 1:3 All praise to God, the Father of our Lord Jesus Christ, who has blessed us with every spiritual blessing in the heavenly realms because we are united with Christ. Page 49

Ephesians 3:14-19 When I think of all this, I fall to my knees and pray to the Father, 15 the Creator of everything in heaven and on earth. 16 I pray that from his glorious, unlimited resources he will empower you with inner strength through his Spirit. 17 Then Christ will make his home in your hearts as you trust in him. Your roots will grow down into God's love and keep you strong. 18 And may you have the power to understand, as all God's people should, how wide, how long, how high, and how deep his love is. 19 May you experience the love of Christ, though it is too great to understand fully. Then you will be made complete with all the fullness of life and power that comes from God. Page 52

Esther 4:16 "Go and gather together all the Jews of Susa and fast for me. Do not eat or drink for three days, night or day. My maids and I will do the same. And then, though it is against the law, I will go in to see the king. If I must die, I must die." Pages 44, 46

Exodus 34:28 Moses remained there on the mountain with the LORD forty days and forty nights. In all that time he ate no bread and drank no water. And the LORD wrote the terms of the covenant—the Ten Commandments—on the stone tablets. Page 46

Ezra 8:21 And there by the Ahava Canal, I gave orders for all of us to fast and humble ourselves before our God. We prayed that he would give us a safe journey and protect us, our children, and our goods as we traveled. Pages 44, 46

Isaiah 7:14-15 All right then, the Lord himself will give you the sign. Look! The virgin will conceive a child! She will give birth to a son and will call him Immanuel (which means 'God is with us'). 15 By the time this child is old enough to choose what is right and reject what is wrong, he will be eating yogurt and honey. Page 49

Isaiah 40:31 But those who trust in the LORD will find new strength. They will soar high on wings like eagles. They will run and not grow weary. They will walk and not faint. Page 52

Isaiah 44:22 I have swept away your sins like a cloud. I have scattered your offenses like the morning mist. Oh, return to me, for I have paid the price to set you free. Page 16

Isaiah 58:6-9 "No, this is the kind of fasting I want: Free those who are wrongly imprisoned; lighten the burden of those who work for you. Let the oppressed go free, and remove the chains that bind people. 7 Share your food with the hungry, and give shelter to the homeless. Give clothes to those who need them, and do not hide from relatives who need your help. 8 "Then your salvation will come like the dawn, and your wounds will quickly heal. Your godliness will lead you forward, and the glory of the LORD will protect you from behind. 9 Then when you call, the LORD will answer. 'Yes, I am here,' he will quickly reply. "Remove the heavy yoke of oppression. Stop pointing your finger and spreading vicious rumors! Page 46

Isaiah 59:2 It's your sins that have cut you off from God. Because of your sins, he has turned away and will not listen anymore. Page 16

Jeremiah 1:12 And the LORD said, "That's right, and it means that I am watching, and I will certainly carry out all my plans." Page 52

Jeremiah 29:12-13 In those days when you pray, I will listen. 13 If you look for me wholeheartedly, you will find me. Page 52

Jeremiah 31:34 And they will not need to teach their neighbors, nor will they need to teach their relatives, saying, 'You should know the LORD.' For everyone, from the least to the greatest, will know me already," says the LORD. "And I will forgive their wickedness, and I will never again remember their sins." Page 16

Jeremiah 36:9 He did this on a day of sacred fasting held in late autumn, during the fifth year of the reign of Jehoiakim son of Josiah. People from all over Judah had come to Jerusalem to attend the services at the Temple on that day. Page 46

Joel 2:12 That is why the LORD says, "Turn to me now, while there is time. Give me your hearts. Come with fasting, weeping, and mourning." Page 46

John 8:31-32 Jesus said to the people who believed in him, "You are truly my disciples if you remain faithful to my teachings. 32 And you will know the truth, and the truth will set you free." Pages 50, 52

John 11:41-42 So they rolled the stone aside. Then Jesus looked up to heaven and said, "Father, thank you for hearing me. 42 You always hear me, but I said it out loud for the sake of all these people standing here, so that they will believe you sent me." Page 19

John 14:13-14 You can ask for anything in my name, and I will do it, so that the Son can bring glory to the Father. 14 Yes, ask me for anything in my name, and I will do it! Page 24

John 15:7 But if you remain in me and my words remain in you, you may ask for anything you want, and it will be granted! Page 52

John 15:16-17 You didn't choose me. I chose you. I appointed you to go and produce lasting fruit, so that the Father will give you whatever you ask for, using my name. 17 This is my command: Love each other. Page 49

Jonah 3:5 The people of Nineveh believed God's message, and from the greatest to the least, they declared a fast and put on burlap to show their sorrow. Page 47

Joshua 1:8 Study this Book of Instruction continually. Meditate on it day and night so you will be sure to obey everything written in it. Only then will you prosper and succeed in all you do. Page 49

1 Kings 19:11-12 "Go out and stand before me on the mountain," the LORD told him. And as Elijah stood there, the LORD passed by, and a mighty windstorm hit the mountain. It was such a terrible blast that the rocks were torn loose, but the LORD was not in the wind. After the wind there was an earthquake, but the LORD was not in the earthquake. 12 And after the earthquake there was a fire, but the LORD was not in the fire. And after the fire there was the sound of a gentle whisper. Page 52

Lamentations 3:25 The LORD is good to those who depend on him, to those who search for him. Page 52

Leviticus 11:2-6 "Give the following instructions to the people of Israel. "Of all the land animals, these are the ones you may use for food. 3 You may eat any animal that has completely split hooves and chews the cud. 4 You may not, however, eat the following animals that have split hooves or that chew the cud, but not both. The camel chews the cud but does not have split hooves, so it is ceremonially unclean for you. 5 The hyrax chews the cud but does not have split hooves, so it is unclean. 6 The hare chews the cud but does not have split hooves, so it is unclean. Page 30

Luke 4:1-2 Then Jesus, full of the Holy Spirit, returned from the Jordan River. He was led by the Spirit in the wilderness, 2 where he was tempted by the devil for forty days. Jesus ate nothing all that time and became very hungry. Page 47

Matthew 4:1-4 Then Jesus was led by the Spirit into the wilderness to be tempted there by the devil. 2 For forty days and forty nights he fasted and became very hungry. 3 During that time the devil came and said to him, "If you are the Son of God, tell these stones to become loaves of bread." 4 But Jesus told him, "No! The Scriptures say, 'People do not live by bread alone, but by every word that comes from the mouth of God.'" Pages 44, 49

Matthew 6:12 and forgive us our sins, as we have forgiven those who sin against us. Page 16

Matthew 9:15 Jesus replied, "Do wedding guests mourn while celebrating with the groom? Of course not. But someday the groom will be taken away from them, and then they will fast. Page 47

Matthew 17:21 NASB "But this kind does not go out except by prayer and fasting." Page 47

Nehemiah 9:1-2 On October 31 the people assembled again, and this time they fasted and dressed in burlap and sprinkled dust on their heads. 2 Those of Israelite descent separated themselves from all foreigners as they confessed their own sins and the sins of their ancestors. Page 46

Numbers 23:19 God is not a man, so he does not lie. He is not human, so he does not change his mind. Has he ever spoken and failed to act? Has he ever promised and not carried it through? Page 52

Philippians 3:13-14 No, dear brothers and sisters, I have not achieved it, but I focus on this one thing: Forgetting the past and looking forward to what lies ahead, 14 I press on to reach the end of the race and receive the heavenly prize for which God, through Christ Jesus, is calling us. Page 16

Philippians 4:8 And now dear brothers and sisters, one final thing. Fix your thoughts on what is true, and honorable, and right, and pure, and lovely and admirable. Think about things that are excellent and worthy of praise. Page 49

Psalm 19:7-10 The instructions of the LORD are perfect, reviving the soul. The decrees of the LORD are trustworthy, making wise the simple. 8 The commandments of the LORD are right, bringing joy to the heart. The commands of the LORD are clear, giving insight for living. 9 Reverence for the LORD is pure, lasting forever. The laws of the LORD are true; each one is fair. 10 They are more desirable than gold, even the finest gold. They are sweeter than honey, even honey dripping from the comb. Page 52

Psalm 35:13 Yet when they were ill, I grieved for them. I denied myself by fasting for them, but my prayers returned unanswered. Page 46

Psalm 37:4-7 Take delight in the LORD, and he will give you your heart's desires. 5 Commit everything you do to the LORD. Trust him, and he will help you. 6 He will make your innocence radiate like the dawn, and the justice of your cause will shine like the noonday sun. 7 Be still in the presence of the LORD, and wait patiently for him to act. Don't worry about evil people who prosper or fret about their wicked schemes. Page 52

Psalm 51:1 Have mercy on me, O God, because of your unfailing love. Because of your great compassion, blot out the stain of my sins. Page 16

Psalm 51:10-12 Create in me a clean heart, O God. Renew a loyal spirit within me. 11 Do not banish me from your presence, and don't take your Holy Spirit from me. 12 Restore to me the joy of your salvation, and make me willing to obey you. Page 16

Psalm 77:6-9 when my nights were filled with joyful songs. I search my soul and ponder the difference now. 7 Has the Lord rejected me forever? Will he never again be kind to me? 8 Is his unfailing love gone forever? Have his promises permanently failed? 9 Has God forgotten to be gracious? Has he slammed the door on his compassion? Page 49

Psalm 103:12 He has removed our sins as far from us as the east is from the west. Page 16

Psalm 105:1-5 Give thanks to the LORD and proclaim his greatness. Let the whole world know what he has done. 2 Sing to him; yes, sing his praises. Tell everyone about his wonderful deeds. 3 Exult in his holy name; rejoice, you who worship the LORD. 4 Search for the LORD and for for his strength; continually seek him. 5 Remember the wonders he has performed, his miracles, and the rulings he has given. Page 52

Psalm 109:24 My knees are weak from fasting, and I am skin and bones. Page 46

Psalm 113:1-9 Praise the LORD! Yes, give praise, O servants of the LORD. Praise the name of the LORD! 2 Blessed be the name of the LORD now and forever. 3 Everywhere—from east to west— praise the name of the LORD. 4 For the LORD is high above the nations; his glory is higher than the heavens. 5 Who can be compared with the LORD our God, who is enthroned on high? 6 He stoops to look down on heaven and on earth. 7 He lifts the poor from the dust and the needy from the garbage dump. 8 He sets them among princes, even the princes of his own people! 9 He gives the childless woman a family, making her a happy mother. Praise the LORD! Page 10

Psalm 115:1-18 Not to us, O LORD, not to us, but to your name goes all the glory for your unfailing love and faithfulness. 2 Why let the nations say, "Where is their God?" 3 Our God is in the heavens, and he does as he wishes. 4 Their idols are merely things of silver and gold, shaped by human hands. 5 They have mouths but cannot speak, and eyes but cannot see. 6 They have ears but cannot hear, and noses but cannot smell. 7 They have hands but cannot feel, and feet but cannot walk, and throats but cannot make a sound. 8 And those who make idols are just like them, as are all who trust in them. 9 O Israel, trust the LORD! He is your helper and your shield. 10 O priests, descendants of Aaron, trust the LORD! He is your helper and your shield. 11 All you who fear the LORD, trust the LORD! He is your helper and your shield. 12 The LORD remembers us and will bless us. He will bless the people of Israel and bless the priests, the descendants of Aaron. 13 He will bless those who fear the LORD, both great and lowly 14 May the LORD richly bless both you and your children. 15 May you be blessed by the LORD, who made heaven and earth. 16 The heavens belong to the LORD, but he has given the earth to all humanity. 17 The dead cannot sing praises to the LORD, for they have gone into the silence of the grave. 18 But we can praise the LORD both now and forever! Praise the LORD! Page 10

Psalm 119:11 I have hidden your word in my heart, that I might not sin against you. Pages 49, 52

Psalm 119:38-46 Reassure me of your promise, made to those who fear you. 39 Help me abandon my shameful ways; for your regulations are good. 40 I long to obey your commandments! Renew my life with your goodness. 41 LORD, give me your unfailing love, the salvation that you promised me. 42 Then I can answer those who taunt me, for I trust in your word. 43 Do not snatch your word of truth from me, for your regulations are my only hope.
44 I will keep on obeying your instructions forever and ever. 45 I will walk in freedom, for I have devoted myself to your commandments. 46 I will speak to kings about your laws, and

I will not be ashamed. Page 52

Psalm 119:97-98 Oh, how I love your instructions! I think about them all day long. 98 Your commands make me wiser than my enemies, for they are my constant guide. Page 49

Psalm 139:23-24 Search me, O God, and know my heart; test me and know my anxious thoughts. 24 Point out anything in me that offends you, and lead me along the path of everlasting life. Page 16

Psalm 145:1-13 I will exalt you, my God and King, and praise your name forever and ever. 2 I will praise you every day; yes, I will praise you forever. 3 Great is the LORD! He is most worthy of praise! No one can measure his greatness. 4 Let each generation tell its children of your mighty acts; let them proclaim your power. 5 I will meditate on your majestic, glorious splendor and your wonderful miracles. 6 Your awe-inspiring deeds will be on every tongue; I will proclaim your greatness. 7 Everyone will share the story of your wonderful goodness; they will sing with joy about your righteousness. 8 The LORD is merciful and compassionate, slow to get angry and filled with unfailing love. 9 The LORD is good to everyone. He showers compassion on all his creation. 10 All of your works will thank you, LORD, and your faithful followers will praise you. 11 They will speak of the glory of your kingdom; they will give examples of your power. 12 They will tell about your mighty deeds and about the majesty and glory of your reign. 13 For your kingdom is an everlasting kingdom. You rule throughout all generations. Page 10

Psalm 145:17-21 The LORD is righteous in everything he does; he is filled with kindness. 18 The LORD is close to all who call on him, yes, to all who call on him in truth. 19 He grants the desires of those who fear him; he hears their cries for help and rescues them. 20 The LORD protects all those who love him, but he destroys the wicked. 21 I will praise the LORD, and may everyone on earth bless his holy name forever and ever. Page 10

Revelation 7:12 Amen! Blessing and glory and wisdom and thanksgiving and honor and power and strength belong to our God forever and ever! Amen Page 24

Romans 5:1 Therefore, since we have been made right in God's sight by faith, we have peace with God because of what Jesus Christ our Lord has done for us. Page 49

Romans 6:1-6 Well then, should we keep on sinning so that God can show us more and more of his wonderful grace? 2 Of course not! Since we have died to sin, how can we continue to live in it? 3 Or have you forgotten that when we were joined with Christ Jesus in baptism, we joined him in his death? 4 For we died and were buried with Christ by baptism. And just as Christ was raised from the dead by the glorious power of the Father, now we also may live new lives. 5 Since we have been united with him in his death, we will also be raised to life as he was. 6 We know that our old sinful selves were crucified with Christ so that sin might lose its power in our lives. We are no longer slaves to sin. Page 49

Romans 8:17 And since we are his children, we are his heirs. In fact, together with Christ we are heirs of God's glory. But if we are to share his glory, we must also share his suffering. Page 49

Romans 10:17 So faith comes from hearing, that is, hearing the Good News about Christ. Page 42

1 Samuel 3:9-10 So he said to Samuel, "Go and lie down again, and if someone calls again, say, 'Speak, LORD, your servant is listening.'" So Samuel went back to bed. 10 And the LORD came and called as before, "Samuel! Samuel!" And Samuel replied, "Speak, your servant is listening." Page 52

1 Samuel 7:6 So they gathered at Mizpah and, in a great ceremony, drew water from a well and poured it out before the LORD. They also went without food all day and confessed that they had sinned against the LORD. (It was at Mizpah that Samuel became Israel's judge.) Page 46

2 Samuel 12:16 David begged God to spare the child. He went without food and lay all night on the bare ground. Page 46

1 Thessalonians 1:4 We know, dear brothers and sisters, that God loves you and has chosen you to be his own people. Page 49

2 Timothy 3:16 All Scripture is inspired by God and is useful to teach us what is true and to make us realize what is wrong in our lives. It corrects us when we are wrong and teaches us to do what is right. Page 52

Zechariah 2:5 Then I, myself, will be a protective wall of fire around Jerusalem, says the LORD. And I will be the glory inside the city!'" Page 49

Additional Resources

The following reference section of sources contains information on the subject of prayer, meditation, meditative prayer and fasting for continued and accelerated study of these subjects.

References and Resources

- A Passion for Prayer by Tom Elliff
- ACTS in Prayer by E. W. Price, Jr.
- Christian Meditation the Better Way by Doris Moffat
- Disciple's PrayerLife. T.W. Hunt and Catherine Walker
        Small group 12-week study course and workbook.

- The Doctrine of Prayer, T.W. Hunt
- Experiencing God through Prayer, Madame Guyon
- Fasting and Eating for Health, Joel Fuhrman, M.D.
- Fasting Can Save Your Life, Herbert Shelton
- Fasting, Jentezen Franklin
- God's Chosen Fast, Arthur Wallis
- How to Have a Quiet Time, Warren and Ruth Myers
- How to be a Child of God, David Howell
- Meditative Prayer, Richard J. Foster
- Meditation: A Practical Guide to a Spiritual Discipline,
        Thomas McCormick and Sharon Fish

- Prayer, John White
- Prayer, A Holy Occupation, Oswald Chambers
- Promised Land Living, J. Oswald Sanders
- The Complete Works of E. M. Bounds on Prayer, E. M. Bounds
- The Grace Discipleship Course, Lee C. Turner
        Workbook for course in exchanged life teachings
        Order through www.GraceFellowshipIntl.com

- The Purpose Driven Life: What on Earth am I Here For, Rick Warren
- Praying God's Word, Beth Moore
- The Roots and Fruits of Fasting, Dr. Mary Ruth Swope
- The School of Prayer, Dr. James R. DeLoach
        Radio series of lessons on prayer with Ralph Neighbor on CARPOOL,
        program on station KHCB, 1987.
        Interviews, conversations, memories and Bible study notes taken
        from Dr. James R. DeLoach, the praying warrior, over a thirty-
        year period at Second Baptist Church, Houston, Texas.
- Holy Bible, New Living Translation, Tyndale House

Quiet Time

THIRTY-ONE DAY DEVOTIONAL

I am in my Father, and you are in me, and I am in you. John 14:20

The following section contains 31 pages of illustrations, instructions and verses designed to pave the way to a more abundant life for you as a child of God. Carefully review each message on a daily basis. Reading only one per day allows you to focus, think, concentrate and meditate on the content for each devotional. Prayerfully do this as instructed and God will transform your life.

Day 1 — THE OTHER SIDE OF JORDAN

Each of us have within ourselves, a longing to be with our heavenly Father. The natural father we have on this earth will never measure up or meet our spiritual needs. We devise many ways to get to the other side and have everlasting peace with our heavenly Father, but none work. Only when we surrender to Jesus Christ and trust Him, can we find a way to be with our real Father. Jesus is the only way; trust and obey.

Yet God has made everything beautiful for his own time. He has planted eternity in the human heart, but even so, people cannot see the whole scope of God's work from beginning to end. Ecclesiastes 3:11 NLT

Day 2 — GOD AS MAN

God became a man and was born of a woman so we could identify with Him and form a relationship with Him. One difference; He did not sin. We as humans inherited Adam's sinful tendencies and have gone our own way. God came to earth to change all that and arrange for us to be forgiven and form a union with Him. Jesus as human and divine did it His way and on His terms. When He finished His ministry, He gave His life for us on the cross. The blood He shed washed away the sins of each of us once and for all, so that we could have a perfect sinless union with our Father. When He died, we died. He is in us and we are in Him forever.

For in Christ lives all the fullness of God in a human body. Colossians 2:9 NLT

You must have the same attitude that Christ Jesus had. Though he was God, he did not think of equality with God as something to cling to. Instead, he gave up his divine privileges; he took the humble position of a slave and was born as a human being. When he appeared in human form, he humbled himself in obedience to God and died a criminal's death on a cross. Philippians 2:5-8 NLT

So the Word became human and made his home among us. He was full of unfailing love and faithfulness. And we have seen his glory, the glory of the Father's one and only Son. John 1:14 NLT

61

Day 3 — HALLELUJAH! WHAT A SAVIOR!

"Man of Sorrows!" what a name. For the Son of God who came Ruined sinners to reclaim. Hallelujah! What a Savior!

Bearing shame and scoffing rude, In my place condemned He stood; Sealed my pardon with His blood. Hallelujah! What a Savior!

Guilty, vile, and helpless we; Spotless Lamb of God was He; "Full atonement!" can it be? Hallelujah! What a Savior!

Lifted up was He to die; "It is finished!" was His cry; Now in heaven exalted high, Hallelujah! What a Savior!

When He comes, our glorious King, All His ransomed home to bring, Then anew this song we'll sing, Hallelujah! What a Savior!

"Hallelujah! What a Savior!" Phillip P. Bliss

Confession, surrender, yielding and submission are all terms we must consider when we come to the end of self and make up our minds to trust Jesus as our Lord, God, Savior and Life. Acceptance of Him and His way of doing things is a form of surrender. We give up our independent way to have His life. The old gives way to the new. The old self has died and we are cleansed and made righteous with a new spiritual nature.

Because of the weakness of your human nature, I am using the illustration of slavery to help you understand all this. Previously, you let yourselves be slaves to impurity and lawlessness, which led ever deeper into sin. Now you must give yourselves to be slaves of righteous living so that you will become holy. Romans 6:19 NLT

Then Jesus said to his disciples, "If any of you wants to be my follower, you must turn from your selfish ways, take up your cross and follow me. If you try to hang on to your old life, you will lose it. But if you give up your life for my sake, you will save it." Matthew 16:24-25 NLT

Day 5 — LEAVE THE JUNK WITH JESUS

On our way to peace with our heavenly Father, we dump our garbage off. We humbly ask Jesus to take it. He graciously accepts it as He has taken on the sins of mankind once and for all. Our junk of the past, present and future is buried at the foot of the cross where it will remain forever.

And what do you benefit if you gain the whole world but lose your own soul? Is anything worth more than your soul? Matthew 16:26 NLT

All to Jesus I surrender, All to Him I freely give. I will ever love and trust Him, in His presence daily live. I surrender all. ("I Surrender All," hymn by Judson W. Van DeVenter)

Day 6 — THE END OF SELF

We reach a point in life where we can no longer carry the baggage of past generations and our own as well. If we have a heart for God, we trust and believe and He (Father, Son, and Holy Spirit) comes to live in us. With that comes eternal life, the life that has no beginning and no end. It is forever in the past and forever in the future. Possessing eternal life allows us to go to the cross of Christ 2000 years ago where we were crucified with Christ and the old self died. (Galatians 2:20) We are born again as new creatures in Christ! Hallelujah! What a Savior!

Yes, Adam's one sin brings condemnation for everyone, but Christ's one act of righteousness brings a right relationship with God and new life for everyone. Because one person disobeyed God, many became sinners. But because one other person obeyed God, many will be made righteous. Romans 5:18-19 NLT

Just as everyone dies because we all belong to Adam, everyone who belongs to Christ will be given a new life. 1 Corinthians 15:22 NLT

And Christ lives within you, so even though your body will die because of sin, the Spirit gives you life because you have been made right with God. Romans 8:10 NLT

"My old self has been crucified with Christ. It is no longer I who live, but Christ lives in me. So I live in this earthly body by trusting in the Son of God, who loved me and gave Himself for me." (Galatians 2:20 NLT)

Our old self is what is left over after the spiritual death of Adam in the Garden of Eden. There isn't much, but that self has to die so you can receive the Spirit of God and become a new creation. It happens when you trust Jesus as Lord of your life and savior of your soul. Appropriation of this truth is the cornerstone of abundant living on this earth. Your new spiritual life begins and your old self dies with Jesus on the cross. When He came back to life, so did you. You are born again! You will now live forever as a child of God in Christ and Christ in you.

For we died and were buried with Christ by baptism. And just as Christ was raised from the dead by the glorious power of the Father, now we also may live new lives. Romans 6:4 NLT

Day 8 — OUR CO-CRUCIFIXION, CO-BURIAL, AND CO-RESURRECTION IN CHRIST

We were crucified with Christ (Galatians 2:20) buried with Him (Romans 6:4) and resurrected with Him (Romans 6:5).

For we died and were buried with Christ by baptism. And just as Christ was raised from the dead by the glorious power of the Father, now we may also live new lives. Since we have been united with him in his death, we will also be raised to life as he was. We know that our old sinful selves were crucified with Christ so that sin might lose its power in our lives. We are no longer slaves to sin. Romans 6:4-6 NLT

And since we died with Christ, we know we will also live with Him. Romans 6:8 NLT

For you were buried with Christ when you were baptized. And with him you were raised to new life because you trusted the mighty power of God, who raised Christ from the dead. You were dead because of your sins and because your sinful nature was not yet cut away. Then God made you alive with Christ, for He forgave all our sins. He canceled the record of the charges against us and took it away by nailing it to the cross. Colossians 2:12-14 NLT

67

It might be difficult to imagine that we could be sitting with our Savior Jesus Christ beside our Father in heaven. But that is just where we are. He is seated at the right hand of the Father and we are there with Him. We are in Christ and that will never change. When He died, we died. As He lives, we live. He sits at the right hand of the Father and so do we. We are in Christ!

For he raised us up from the dead along with Christ and seated us with him in the heavenly realms because we are united with Christ Jesus. Ephesians 2:6 NLT

Since you have been raised to new life with Christ, set your sights on the realities of heaven, where Christ sits in the place of honor at God's right hand. Think about the things of heaven, not the things of earth. For you died to this life, and your real life is hidden with Christ in God. Colossians 3:1–3 NLT

Why is it that so few enjoy the abundant life? Do we seek an easier softer way? Do we fear the hardships of living a Christ-centered life. Trying to live our lives for Christ is impossible and filled with pitfalls and failure every step of the way. Remember we died with Him on the cross (Galatians 2:20) and our role now is to allow Him to live His life through us. That gateway to life is very narrow and only a few ever find it. Surrender is the only way. Give up the fight and He will take you on your spiritual journey.

You can enter God's kingdom only through the narrow gate. The highway to hell is broad and its gate is wide for the many who choose that way. But the gateway to life is very narrow and the road is difficult, and only a few ever find it. Matthew 7:13-14 NLT

Day 11 — ACCEPTANCE MEANS SURRENDER

Accepting the love of Jesus motivates us to surrender to Him. Give your heart, mind, will, and emotions over to the Lord Jesus Christ and let Him direct your life. He died for you and you died with him. He now seeks to live his life in you and through you to expand the Kingdom using your circle of friends, family and acquaintances. His life becomes your source of living.

Yes, I am the vine and you are the branches. Those who remain in me, and I in them, will produce much fruit. For apart from me you can do nothing. Anyone who does not remain in me is thrown away like a useless branch and withers. Such branches are gathered into a pile to be burned. But if you remain in me and my words remain in you, you may ask for anything you want, and it will be granted! When you produce much fruit, you are my true disciples. This brings great glory to my Father.
John 15:5-8 NLT

Changes start when you first come to know Jesus Christ. The Spirit of God literally comes to live in you and you become spiritually alive. The new Spirit of God dwelling within begins to change you and you become more like Christ. You have a new identity as a child of the living God!

Don't copy the behavior and customs of this world, but let God transform you into a new person by changing the way you think. Then you will learn to know God's will for you, which is good and pleasing and perfect. Romans 12:2 NLT

Since you have heard about Jesus and have learned the truth that comes from him, throw off your old sinful nature and your former way of life, which is corrupted by lust and deception. Instead, let the Spirit renew your thoughts and attitudes. Put on your new nature, created to be like God — truly righteous and holy Ephesians 4:21-24 NLT

Day 13 — THE FAMILY OF GOD

Include the Lord Jesus in every facet of your life. He desires to be your counselor, friend, prayer partner, companion, husband, brother and Father. Love Him with all your heart, mind and soul. He is your life. There is nothing of value without Him. You are nothing without Him.

You didn't choose me. I chose you. I appointed you to go and produce lasting fruit, so that the Father will give you whatever you ask for, using my name. John 15:16 NLT

But to all who believed him and accepted him, he gave the right to become children of God. They are reborn—not with a physical birth resulting from human passion or pain, but a birth that comes from God. John 1:12-13 NLT

And I will be your Father, and you will be my sons and daughters, says the Lord Almighty. 2 Corinthians 6:18 NLT

Day 14 — GOOD-BYE TO ADAM

For, "Who can know the Lord's thoughts? Who knows enough to teach him?" But we understand these things, for we have the mind of Christ. 1 Corinthians 2:16

The sooner we can understand that we have become children of God, the sooner we will be able to grow in Christ. Then we will be able to develop the character qualities God intended us to have when He adopted us into His family. We will be able to say good-bye to the family of Adam and hello to the family of God. Good-bye Adam, hello Jesus. After all, we are now new creatures with the Spirit of the Living God living within.

When Adam sinned, sin entered the world. Adam's sin brought death, so death spread to everyone, for everyone sinned. Romans 5:12 NLT

For the sin of this one man, Adam, caused death to rule over many. But even greater is God's wonderful grace and his gift of righteousness, for all who receive it will live in triumph over sin and death through this one man, Jesus Christ. Romans 5:17 NLT

Day 15 — GIFTS FROM GOD

The Holy Spirit imparts to you at least one special spiritual gift when you become a child of God and a spiritual creature. The broader categories of these gifts are; prophecy, serving, teaching, exhortation, giving, organizing, and mercy.

A spiritual gift is a supernatural ability to accomplish something that is not within you and it is a means of reminding you of your new spiritual nature. It is a means by which God intends for you to help others and to bring others to know and trust Jesus. Chances are, the gift you receive is closely related to something you already do or desire to do in service to the Kingdom of God. As you mature in your trust and knowledge of Jesus, you might discover one or more additional gifts God has provided for you.

There are different kinds of spiritual gifts, but the same Spirit is the source of them all. There are different kinds of service, but we serve the same Lord. God works in different ways, but it is the same God who does the work in all of us. A spiritual gift is given to each of us so we can help each other. To one person the Spirit gives the ability to give wise advice; to another the same Spirit gives a message of special knowledge. The same Spirit gives great faith to another, and to someone else the one Spirit gives the gift of healing. He gives one person the power to perform miracles, and another the ability to prophesy. He gives someone else the ability to discern whether a message is from the Spirit of God or from another spirit. Still another person is given the ability to speak in unknown languages, while another is given the ability to interpret what is being said. It is the one and only Spirit who distributes all these gifts. He alone decides which gift each person should have. 1 Corinthians 12:4-11 NLT

74

Day 16 — WRITE IT DOWN AND GIVE IT TO JESUS

We all have things in our past that we wish we had never done. One way to deal with it permanently is to make an inventory, write it down and hand it over to Him. Jesus dealt with these sins once and for all at the cross when He died. Understand when you trusted Jesus as your Lord and God, you gained His eternal life and died with Him. All of the garbage you picked up in your past life is buried at the cross. He died to relieve you of all that junk! Give all to Him now, any regrets and guilt, and be done with it forever.

This means that anyone who belongs to Christ has become a new person. The old life is gone; a new life has begun! 2 Corinthians 5:17 NLT

And this is the secret: Christ lives in you. This gives you assurance of sharing his glory Colossians 1:27 NLT

When we become children of God, we start thinking a new way. We are being transformed because we have been given the mind of Christ and Jesus lives in us. We just have to start thinking of what our true identity is now. Practice saying and thinking the following, and believe that your heavenly Father is always with you.

Set your minds on things above, not on earthly things. For you died, and your life is now hidden with Christ in God. Colossians 3:2-3 NIV

So we don't look at the troubles we can see now; rather, we fix our gaze on things that cannot be seen. For the things we see now will soon be gone, but the things we cannot see will last forever. 2 Corinthians 4:18 NLT

For God has not given us a spirit of fear and timidity, but of power, love, and self-discipline. 2 Timothy 1:7 NLT

So letting your sinful nature control your mind leads to death. But letting the Spirit control your mind leads to life and peace. Romans 8:6 NLT

For all who are led by the Spirit of God are children of God.
Romans 8:14 NLT

For, "Who can know the Lord's thoughts? Who knows enough to teach Him?" But we understand these things, for we have the mind of Christ. 1 Corinthians 2:16 NLT

We all could benefit from an accountability partner. That is someone we can pour out our triumphs and sorrows to, trusting that we will be heard and truth will emerge from the conversation. When you are sincere, the Lord Jesus will always be present to listen and respond directly through a Christian friend.

Confess your sins to each other and pray for each other so that you may be healed. The earnest prayer of a righteous person has great power and produces wonderful results. James 5:16 NLT

But if we confess our sins to him, he is faithful and just to forgive us our sins and to cleanse us from all wickedness (unrighteousness).
1 John 1:9 NLT

Day 19 — OUR FATHER

You are never alone when you seek your Father in heaven. Call out to Jesus. Practice His presence and seek His companionship. Experience His love and protection. He desires to devote His life to you and live His life through you. You are a co-heir with your elder brother Jesus.

So now Jesus and the ones he makes holy have the same Father. That is why Jesus is not ashamed to call them his brothers and sisters.
Hebrews 2:11 NLT

Father to the fatherless, defender of widows — this is God, whose dwelling is holy. God places the lonely in families; he sets the prisoners free and gives them joy. But he makes the rebellious live in a sun-scorched land.
Psalm 68:5-6 NLT

But to all who believed him and accepted him, he gave the right to become children of God. They are reborn — not with a physical birth resulting from human passion or pain, but a birth that comes from God. John 1:12-13 NLT

Never hesitate to pray with or for someone else, giving thanks to your heavenly Father. God is always there to love, comfort and to intercede for you. There is no better way to express the love of God to a friend than through prayer. You can say things in prayer that only the Lord Jesus can interpret for you. And He is always there to give you the words to say and the thoughts to express.

And they will pray for you with deep affection because of the deep overflowing grace God has given to you. Thank God for this gift too wonderful for words. 2 Corinthians 9:14-15 NLT

And the Holy Spirit helps us in our weakness. For example, we don't know what God wants us to pray for. But the Holy Spirit prays for us in groanings that cannot be expressed in words. And the Father who knows all hearts knows what the Spirit is saying, for the Spirit pleads for us believers in harmony with God's own will. Romans 8:26-27 NLT

Create the habit of being sensitive to His presence. Understand the Lord Jesus Christ is not just God on an as-needed basis, but He seeks to be with you day and night, participating in all that you do. Look for reasons to glorify and praise Him in prayers of thanksgiving whoever you are with and wherever you go. He is the Living God of your life and indeed He is your life. Include Him in everything that happens. He is your friend, companion, and confidante. When you are constantly thanking God, you are never thanking your self.

Always be joyful. Never stop praying. Be thankful in all circumstances for this is God's will for you who belong to Christ Jesus.
I Thessalonians 5:16-18 NLT

And give thanks for everything to God the Father in the name of our Lord Jesus Christ. Ephesians 5:20 NLT

Can it be? Does Christ, the Living God, really desire to live his life in us and through us?

The Lord Jesus Christ wants to live His life through each of us all the time. He seeks to show Himself through us to others we know and with whom we associate. As children of God, we can show Jesus in everything we as Christians do. As believers, we are or should be Christ on display

---

And I will give you a new heart, and I will put a new spirit in you. I will take out your stony, stubborn heart and give you a tender, responsive heart. And I will put my Spirit in you so that you will follow my decrees and be careful to obey my regulations. Ezekiel 36:26-27 NLT

And this is the secret: Christ lives in you. This gives you assurance of sharing His glory Colossians 1:27 NLT

Day 23 — JESUS LIVING HIS LIFE THROUGH US

It helps to understand that when we came to know Jesus Christ and trusted Him to take over our will and our lives, we literally invited the Living God into our being. In fact, His Spirit entered when we were adopted into the family of God and we became spiritually alive. That is how we died; got eternal life, and cannot die again. (Galatians 2:20) Our physical bodies will expire, but our souls / personalities will live forever. In the interim, Jesus Christ seeks to be in every part of our lives every minute of the day. He wants all of us to have a good life, an abundant life on this earth while we are waiting to go home. He needs to use all of us to reach others to build the kingdom.

For we are God's masterpiece. He has created us anew in Christ Jesus, so we can do the good things he planned for us long ago.
Ephesians 2:10 NLT

Our lives are a Christ-like fragrance rising up to God. But this fragrance is perceived differently by those who are saved and by those who are perishing. 2 Corinthians 2:15 NLT

Day 24 — PORTABLE PRAYER

ACTS in Prayer by E. W. Price, Jr. contains a useful prayer that is portable enough to carry around and use anytime and anyplace.

A = **Adoration and Praise.** Tell God you love Him.

C = **Confession.** Keep short accounts. Confess to Him and admit to yourself today's wrongdoings.

T = **Thankfulness.** You could spend all day thanking Him for everything He has provided for you. (food, shelter, transportation)

S = **Seeking.** When you have cleaned up and feel better about yourself, feel free to start asking for yourself and others. Keep the asking on a spiritual level for best results. (salvation, forgiveness, amends to others)

Begin the prayer by addressing God as your Heavenly Father and end by praying in the name of Jesus. Finally use Amen or "So be it!" Use A.C.T.S. in between. Practice this simple acronym and you will find yourself readily praying as you drive, work, prepare for a task, or prior to speaking anything. You will find yourself always saying the right thing.

I tell you, you can pray for anything, and if you believe that you've received it, it will be yours. But when you are praying, first forgive anyone you are holding a grudge against, so that your Father in heaven will forgive your sins too. Mark 11:24-25 NLT

83

Day 25 — PRAY FOR THE LOST

Remember in your prayers, those who are lost. God has put at least ten persons in your heart that He wants to reach through you. Chances are you already know them as friends, co-workers, and family members. Prepare for your mission by praying for the salvation of each. Pray that they will be open when you tell them your story of how you became a child of God. It is not by your ability, but the person, the power and the presence of the Living God, Jesus Christ, seeking to live His life through you. Be available.

I urge you, first of all, to pray for all people. Ask God to help them; intercede on their behalf, and give thanks for them...This is good and pleases God our Savior, who wants everyone to be saved and to understand the truth.
1 Timothy 2:1, 3-4 NLT

For the Son of Man came to seek and save those who are lost.
Luke 19:10 NLT

But you will receive power when the Holy Spirit comes upon you. And you will be my witnesses, telling people about me everywhere---in Jerusalem, throughout Judea, in Samaria, and to the ends of the earth.
Acts 1:8 NLT

Remember the least, the last and the lost in your prayers. Pray they come to the end of self. Pray for proclaimers to go into the prisons and teach about freedom in Christ.

Remember those in prison, as if you were there yourself. Remember also those being mistreated, as if you felt their pain in your own bodies. Hebrews 13:3 NLT

You will open the eyes of the blind. You will free the captives from prison, releasing those who sit in dark dungeons. Isaiah 42:7 NLT

For I was hungry, and you fed me. I was thirsty, and you gave me a drink. I was a stranger, and you invited me into your home. I was naked and you gave me clothing. I was sick, and you cared for me. I was in prison and you visited me. Matthew 25:35-36 NLT

Day 27 — CHRISTIAN MEDITATION

Meditation in the Christian context is focusing on, thinking about, and reviewing God's Word. By meditating on Bible verses and passages, we start a process of eliminating wrong thoughts, habits, and attitudes. We begin to replace those thoughts with godly thinking and biblical teachings. Deep concentration on the Word of God will change our thinking and how we look at life.

Then the angel showed me a river with the water of life, clear as crystal, flowing from the throne of God and of the Lamb. It flowed down the center of the main street. On each side of the river grew a tree of life, bearing twelve crops of fruit, with a fresh crop each month. The leaves were used for medicine to heal the nations. Revelation 22:1-2 NLT

Fix your thoughts on what is true, and honorable, and right, and pure, and lovely, and admirable. Think about the things that are excellent and worthy of praise. Keep putting into practice all you learned and received from me — everything you heard from me and saw me doing. Then the God of peace will be with you. Philippians 4:8-9 NLT

I heard a shout from the throne, saying, "Look, God's home is now among his people! He will live with them and they will be his people. God himself will be with them. He will wipe every tear from their eyes, and there will be no more death or sorrow or crying or pain. All these things are gone forever." Revelation 21:3-4 NLT

Try group meditation some time when a few friends or like-minded people are gathered or make the meeting a regular event. Pick a spiritual subject like surrender, confession, forgiveness, or unconditional love. Open the time in prayer and ask the Lord Jesus to speak through each of you on the subject designated. You will get new insights as you find yourself contemplating (meditating) on the subject at hand.

For where two or three are gathered together as my followers, I am there among them. Matthew 18:20 NLT

Finally, all of you should be of one mind. Sympathize with each other. Love each other as brothers and sisters. Be tenderhearted, and keep a humble attitude. 1 Peter 3:8 NLT

It is important to look at fasting as an aid to worship, prayer, and meditation. Jesus was baptized by John and then went into the wilderness where He fasted for forty days. He spoke Scripture and His strength came from meditating on the Word of God. Fasting is mentioned many times in the Bible as a means of healing ourselves spiritually and physically There are many types of fasting and durations, and all will help in your concentration, focus and problem solving. Jesus is our model.

Then Jesus was led by the Spirit into the wilderness to be tempted there by the devil. For forty days and forty nights he fasted and became very hungry During that time the devil came and said to him, "If you are the Son of God, tell these stones to become loaves of bread." But Jesus told him, "No, the scriptures say, 'People do not live by bread alone, but by every word that comes from the mouth of God.'" Matthew 4:1-4 NLT

So after more fasting and prayer, the men laid their hands on them and sent them on their way Acts 13:3 NLT

And there by the Ahava Canal, I gave orders for all of us to fast and humble ourselves before our God. We prayed that he would give us a safe journey and protect us, our children, and our goods as we traveled. Ezra 8:21 NLT

Day 30 — GUARD YOUR HEARTS

It is one thing to be a child of God. It is another to be in the Devil's family. But that would be before you surrendered your life to Christ. Satan comes disguised as an angel of light at times. So guard you hearts, call out to Jesus and seek His protection. We are either children of God or we are children of Satan. We are either children of the light or children of the darkness.

His peace will guard your hearts and minds as you live in Christ Jesus. Philippians 4:7 NLT

Guard your hearts above all else, for it determines the course of your life. Proverbs 4:23 NLT

If we had forgotten the name of our God or spread our hands in prayer to foreign gods, God would certainly have known it, for he knows the secrets of every heart. Psalm 44:20-21 NLT

Dear children, keep away from anything that might take God's place in your hearts. 1 John 5:21 NLT

Dear children, do not let anything lead you astray. He who does what is right is righteous, just as he is righteous. He who does what is sinful is of the devil, because the devil has been sinning from the beginning. The reason the Son of God appeared was to destroy the devil's work. 1 John 3:7-8 NIV

And no wonder, for even Satan disguises himself as an angel of light. 2 Corinthians 11:14 NASB

Day 31 — MAKING THE SONG COME TRUE

The mind and how we use it can be the most influential aspect of our personality. Our hearts, emotions, and will are dependent of what we think about and what we allow to enter our minds. Now we are eternally in Christ and He is eternally in us as we have become spiritual creatures. Our finite thinking and still-maturing minds can hold us captive to the lies of Satan. He prowls around this earth where our physical presence remains in these earth-suits until Jesus comes, but we have the victory!

So we don't look at the troubles we can see now; rather, we fix our gaze on things that cannot be seen. For the things we see now will soon be gone, but the things we cannot see will last forever. 2 Corinthians 4:18 NLT

And we believers also groan, even though we have the Holy Spirit within us as a foretaste of future glory, for we long for our bodies to be released from sin and suffering. We, too, wait with eager hope for the day when God will give us our full rights as his adopted children, including the new bodies he has promised us. We were given this hope when we were saved. Romans 8:23-24 NLT

Set your minds on things above, not on earthly things. For you died, and your life is now hidden with Christ in God. Colossians 3:2-3 NIV

For we died and were buried with Christ by baptism. And just as Christ was raised from the dead by the glorious power of the Father, now we also live new lives. Since we have been united with him in his death, we will also be raised to life as he was. We know that our old sinful selves were crucified with Christ so that sin might lose its power in our lives. We are no longer slaves to sin. Romans 6:4-6 NLT

For he raised us from the dead along with Christ and seated us with him in the heavenly realms because we are united with Christ Jesus. Ephesians 2:6 NLT

Many have had close calls through-out their lives and wondered how they survived. They tried successfully and unsuccessfully to balance material things in their lives believing they were smart, lucky or indestructible. They never understood that God knew their hearts and had sent angels to protect them until the time they would make a decision for Him. Therefore, angels are only servants-who will inherit salvation. Hebrews 1:14 NLT. Even before he made the world, God loved us and chose us in Christ to be holy and without fault in his eyes. Ephesians 1:4 NLT. For everyone has sinned; we all fall short of God's glorious standard. Romans 3:23 NLT When we were utterly helpless, Christ came at just the right time and died for us sinners. Romans 5:6 NLT

We know that our old sinful selves were crucified with Christ so that sin might lose its power in our lives. We are no longer slaves to sin. For he who has died is freed from sin. Romans 6:6-7 NLT. So you should consider
yourself dead to the power of sin and alive to God through Christ Jesus. Romans 6:11 NLT. We know that God's children do not make a habit of sinning, for God holds them securely, and the evil one cannot touch them. We know that we are children of God and that the world around us is under the control of the evil one. 1 John 5:18-19 NLT

Don't you realize that your body is the temple of the Holy Spirit, who lives in you and was given to you by God? You do not belong to yourself, for God bought you with a high price.
So you must honor God with your body 1Corinthians 6:19, 20. NLT
We are carefully joined together in him, becoming a holy temple for the Lord. Ephesians 2:21 NLT

Do not conform any longer to the pattern of the world, but be transformed by the renewing of your mind. Then you will be able to test and approve what God's will is---his good, pleasing and perfect will. Romans 12:2 NIV. My dear children, I am writing this to you so that you will not sin. But if anyone does sin, we have an advocate who pleads our case before the Father. He is Jesus Christ, the one who is truly righteous. He himself is the sacrifice that atones for our sins---and not only our sins, but the sins of all the world. 1John 2:1-2 NLT.

So the trouble is not with the law, for it is spiritual and good. The trouble is with me, for I am all too human, a slave to sin. I don't really understand myself, for I want to do what is right, but I don't do it. Instead, I do what I hate. But if I don't know that what I am doing is wrong; it is sin living in me that does it. And I know that nothing good lives in me, that is in my sinful nature. I want to do what is right, but I can't. I want to do what is good, but I don't. I don't want to do what is wrong, but I do it anyway. But if I do what I don't want to do, I am not really the one doing wrong; it is sin living in me that does it. Romans 7:14-25 NLT

93

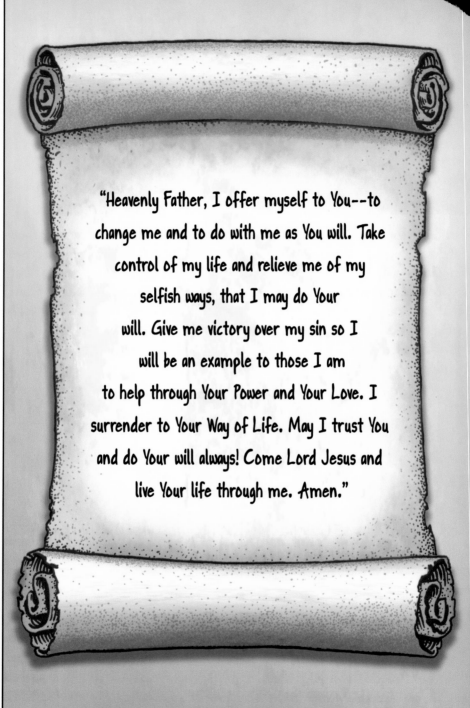

"Heavenly Father, I offer myself to You--to change me and to do with me as You will. Take control of my life and relieve me of my selfish ways, that I may do Your will. Give me victory over my sin so I will be an example to those I am to help through Your Power and Your Love. I surrender to Your Way of Life. May I trust You and do Your will always! Come Lord Jesus and live Your life through me. Amen."

M000073632

Political Wives
Veiled Lives

Political Wives
Veiled Lives

Joyce Schuck

Madison Books
Lanham • New York • London

Published by Madison Books
4720 Boston Way
Lanham, Maryland 20706

3 Henrietta Street
London WC2E 8LU England

Distributed by National Book Network

The paper used in this publication meets the minimum
requirements of American National Standard for
Information Sciences—Permanence of Paper for
Printed Library Materials, ANSI Z39.48–1984. ∞™
Manufactured in the United States of America.

Library of Congress Cataloging-in-Publication Data

Schuck, Joyce
Political wives, veiled lives / Joyce Schuck.
p.   cm.
Includes index.
1. Electioneering—United States.
2. Politicians' wives—United States.   I. Title.
JK1971.S38   1991
324.7'0973—dc20   91–9795 CIP

ISBN 0–8191–8068–8

British Cataloging in Publication Information Available

To Annie

Contents

Introduction   **ix**

1. On the Campaign Trail   **1**

Hectic pace and scheduling. Speech-making.
Demands placed on the political wife and her family

2. Rules of the Game   **35**

Dealing with the press. The merging of politics
with the worlds of entertainment and mass
communications. Illusions and perceptions of
political power

3. All the People You Meet Along the Way   **75**

Media consultants, campaign managers, etc. Staff
members. Friends—old and new. Users and abusers.
Designing women

4. From White Gloves to Bare Hands   **109**

Historical perspective. The political system's
expectations of the political wife

5. Whose Life Is This Anyway?   **147**

The rewards of political life. Emotional and physical
effects of political life on the wives of politicians

6. No More Pizza at Midnight   **187**
   Experiencing the loss of an election

Afterword   **209**
   Includes a survival guide for political wives
Index   **219**

Introduction

During my husband's 1986 gubernatorial campaign in Colorado, I discovered that politics essentially mirrors the entertainment world and is a system not yet in sync with women's evolution. Actually, the politician has taken on star status, and politics has become a game of illusions. In many cases, the election's victor, regrettably, is the politician who best portrays the image.

In 1976, Virginia's Senator John Warner described what was in store for his future bride, Elizabeth Taylor, when she stepped into the role of the political wife—campaigning endlessly, shaking thousands of hands, smiling, and kissing babies, whatever it would take to win the 1978 GOP nomination at the state convention. To appeal to voters, Warner intended to present himself as "a simple country farmer. She would be the farmer's wife."[1] Though Liz, in the year and a half that she campaigned for her husband, could never have been described as "the farmer's wife," she certainly deserved another Oscar for her performance. Indeed, the life of the political wife takes on the aura of a theatrical production the moment she dons her political hat and becomes a partner in the whistle-stop masquerade.

When I became a political wife, I assumed that the political system would reflect the progress women have made in their struggle to achieve personal and economic independence. Instead, I was appalled to learn that the wife of a politician is expected to present herself as a supportive "traditional" wife who stays at home raising the children, one who possesses no ambitions of her own except to dutifully subordinate herself for the sake of her husband's career. The system also demands that the political wife shout her strength of character with confidence, but with her mouth closed! Though many former first ladies fit this profile, Pat Nixon will be remembered for best epitomizing the role of the dutiful wife, discounting herself right up to and including President Nixon's forced resignation from public office.

In contrast, the general public encourages the political wife to present herself as the strong, independent type with her own career direction, an autonomous or "modern" individual whose own ambitions only complement her husband's and in no way will be sacrificed for his political ambitions. Many of the wives of the 1988 presidential contenders fit this profile; among them were lawyers, writers, activists, and even a cabinet officeholder.

The political wife faces a real dilemma. She must contend with the expectations of the political system and those of the general public, as well as her own personal expectations and ambitions. Consequently, she can easily fall into the trap of trying to be all things to all people. If she decides to play by the political system's rules, the erosion of both her identity and her personal ambitions and expectations will most definitely occur to some degree. Adding insult to injury, she will be known as the "wife of." And because the political system is such a direct and visible reflection of our lives at the most personal level, all of the political family's energies go toward convincing the public that all is well in politicaland.

Some political wives find it easier to adopt Scarlett

O'Hara's philosophy and worry about things tomorrow rather than resisting the system's rules. Indeed, a number of political wives even have suggested that they can be themselves when the election is over. But tomorrow comes too soon, bringing along with it a disturbing portrait of a woman whose evolving sense of self may be suffocated by a process and a system that is neither reality-based nor in sync with the changing times. Only the political establishment sets such unrealistic expectations for women while totally discounting their worth.

After an 18-month-long political campaign and my husband's defeat in the primary election, I was afforded the opportunity to reflect on my experience as a political wife. A good deal of my time was spent distancing myself from a political system that demands the participation of the politician's spouse but disregards her opinions and contributions—and her right to pursue her own ambitions. My time and purpose no longer were oriented around a series of political events or toward upholding an image, whether it be his or mine. And our life, previously chronicled in the newspapers, again was private.

Despite this self-imposed retirement from things "political," dealing with the loss evoked a multitude of emotions within me—anger, sadness, and frustration being the most common. I was angry with myself for allowing my participation in my husband's campaign to nearly destroy my individuality. I was frustrated with the political system for requiring that women subordinate themselves. Sometimes I laughed about the absurdity of it all, which only rekindled my emotions. Moreover, I was confused about why and how political wives allow the situation to exist, even questioning whether my experience as a political wife might be unique. And I didn't know what, if anything, to do about it.

Needing to take a closer look at the entire process of

campaigning, I began reading the journal I had compiled during my husband's campaign. Journal keeping was my outlet after those 18-hour days when Steve and I were either separated or too tired to talk to each other. In a world where honesty and friendship are precious, rare commodities, the journal became my unconditional friend. As the campaign progressed, my moments of joy, sadness, concern, and optimism were recorded. The hard work, months of planning, little sleep, and constant travel which are the reality of campaigning were also recorded. Initially, all those unexpressed concerns and frustrations found their way onto the pages of the journal. My very first entry included these words: "I neglected to introduce myself. I'm the candidate's wife. You know—Ole What'sername. . . ."

In time, some very strong feelings and statements began cropping up on the journal pages regarding the political system and the political wife's role in it. Too, my journal entries reflected that the more involved I became in my husband's campaign the wider the gap between reality and illusion. Not knowing if I was alone with my thoughts, I decided to talk to other women who were married to political candidates and incumbents, women who live, or have lived, the same life I had only briefly experienced.

At first, all my efforts were directed toward meeting and informally interviewing the wives of senators, congressmen, and governors. Later, the opportunity to interview Native American first ladies was made available to me as well. My sense was, despite the fact that Native Americans have a one-party system, these first ladies must encounter similar experiences in their election process. Therefore, I enthusiastically accepted my self-imposed challenge.

I was determined to meet with equal numbers of Democrats and Republicans. Although the reader will find that there are conservatives, liberals, Republicans, Democrats, and Native Americans all represented here, my efforts to uphold that democratic ideal of equal representation quickly proved to be unnecessary. It became clear, after several interviews, that a woman's political affiliation has little to do with her thoughts and feelings about being a political wife. First Lady Barbara Bush; Marilyn Quayle, wife of the U.S. vice president; first lady of the Navajo nation, Wanda MacDonald; first lady of the Zuni nation, Virginia Lewis; Dottie Lamm, wife of the former Democratic governor of Colorado, Dick Lamm; Joanne Kemp, wife of Jack Kemp, former Republican congressman and currently Secretary of Housing and Urban Development; and Wren Wirth, wife of Democratic Senator Tim Wirth, are just a few of the numerous political wives interviewed.

I expected other women to be as interested in relating the political wife's story as I was. I expected others to welcome and encourage my attempts to sympathetically portray the political wife. And I expected the women to be candid. In many instances, what I encountered was a wall of suspicion. Very few of the political wives who agreed to meet with me were candid about their personal and political lives. Most were extremely careful not to damage their own or their husbands' image. Having been a political wife, I could understand their caution; however, it didn't prevent me from wanting to remove those protective barriers the women appeared to be hiding behind. In fact, those guarded encounters only deepened my resolve to find a way to present a realistic portrait of both the political wife and her bittersweet political life.

It wasn't until after all the interviews were completed and my notes were pored over again that I discovered fragility behind the image. Some women had a friend or staff person join us for the interview to provide encouragement and support. Usually, this extra person would assure the guest "reporter" of the political wife's humility. Often, the administrative aide or friend would answer questions, give affirmative nods of her head, or, on occasion, intimate, "She won't tell you how terrific she is, so I'm here to do that for her. Now put that in your book." These encounters revealed the insecurity and guardedness of many political wives when in the presence of a "political reporter."

Still, similarities surfaced. For instance, all the women were raised with traditional values, desired to take more time for themselves, and had strong personalities. The viewpoints of all the women were deeply rooted in their various generational experiences. Wives of the pre-fifties generation, for example, believe women belong in the home, even after the children are grown and gone. The majority of wives from the fifties generation are caught between wanting and/or having a career and being "just a housewife." The women of the post-sixties, however, want it all. They simply take time out from their careers to have children. In fact, one young woman's 19-day-old baby joined us for the interview. The woman expressed the conflicts inherent in being a modern political wife when she said she would "love to have a career and know that I was meeting all my daughter's needs and my needs at the same time."

A question that produced some startling remarks was, "What would you change about your life if you had the opportunity?" Kathy Carruthers, New Mexico's former first lady, reflecting on the demands of her position, said she would "ask for a salary." After relating that she feels as though she is living her life in a fishbowl, another first lady said she would like to "take back my maiden name and not be recognized." A former congressman's wife said she wanted her husband "to be the winner instead of the loser." And the wife of a senator responded cheerfully that her "life is so perfect" she would change only the kind of car she drives!

In order for the interviews to be conducted in surroundings that would be comfortable for the political wives, each woman was asked to select the meeting place. Their requests, a point of interest to me, led me to some very interesting places and introduced me to several equally interesting people. In Topeka, Kansas, for example, I met a cab driver named J.J. who said he knew the governor. "Old tough Mike Hayden? Yes, I do. I'm a Democrat," he went on to say, "but I knew he'd win." After impressing me with his depth of knowledge on the governor's background, J.J. added, "The other governor was married three times. That house does it to you! See it over there? A castle. The house is across the street from Menninger's Clinic, just in case he needs it!" We shared a laugh before J.J. deposited me at the castle's front door.

Most governors' wives proposed the mansion as our meeting place. One first lady answered the doorbell herself. Another had a "bone cruncher" (that's Indian for chiropractor) work on my pinched nerve before sending me home. The wives of congressmen and senators were different, though. If they had their own careers, it was "at my office." If they didn't, it was "at our home," "in the Senate dining room," "in the House dining room," or "at my husband's office."

"At my husband's office" sometimes produced a brief encounter with the politician. During one interview, while the political wife and I were deeply engrossed in conversation, the door opened, admitting a well-dressed, exuberant man. The congressman, it seemed, was checking on his wife! After introductions and some discussion about the past election, he asked how our interview was progressing. To my amusement, the congressman's wife gave him a silent smile, that classic non-verbal exchange that states in no uncertain terms: "I am fine, thank you, and can do very well without any assistance from you, dear!"

As was the case with most of the other husbands who made their presence known, the politician hurriedly took his leave.

Another husband who listened to a portion of the interview tried answering some questions for his wife. In this instance, I had to remind the politician whose interview it was. Yet another politician wanted me to know how delighted *he* was that I was interviewing his wife. She, however, was one of the most guarded political wives I encountered.

Several women refused to be interviewed. One Native American woman asked, "Do I have to do it?" One Native American husband accepted for his wife, then sheepishly called me back to decline for her. "It's her prerogative," he said. Another time, one former congressman's wife would not agree to an interview because "people will recognize me." Another woman responded to my request for an interview with, "No, I'll get in trouble." Former Governor Evan Mecham's wife said, "I don't give interviews, and especially not now." Lee Hart's press secretary initially said yes for her; later, apparently due to Gary Hart's public embarrassment regarding his tryst with Donna Rice, my phone calls were not returned.

Some women would sign the release form only after the interview was completed. Several women asked, after their interview, "I didn't say anything wrong, did I?" In fact, one first lady taped our interview herself and then delayed signing the release form for several weeks; it seemed she wanted to write her own release form. Some women who agreed to be interviewed refused to have their words attributed to them. And other women agreed to be interviewed but refused to be identified as a respondent. Consequently, the reader will not be introduced to all of the political wives with whom I have spoken, though where appropriate and when consent has been given, each woman's name is noted in the text.

When I discovered that the Native American women struggle with the same issues and challenges as other political wives, there seemed to be no reason to isolate their comments. However, there was one area where the Native American first ladies and all the other political wives did have a distinct difference of opinion. That difference, regarding how the women define power, is discussed in the chapter entitled "Rules of the Game."

In the process of campaigning and interviewing, I met many fascinating, intelligent women who have spent a great number of years maneuvering from one election to the next. Some women assume their prescribed role, accept themselves as an afterthought, and have little or no voice in the political system. I also discovered that many political wives are at a loss to describe themselves independently of their husbands. They define their identities externally and passively through the successes and failures and present standing of their husbands' political careers.

The expectations and demands of the public, the political system, and the media quickly overwhelm the newcomer to the world of politics. If he is to be elected, the politician and his spouse must meet as many of those expectations as possible, which requires that the political family assume prescribed roles. The obvious result of this transformation, of course, is that reality and substance are replaced with false images and illusions. And until the political world reflects a more realistic picture, the general public cannot expect authenticity from its leaders or their wives.

Since the political wife generally sacrifices the most and yet has the least to gain from the present political system, she appears the most likely to promote major changes within it. A few political wives have boldly stepped outside the prescribed role, but these women form a small minority. Barbara Bush may be in a category by herself, as she seems to have met the difficult challenges of "political wifedom" without sacrificing her identity, her opinions, her honesty, or her graceful and easy sense of humor. Political wives with their own careers have a more treacherous course to navigate, obviously. But when enough women start to refuse to be bullied and suppressed by the system and finally break through its restraints, the political world will never be the same.

While there exist large numbers of publications on politicians and politics, and even a few that focus on women politicians and selected wives of politicians, no other book presents the collective views of political wives and examines their position and status in the political world. Their past experiences with the press have conditioned political wives to resist revealing their true feelings and opinions. Understandably, they are cautious and guarded when in the presence of those who might "spill the beans" to the public. No doubt, it is due to this reserve that no previous book has attempted to examine "the life and times of the political wife."

Having experienced the brutal world of politics myself, this resistance on the part of the political wives simply increased my resolve to both dispel the myths and gain a better understanding of their plight. To that end, I have explored the issues confronting political wives, presented and analyzed the responses obtained through my interviews with the women, and shared my own views and firsthand experiences as a political wife. This book offers a glimpse into the bittersweet world of politics from the vantage point of those who reside there. Let readers beware: by the time they turn over the last page, many of their illusions about the powerful and glamorous inhabitants of the political realm will have been toppled.

Each chapter is organized in two sections. The first section examines the material collected from the interviews with political wives as well as the research amassed from secondary sources. The second section of each chapter contains my own journal entries recorded during my husband's political campaign in 1985 and 1986, entered sequentially without regard to the year.

The entire book refers to different aspects of the political campaign because when all is said and done, the reality of political life is wrapped up in the rigors of campaigning. Chapter One, "On the Campaign Trail," though, focuses primarily on the frantic pace of campaigning, the torturous 18-hour days of travel, interviews, and speechmaking, and other demands that campaigning places on the political wife and her family. "Rules of the Game" examines glamour and power as portrayed by the politician, his wife, and the media, as well as the merging of politics with the worlds of entertainment and mass communications. The users, abusers, designing women, political media consultants, staff members, and old and new friends who form the world of the politician and his wife are discussed in "All the People You Meet Along the Way." "From White Gloves to Bare Hands" presents the historical perspective, including the political system's changing expectations of the political wife. "Whose Life Is This Anyway?" reveals the emotional and physical effects of political life on the wives of politicians, including isolation, loss of identity, drug and alcohol addiction, and other health problems. "No More Pizza at Midnight" describes the experiences and feelings of those wives whose husbands lost their elections. And finally, the book offers a concise survival guide for the political wife.

I would like to thank those individuals who assisted me in arranging interviews with political wives, and especially Ellen Armstrong for her helpful suggestions and her confidence in me to relate the information as a political wife rather than as a probing reporter. I am grateful to my

children—Ann, Tom and Carol, Bill and Dede—and to
my husband, Steve, who not only were understanding but
also were especially supportive of my commitment to this
project. Special appreciation is extended to the late Patty
Ash, John Jackson, Dick Blair, Steve Shwiff, Artie Ken-
singer, Rita Walker, Joan Donner, Sandy Price, Dick
Schmidt, Bill Wallisch, Esther Lanigan, and Susan Holte
for providing encouragement when I needed it most. The
library staff at the University of Colorado provided assistance in locating books and articles about political wives.
Thanks are also due Susan Duffey Campbell and Don
Walker for their special expertise. I would also like to
express enormous gratitude to all the people who worked
on and for my husband's political campaign. Finally,
because I feel so strongly about sharing the story of the
political wife, my thanks to all the women who consented
to be interviewed. Their cooperation allowed this project
to become a reality, and I am forever grateful.

NOTES

1. Kitty Kelley, *Elizabeth Taylor: The Last Star* (New York:
Dell, 1981), 341.

Chapter One

On the Campaign Trail

> Always be on time. Do as little talking as humanly possible. Remember to lean back in the parade car so everybody can see the President. Be sure not to get too fat, because you have to sit three in the back seat.
>
> —*Eleanor Roosevelt*

For 18 months we traveled our state, as candidate and political spouse, urging the public to consider my husband's candidacy and to vote for him first at the state assembly and later in the primary election. Together and separately we attended dinners, picnics, breakfasts, and parades in as many of Colorado's 63 counties as time would permit. There were untold meet-the-candidate events, fund-raisers, and media events and interviews on our schedules. Gradually, one day flowed into the next, until we had no idea what day or month it was without a calendar to remind us.

Family life with our three grown children became practically non-existent, because most of the time we were all going in different directions. Whether or not Bill, Tom, or Ann campaigned, there was no time for them to be alone with their father. Our family gatherings consisted of discussions about political strategy, Steve's standing in the polls, and who was going to attend the next event.

Every article and book that discusses campaigning for high political office makes note of the rigorous pace required of candidates as well as the importance of spousal participation, and our experience bore this out. Political wives, realizing the importance of their participation, usually become active campaigners, with some women enjoying it more than others.

It seems the wives of politicians have a definite role to fulfill—the traditional role. At the start of our 18-month campaign stint, I knew nothing about expectations for political wives and wanted as much information as I could absorb. Consequently, I was grateful to receive from one of the members of the campaign staff a booklet entitled "The Candidate's Wife," a guide to "finding and carrying out your role in the campaign."[1] It took me only a few minutes to detect the message that campaigning, like other phases of political life, is based on an unwritten code. Image is everything.

The booklet defined the role of the candidate's wife, with such basic image-provoking directives as: "Remember you are NOT the candidate. . . . Whether or not you work in your husband's campaign office, you can help rally the troops by being cordial with campaign workers. . . . Campaigning, especially in a hotly contested race, can be very nervewracking. If you do go into it, keep your cool. . . . If you have a speaking schedule of your own, you must be well informed on campaign issues. . . . If an issue is raised with which you are unfamiliar . . . it is perfectly all right to say that you would rather discuss the matter with your husband before you comment."

The manual goes on to note: "Even though you are married to the man and your stake in his success is as great as his, you are not the best judge of how his campaign should be run. Defer to the experts." Does this profile fit the independent, free-thinking woman of today? These comments, I acknowledge, might be helpful to some women. However, they offered very little to me. In fact, I wondered at the time if the guide was a satire, an irreverent comedy. The authors' outdated view of women most definitely centers around the subordination and compliance of political wives.

Sadly, though, the truth of the matter is that many political wives continue to comply with such condescending directives. They publicly present themselves only as traditional wives and loyal spouses; they stand by their man. Lee Hart is a prime example of the dutiful, ever-loyal political wife. When she was at the airport, having to face the TV cameras after her husband's political candidacy was all but over, she looked so pale, tired, and pained as she attempted composure. I wondered what she was going to say about the man who had publicly embarrassed her by making front-page headlines with his relationship with Donna Rice. In short order, she did what most political wives have been trained to do. She defended her husband's behavior and her own role as victim, even making light of his treatment of her.

Most of today's women have much more to offer than a pleasant smile and everlasting loyalty. Political wives spend a great deal of their time representing their husbands. Many also have children to raise and their own careers to manage. And politicians' wives who choose to fill the role of traditional wife find themselves in conflict a good deal of the time, with balance eluding them.

The husband, on the other hand, is expected to know all the issues confronting his district, state, or country. Moreover, the candidate is expected to have simple, quick, no-pain solutions to the problems confronting the voters. He is to be available to every person wanting his attention, to have the stamina to address numerous audiences each day without losing his enthusiasm or concentration, and to pay his dues, so to speak, to his political party. If that isn't enough, the candidate is also expected to do all this with a charismatic flair that says he is witty, bright, caring, and gracious. In the end, however, even that candidate who has accomplished all these feats may lose the election. In fact, according to the Congressional Research Service of the Library of Congress fewer than 25% of all the candidates who run for Congress are elected.

No, there simply are no guarantees in politics, and there's never enough time in each day for a candidate to accomplish what has to be done in order to win a race. He cannot be in all places at once, and he cannot do all the campaigning himself. Therefore, spousal participation clearly becomes an important ingredient in any campaign, with the wife being, in many instances, the politician's strongest asset. Just as a man's financial status is equated by others with the way his wife is adorned, so does a candidate's perceived public image have a lot to do with the way his wife looks and conducts herself. And many people make erroneous assumptions about the candidate based on their perceptions of his wife. For example, if she appears to be the traditional wife, he must be a family man. And if he cannot handle his "errant" or non-traditional wife, how can he possibly manage the country, state, or country?

I am reminded of an interview I conducted with a congressional wife from Texas who suggested that a wife's participation in a political campaign can do more damage than good to her husband's career. Christine Delay remarked: "If she pulls a stupid stunt or says the wrong things, rather than saying something wonderful to turn people on, she can hurt him." Clearly, one slip-up by the wife can undo all the effects of months of posturing and image-building. Consequently, most political wives play the game very carefully, creating and polishing an image that ultimately results in praise being showered upon their husbands. After all, the political wife is often viewed as an extension of her husband, and she offers the public a glimpse into the "private life" of her man.

But in order to participate in campaigning at any level, with a high or low profile, the political wife must be aware of her strengths and weaknesses, as well as possess an awareness of her own needs and desires. During our 1987 interview in Maine, Barbara Bush, the first lady and veteran campaigner, remarked: "At my age I don't have to pretend to be something I'm not." Barbara Bush certainly does not subscribe to playing the image game! She is candid, caring, fun-loving, and gracious. And though she is comfortable in the traditional role, she is a lady who knows herself, a lady who may well encourage other women to allow the public to know who they really are instead of constantly portraying "the image."

It stands to reason that the degree to which political wives become involved in their husbands' campaigns varies greatly. A few women are graduate students, doing a minimum of campaigning. Others have careers, with no intention of relinquishing their positions should their husbands be elected. And there are those who, by their own admission, simply choose to do as little as possible during a campaign, often with a great deal of guilt. But one candid congressional wife with whom I spoke suffered no guilt whatsoever. She avoided as much of the campaign as possible, preferring instead to show her horses. No, Linda Campbell, wife of Colorado's Congressman Ben Nighthorse Campbell, does not like campaigning. In fact, she "totally hated the campaign." Linda Campbell keeps a low profile, apparently with no negative effect on her husband's career. So why do women continue to put themselves through the hoops, if it doesn't affect their husbands' campaigns anyway? Then, at the other end of the spectrum, there are those women who mirror the candidate, doing as much as is humanly possible to get their husbands elected. These are the women who preface most statements with "We are planning" this or that.

Some women, the extraverted, politically minded wives, debate for their candidate husbands. Most wives who debate do so because they enjoy the competition as well as being deeply concerned about the issues, and yes, because they enjoy the limelight, too. When interviewing those few women who chose to debate for their husbands, I wondered if they themselves had any desire to be political candidates. Perhaps debating is one way of portraying the role of a candidate without actually being the candidate.

During one of my interviews, however, an outspoken senator's wife intimated that on occasion her debating would be incorporated into her husband's campaign strategy for the express purpose of drawing the opponent off guard. Obviously, it would be difficult to debate issues with another person who has the option of begging ignorance to a detail when things seem to be going awry. Of course, part of the strategy might be to totally frustrate the opponent. After all, how can a man who was raised to open the door for a lady lambaste her with a verbal right hook—especially in public?

The majority of women, I learned, choose the middle ground when campaigning for their political office-seeking husbands. One aspect of campaigning that troubles many women is their time away from their spouses, so most women travel with their candidate husbands a good portion of the time. And some women travel exclusively with their husbands, having no programmed schedule of their own; these are the women who often declare, "I am *not* the candidate." But if the candidate's wife has a separate schedule, conflicts inevitably arise, with or without scheduling coordination.

For example, Marilyn Quayle, wife of Vice President Dan Quayle, recalls being pregnant with their oldest child the first time her husband ran for political office. She delivered the baby three days after the election and then tackled the bar exam while "sitting on a pillow." During the interview with Marilyn Quayle, which was conducted in the Senate Dining Room in December 1986, I asked if she would ever want her husband to run for president. Curiously, that question never came up during interviews with other political wives, and I am still not sure why I queried her on the subject. I did sense, though, that she had ambitions for her husband beyond the U.S. Senate. Her very non-committal response to my question was, "If the people want it. The presidency is a thankless job."

Over time, I talked with a number of women who choreographed their husbands' campaign publicity and organized volunteers, and a few, like Marilyn Quayle, managed their husbands' entire campaign. Working behind the scenes can be very fulfilling to those who prefer being the king-maker to being the king. My sense is that most women accept the responsibility because it is a safe, yet powerful, position, placing the candidate rather than his wife on the line. Indeed, a congressional wife who helped strategize her husband's campaign said, after his loss: "I've lost my power."

Marilyn Quayle, however, lost her safe position behind the scenes when her special skills and talents were brought to light in newspaper and magazine interviews conducted after George Bush selected Dan Quayle as his running mate. The consensus was that she might well be a viable candidate in her own right. According to pollster Claibourne Darden, "She's the one who should be vice president."[2]

But whether a wife debates for her husband, has her own schedule, or loves or abhors campaigning, much of her energy is devoted to representing him. And while most women do not debate for their husbands, they do find themselves speaking for them at teas, coffees, luncheons, and dinners, not to mention the events held at county fairgrounds. Each time a wife attends an event by herself, she is expected to speak for and about her husband. The political wife is, after all, his surrogate, his substitute, his stand-in, and emissary. And over time, this process, regardless of the expectations, will eventually take its toll on her because her sense of self, her identity, will erode if she allows it.

It came as no surprise that a number of the political wives I interviewed would like to run for political office. And why shouldn't they? So many of them are well versed on the issues and have a keen understanding of what running for political office entails. Dottie Lamm, wife of Colorado's retired Governor Richard Lamm, indicated that given the opportunity, she would choose to run for political office. However, after pausing briefly, she added, "But probably not, especially since I'm trying to get the family out of politics." A foreign-born wife of one former U.S. congressman indicated that "in my country, I would have run for political office. I've thought about running for Congress, here—I'd like to be a congresswoman." And Joanne Kemp, wife of former Congressman and current Secretary of Housing and Urban Development Jack Kemp from Buffalo, New York, said that she, too, had given some thought to running for public office. However, none has made the move from private citizen to public official, suggesting that their husbands' political ambitions take precedence over their own.

These women, however, are the exception. Indeed, I discovered that most women are decidedly more content playing the role of supporter—no doubt female acculturation's handiwork leaving an indelible impression on women. For example, when Carolyn Moore, married to former Congressman W. Henson Moore of Louisiana, said, "I love the roar of the crowd," she quickly added that "as a little girl I was always on stage, and politics fulfilled a need in me." Later on in our conversation, she admitted that she was responsible for her family's lifestyle because she "encouraged him to run for office in 1974."

In another interview, Mary Andrews remarked that she had been a political science major in college, was intrigued with politics, but was raised thinking a woman's role was to be "the helper," adding that she "didn't ever think of running for office." Instead, she "urged" her husband, Mark Andrews, former U.S. senator from North Dakota, into political life in 1962. My sense is that many of the political wives with whom I spoke would make excellent public officials, were they to follow their heart and venture out on their own political path.

Because most women interested in running for political office choose to believe that their only value is in being someone's helpmate, a great deal of talent in our country is being wasted, discounted, or even ignored. It's unfortunate and disturbing that so many women acquiesce or subordinate their talents and ambitions willingly and allow the opinions of others, whether individuals or institutions, to control their lives.

An article in the New York *Times* addressed the issue of women subordinating their own careers to their husbands' political ambitions. In the article, Nina Solarz, who is executive director of Peace Links and married to Congressman Stephen J. Solarz, a Democrat from Brooklyn, New York, was quoted as saying, "For me, having my own identity and interests has been very important. But that doesn't mean I wouldn't drop everything if my husband needed me. If he had a difficult campaign or was running for higher office, I think I would be very old-fashioned and put my own career on hold."[3]

And then I am reminded of the comments made by Elizabeth Dole after she resigned her cabinet position to campaign with her presidential candidate husband, Senator Robert Dole: "Do George Bush, Jack Kemp, and Bob Dole have to give up their job? Why should the wife of a candidate have to?"[4] Precisely. Why? I had to question what had transpired between that interview in August 1987 and September 1987 when she was again quoted, because this time Elizabeth Dole said: "It is not necessary to leave. It is my personal choice."[5]

Because a wife devotes so much of her time to her husband's campaign, her friends and co-workers are less accessible to her, as she is to them. And she's alone a lot if she has her own schedule or does not accompany her husband to all the events. Understandably, the candidate has his dream to fulfill; he may be preoccupied and unavailable a good deal of the time. A congressman's spouse, commenting on the loneliness of political life and the lack of close female relationships, said, "Even other wives are pointmen for their husbands, although they would deny it."

Furthermore, many women declare that campaigning affects the wife more than it does the hard-driving politician. He is still working 18-hour days, as he did before politics. However, when she enters the political world, not only must she continue doing what she did before, but she now tacks on campaigning to her list of responsibilities— and no longer has a life of her own. For example, a congressional spouse who worked full time commented that she campaigned most evenings and every weekend because the majority of women in their congressional district worked outside the home. So, for the sake of his election, the political wife sacrifices her time as well as her needs. During one of her husband's campaigns, Dottie Lamm said, "A part of me seems to be dying, as I father, mother, organize and campaign—and at such a pace! I am successful, but there is no emotional space for me."[6]

"But you can't go around resenting your husband's career. You have to accept it and get on with it," Lavender Patten is quoted as saying in the article "Political Wives," written by Mary Ann Seighart. Quite true, but easier said than done. The continual focus on the candidate's career, schedule, and needs and the subjugation of all of the wife's interests are bound to result in frustration and anger on the part of the political wife, though generally concealed from the public. Every so often during the interviews, however, a woman's resentment finds its way to the surface. For example, on one occasion a candid spouse remarked, "Indeed we are working together. Together for him." Her tone of voice said it all. Generally, though, when my queries touched on the woman's feelings about campaigning, most responded with the well-worn statement that they were working together as a team, for the same purpose.

When the political wife enters the heat of battle, so to speak, often she is drawn into the frenzied pace of the campaign before she realizes it's happened. Her personal time slips away and is replaced by 18-hour days working to promote her husband's career. She gives speeches and attends events for her candidate husband. She even accepts the absurdity of speaking for him simply because she's married to the candidate and not because she has something of her own to offer. The political wife does what has to be done, which includes internalizing the personal conflicts and humiliation inherent in her position. "No one listens to the candidate's wife. I was the last one they wanted to see," commented Carol Fisher, wife of Pennsylvania's lieutenant governor candidate, Mike Fisher. Jill Biden echoed those words during the last presidential election when she remarked, "People aren't really interested in what I do."[7] And Dottie Lamm expressed the same opinion, but in stronger terms: "I wanted to tell them, 'you've got me buddy, and that's all you're going to see.' "

Veteran campaigner Ellen Armstrong, who is married to retired Senator William Armstrong from Colorado, stated that she travels the rural areas when on her own schedule, "tailoring things to my needs." She is one of the few women interviewed who even mentioned their own needs when discussing campaigning. For most political wives, campaigning is centered around meeting the candidate's needs, the public's needs, and the campaign workers' needs. Such an attitude suggests that these women have no needs, are not aware of their needs, ignore their needs, or are willing to deny them for the sake of upholding the image. And as "The Candidate's Wife" informs us, meeting the candidate's needs means being available; meeting the public's needs means portraying an image; and meeting the campaign workers' needs means "being cordial."[8] In reference to campaigning, Hattie Babbit, wife of Bruce Babbit, the former governor of Arizona, says: "You have to be demented to like all of this."[9]

The experience of being a governor's wife is unique. An advantage many of these women referred to in my interviews with them was having more time to develop as separate individuals. It seems their role and the public's expectations of them are not so rigidly defined, allowing them more latitude to mold their role more to their liking. "At first," says Dottie Lamm, "I did what was expected of me. Later, however, I became more my own person." Yes, in time Dottie Lamm was not only fulfilling her responsibilities as Colorado's first lady, but became a well-known personality in her own right, serving as spokesperson for a number of causes, writing her own column for the *Denver Post,* and even finding time to write a book. Kathy Carruthers, former first lady of New Mexico, suggests that she "can choose what I want to do. I can focus the spotlight on certain projects and set my own schedule."

Congressmen's wives are not as fortunate. They are at a distinct disadvantage because of their husbands' two-year terms, which require them to campaign all the time. The term of office for almost all governors is four years; for senators, six years. Congressmen, however, begin campaigning for the next election immediately following their victory, bringing to mind Sisyphus eternally pushing the rock uphill!

The candidates' families have always been given at least a token role in the election process. Usually the candidate is seen with his wife, children, and maybe a dog or two. But recent elections have placed stronger emphasis on the family, so that children and wives are now playing a much more active role in the candidates' campaigns. It's practically required of them. During one interview, a political wife told me that themes change with each election. "This year," she said, "the theme was the family tradition." If the entire family enjoys campaigning, then the theme of the family tradition works well for them. For example, Caroline McMillan, the wife of J. Alex McMillan, congressman from North Carolina, remarked, "Our children participated; our nieces, nephews, and my mother-in-law participated. It brought about family closeness. We worked together for a common goal." Lynn Waihee, first lady of Hawaii, told me her son not only campaigned but designed the campaign buttons as well. And Wyoming's first lady, Jane Sullivan, remarked: "Our daughter loved campaigning. She debated for her father, traveling with her own schedule."

But a few other political wives said that campaigning adds a tremendous strain to their family life. Actually, if they do not campaign together, there is little time for a normal family life. For example, one woman's teenager couldn't handle the campaign or the constant political talk that dominated their lives, so he eventually left the United States and continued his studies abroad. Another first lady pointed out the differences between her children: "Our oldest worked in our home county, but our middle child didn't like it." Still another political wife remarked that their children never campaigned.

Marital relationships, however, are harder to discuss. And owing to the importance placed on projecting an image, most political wives feel pressured to represent themselves as having the perfect marriage. In fact, a good portion of my time interviewing wives of politicians was expended trying to read between the lines, that is, if we weren't deadlocked. For example, when I asked the question: "How were decisions made regarding the campaign?" the response generally was: "All of our decisions are made jointly." Period. They offered no elaboration. A rather outspoken political wife did, however, comment that "the decision to run was mine—I could not live with the guilt of saying no." And then realizing what she had just said, she quickly directed me not to use her name. Or if I asked, "Do you and your husband have any disagreements about money, children, or your attempts to pursue your own goals?" the response generally was: "We don't disagree on anything." But then another, more candid political wife remarked, "We have a very competitive relationship. We disagree on those subjects a lot of the time."

Sometimes when I did not know where to locate the answers, an insightful politician filled in the blanks to difficult questions. The following citation demonstrates that at least one politician is keenly aware of the havoc that political life played on his family life. In 1980, upon deciding not to run again for political office, Nebraska's Democratic Congressman John Cavanaugh declared: "There were times when I would go a week to 10 days without seeing my kids. You're not there to be with them, and appreciate them, and grow with them, and influence them, and all those things you want to do. . . . And for me at that point in time, it was too demanding in terms of the sacrifice."[10]

Campaigning is strenuous. It's hard work, all-consuming, leaving little time for any relaxation, unless sleeping in the car between events is considered relaxing. And the candidate's wife is expected to dispose of all her other responsibilities so that she is available at any given moment to speak intelligently about her husband and about his positions on political issues. According to Wren Wirth, wife of Colorado Senator Tim Wirth, "Politics is like a black hole that engulfs your time and energy." Indeed, campaigning is a coming together of absurdities, if you will, for candidate and spouse, in order to get him elected.

The physical act of campaigning, however, can be fun, interesting, educational, sometimes boring, hard work, and also a straightforward exercise. A good deal of the politician's time, and his wife's time, is scheduled before audiences and the press, giving speeches, answering questions, and visiting briefly with more people than you ever thought existed. The people and the press, the speeches, and the questions are all difficult givens in campaigning, and if they could be spread over more reasonable amounts of time they wouldn't be quite so demanding. But our elections are booked decades in advance, and no extensions or do-overs are permitted. So candidate and spouse spend practically every waking hour, separately and together, at a frantic pace trying to get him elected. And that, my friend, is reality.

Despite all the apparent craziness, you can get caught up in the excitement of campaigning. Frequently it's an enthusiastic audience that will hook you. As they cheer you on, accept your statements, liking what they hear, your physical tiredness abates and your adrenalin begins to flow. You radiate, reflecting the audience's enthusiasm. In that moment your frustrations and anguish are forgotten, and you shine. It's amazing, and seductive. No doubt, the bright lights and roar of the crowd have something to do with it.

But between those too infrequent moments of exhilaration are seemingly endless days of frantic commuting from one event to another. Yes, campaigning is an extremely demanding process, both physically and emotionally. There is little glitz and glamour. Joan Kennedy's campaign stop in Iowa in 1980 illustrates the point. At 7:45 a.m., Ted Kennedy's wife and his staff left for a motorcade trip to Indianola. It was two degrees outside. "Joan wanted to look fashionable, even tramping around a hog farm, but it was so cold that she continued to wear her heavy wool red, white, and black plaid suit under a matching plaid coat to almost every event. At one point during our trip, the comedians of the press corps passed a hat to buy her another outfit."[11]

Days are planned long in advance by the staff and candidate, with little or no time remaining for the politician and his wife to be alone. It requires a lot of stamina to regularly endure those 18-hour days. And rightfully so, there is a definite sense of relief when the polls close on election night. If your efforts pay off and the election is won, then perhaps it will all seem worth it. Perhaps.

*   *   *

The following journal entries illustrate the process of campaigning, including the rigorous schedule that every candidate must endure. The reader, I hope, will come away with a visual image of what campaigning is all about. At best, the process is difficult for one and all. And one particular enterprise, the announcement tour, illustrates the craziness of those daze; I mean days.

June 3

A five-day, 17-city tour of Colorado began this morning, placing us briefly in every corner of the state. It started at home in Colorado Springs with an early morning press conference. Then on to Denver for a healthy dose of flesh-pressing and interviews. Two photographers and four reporters joined us in Denver for part of the tour. On our way out of town we passed the governor's mansion. What a majestic old house, but the gardens need tending. . . .

In our banner-clad vans we set out to shake Colorado's hand, stopping just long enough to meet the media, some supporters, and local activists, and smile a lot before moving to the next town. And as we traveled, the press who traveled with us had questions for Steve. As I was observing the reporters and the photographers who were sitting just inches away, the constant flash bulbs and countless questions posed seemed to set my mind awhirl. In fact, at night my dreams must be reflecting newspaper print and flashbulbs, because I'm starting to dream in black and white. What a hoot.

June 5

First stop seemed to go well, despite John not being able to make it. He had some relatives of the Queen (of England) coming to the ranch (really), and the plumbing went out! Told him that he should bring them to the cafe where the press conference was being held, but he said they can't vote.

Second press stop went well, with several people committing on the spot. Then a radio interview before another long drive. All the press people and one of the drivers went on to their homes in one car and one van, while we stopped at home for a few hours before driving to the next stopover.

Going home is a mistake if you have to continue on that same day. There's much too much going on to try to settle down. The children's lives have no structure, and I don't feel that I can handle too much more stress right now. I think I'm very tired.

June 7

Well, it's over. Five 18-hour days, 2,000 miles, every corner of the state. Feet are swollen, body is exhausted, and mind is blank. We had pictures taken at the Lamar newspaper before leaving town and after Steve finished two interviews. Left late, arrived in La Junta with a speeding ticket, and two of the press corps already gone. . . . La Junta press conference was okay, but Steve tried to be funny, taking a big gulp when asked about Colorado's water problems, and no one laughed. He must be tired, too. No, he passed tired and went directly on to punchy. Then on to Pueblo for the last stop before going home. Glamourous life, huh?

July 10

What a day . . . 18 hours long. We woke up in Ft. Collins, after four hours of sleep, and started off with a fairly good turnout and press conference. Drove to Greeley for another media stop. (Never realized how much the aroma of feedlots alters the air in the summertime. But how would I have known that? NYC doesn't have any feedlots. Must remember, though, for future visits.)

Steve's speech and subsequent discussions ran on . . . and on. We were 25 minutes late for our next scheduled stopover before we put our tired bodies in the car. So we were 45 minutes late getting to Ft. Morgan, and it worsened as the day progressed. We did meet some interesting people, though, radio, newspaper, and radio interviews again, with all three reporters having the same first name—Mike.

After that, we moved on to Brush for another newspaper interview. Nice people—Chicago transplants (wonder if they know about feedlots). Sterling was next, with more interviews, arriving for our final radio station meeting only one-and-a-half hours late!

Later, we stopped in Wray and another small town to leave press kits. The newspapers were closed by then, so we had to drop the press kits in the mail slot to let them know we had been there. We did squeeze in a quick dinner during the three-hour drive to a motel room with no windows. It's 1 a.m. now, and I'm still laughing about all the frogs running freely in the lobby when we checked in, no doubt escaping the pool area where they usually reside—then again, maybe not. The desk clerk wasn't alarmed in the least about their presence. We did, however, walk very carefully. . . .

So far, the only things that change are our clothes and the names of the towns. And tomorrow I fly to Alamosa, Montrose, Park, and Routt counties, then meet Steve in Ft. Collins to go on to Yuma. Sunday is Steve's birthday. Hope I'm awake for it!!!

*   *   *

Other entries, those taken from my own separate schedule, give additional illustrations of what is involved in a political campaign. One aspect of campaigning that I came to enjoy after a shaky beginning was public speaking. At first I was reluctant

*to speak for Steve, but with the staff's encouragement I finally
agreed to venture out.*

January 15

My first few speeches have been comedic disasters. I
hardly looked up from my note cards, all 20 of them,
which by the way would have been approved for the
visually impaired! My reading glasses prevent me from
seeing things at a distance—so I was forced to choose
between reading my notes and viewing the audience.
Wouldn't you know it, I chose to see the audience.

January 21

My solo flight. . . . Patty was with us for the first day,
which really helped immensely. Then Mindy and I were
on our own.

Timed my speech last night after I finished writing it—
three minutes. But I am expected to talk for 10 minutes.
Today, in the car, Mindy and Patty timed me at 18
minutes. Now I can't get it short enough. And let that be
my biggest problem! Estes Park went well, though. I was
scheduled to speak before lunch—how nice not to be
nervous for too long a period of time. The people were
very friendly, understanding my anxiety and apprehen-
sion. They gasped and even laughed in all the right places.
And guess what? I left with a check for Steve! They loved
me. . . . I'm on a roll.

Didn't last long. As we were driving to our next stopover—Loveland—Mindy and Patty critiqued my presen-
tation. Seems that Mindy wanted to grab my hands while
I was talking to stop me from shuffling my index cards!
Oh well, if public speaking doesn't work out, maybe I can
get a job as a dealer in Vegas. . . . So who's perfect?

In Loveland, we talked to the press for 30 minutes, took

pictures, and Patty cued me on some things. Thanks. Next stop Ft. Collins Court House to meet some supporters. Checked into the hotel in time to wash my face and mingle with 40 delegates for over an hour before dinner at 9:30 p.m. (It felt like that old skit with Carol Burnett at a cocktail party, where the shy character is offered advice on how to handle herself in crowds. She's instructed to move from group to group uttering the words "mingle, mingle" because nobody really listens to what people have to say.) No speech tonight, just an informal get-together.

Modified my index cards tonight. Went from 20 down to 10. Now I have to explore other options if this doesn't work out—10 cards do not a dealer make. Rats.

January 22

Radio, press, and lunch in Sterling. There were over 25 women at the luncheon. Picked at lunch; could hardly cut the chicken thinking about what I was going to say. Gave the speech without looking at my cards. It was a first! And relatively comfortable. Enjoyed the questions more, though. But I still can't remember what I said, or anyone's name.

After lunch, we went to the Sheltered Workshop, with a photographer from the newspaper following us around snapping pictures. (All of the clients are developmentally disabled.) At one point, the director played some music and I danced with a young girl Annabel's age. She loved dancing, moving freely and rhythmically with no inhibitions. Her dark eyes seemed to twinkle in time with the music. Quite an experience.

After that, we stopped by the newspaper for a short visit—30 minutes. Don't know if they will print anything. We'll see. Then dinner with party officials.

January 23

What a day. My first big blooper. We laughed so hard the tears rolled down our cheeks.

First thing in the a.m., had press interview in Brush. Then on to radio interview. Next, the infamous luncheon in Ft. Morgan. I remember glancing at a woman who reminded me of a friend of my mother's who lives in New York City. Somehow, when I referred to the mayor of Colorado Springs, I relocated him to the Big Apple and, not hearing my own words, blithely continued talking. Mindy interrupted me at that point and asked if I worked in Colorado Springs. I remember looking at her as if she had lost her mind and responded, "Yes, of course." She then informed me of my mistake, and I was left only to make fun of myself and carry on. During our drive, though, we had more fun rehashing the incident. If this keeps up, I may have enough material to do a speech on all my foul-ups!

Next stop was the newspaper. Shared my blooper with the journalist and he shared one with us. The last stop for the day was another radio station. When we were in the car, after the interview, I said to Mindy, "I did not answer one question I was asked. I just said what I wanted to say." And she replied, "That's right, you were great!" What a game this is. I don't know if I'll ever understand it. Now we have to wait for the press results to see if we did any good.

February 12 . . . First dinner speech

Wrote my speech this a.m., since the county chairman wanted me to speak for Steve. Ken drove while I practiced. The Senate candidates went first—all five minutes over their time—and then the surrogates started.

Well, for openers, as I was walking up to the podium I

tripped over an imaginary something on the floor. Real cute! If that weren't enough, my knees trembled as I tried to navigate the stairs in my high heels. Then, when I stood at the microphone and looked out at the sea of faces—250 of them—they all were staring back at me. In my inimitably poised way, I proceeded to virtually blank!!! But I found my trusty cards in time, and my voice shook for only a minute before I finally settled into my talk, getting through it as quickly as possible. But the good news is they laughed in the right places and applauded when I was through. I was a success . . . I think.

* * *

February is a killer month for both Republican and Democratic candidates and their spouses. In February, to commemorate Abraham Lincoln's birthday, the Republican Party in each county conducts a fund-raising event. Usually it's a social event to raise funds for operating expenses for the upcoming year. However, with 63 counties in Colorado, the Lincoln Day circuit continues long after the month of February. Not only is this schedule totally exhausting, but candidates can win or lose delegate votes by their presence or absence at one of these dinners. My journal reflected my mood after one Lincoln Day dinner.

February 4

Now I know what the "downs" in ups and downs feel like. The night was a total bust. The drive up took five hours. Our first media stop, before dinner, was the local newspaper, then on to the radio station for another interview. Our driver could not make contact with the campaign's field coordinator, so we assumed he'd be at the dinner. Wrong. We arrived at the meeting place, after getting lost, to find no materials, no coordinator, no host, no people we knew or anyone who wanted to know us! To make matters worse, when Steve paid for the tickets, the ticket-taker didn't even know Steve was a candidate. (I should have listened to my mother years ago.)

At 8:50 p.m., after dinner and after Steve spilled the reporter's drink, the speeches started. The candidates were each allowed five minutes to relate their life history, their vision for the state, and why they were running for +h⸴. political office. The Senate candidates started first. Not one of the candidates stayed within their five-minute allowance. The gubernatorial candidates were next. Steve went on stage, after two other gubernatorial candidates, and gave a so-so talk, appearing extremely tense. He received polite applause. Nobody even asked him a question during the Q and A portion. Then the county chairman announced that the other gubernatorial candidate couldn't be there because he was off campaigning somewhere else. And in a flash, that took care of him! Next on the agenda, all the county people seeking political office. I couldn't believe it. At 10:45 p.m., they were still giving speeches!

We left at midnight, drove three hours, and got to bed at 3:30 a.m. While I can see the humor in some portions of the evening, I feel so badly for Steve. He doesn't deserve this. No one does. It's absolute craziness. He's sleeping now, readying himself for tomorrow's challenges, and I just want to go home. . . .

* * *

Sometimes an evening of campaigning can be utterly boring, and sometimes there can be moments of serendipity when you least expect it. My journal reminds me of those events, bringing these images to light.

June 24

Saturday night in Denver for a big gathering. There were more candidates there than delegates. The highlight of the evening was running out of gas on the freeway. . . .

August 19

Busy couple of days on the road. Late again, too. Denver County for a baseball game, Arapahoe County for a picnic, and then on to Clear Creek County for another picnic—however, we arrived when it was over! But we did meet the hosts, who were very nice. She was a sketch! A free spirit. I really enjoyed her. She's a Ruth Gordon type who just had the ability to simply "be." . . . If more people like her emerge from this campaign, it will be worth all the traveling and campaigning. They live in the wilderness with their dogs, enjoying a very simple life. Serendipity! Then on to Eagle County where Steve is scheduled to give a speech.

October 20

I think I'm losing it. Tonight as Steve was delivering his speech, and as I was in my usual stance next to him, my mind started to wander. I almost laughed out loud as I envisioned myself breaking into an outrageous soft shoe dance. Still wonder what would have happened had I tried it!

*   *   *

The following journal entries shed additional light on the personal conflicts that arise as campaigning begins taking its toll on everyone. One's relationships and children are directly affected by the candidate's entry into the political world.

January 14

I am slowly but surely coming to the conclusion that candidates represent themselves as having perfect marriages. But there are no perfect marriages, if you live in the public eye. Well, if being apart means perfect, I take back what I said.

Most of my days are spent either campaigning without Steve or staying home with the children, also without him. And when we are together we never can discuss anything other than how the campaign is progressing, because someone from the staff is always with us. Others' lives can't be much different. So why are their marriages so perfect? Hey, maybe our marriage is perfect, too, and I just don't know it.

February 22

Thursday night I drove myself to Douglas County through a blinding, sudden snow storm. Then black ice and dense fog. I was so tense when I finally got there that my speech was easy compared to the drive.

Steve was in Collins, which apparently went well, but he's really run down physically and flies off the handle easily. We've been having a great many arguments lately . . . money, children, and individuality. I guess they're universal problems, though. Still, I don't like what campaigning does to us.

April 14

I am constantly being scheduled to go one place or another. No thought seems to be given to my needs or desires. I either go here or there, and if I choose not to go some place I sense that I am looked upon as not being supportive. Wonder what the staff would say if they knew that I took the afternoon off to spend it playing "hooky" with a friend. It was crazy, though, to be downtown feeling guilty but loving my freedom all the same, and then walking directly into another candidate as we crossed the street. There we both were, making excuses to each other for not working. How ridiculous!!!

April 23

Sometimes he only wants an ear, not advice or feedback. Tonight we went to a large party for Steve, and we disagreed about the tone of the group. He said there was a lot of hostility toward him and his profession (real estate), and I felt that it was a group of very concerned people with one jerk thrown in to spice it all up! He told me to see things more clearly—"It was a hostile group!"

May 5

It's interesting that Steve thinks our marriage is stronger now than ever before. He thought we were going in separate directions before. I can't believe that having separate interests and being separate people is bad for a marriage. But then again, what do I know? I'm only the candidate's wife. He's a hoot!

August 26

I'm so tired right now. Told Steve he better win because I am not going to do this again. Little by little, this campaign is squeezing out the things we enjoy doing and our time with the family. Everyone suffers.

Steve looks pale and needs a rest from all this glamourous high living we call campaigning. Ha! If people only knew, but it probably wouldn't make any difference—the show must go on and all that stuff. He drew a blank when he was giving his speech tonight. I wish he could lighten up and not be so intense when he speaks.

Well, I found out afterwards that although it wasn't his best speech, he didn't lose any supporters and even picked up some new workers. Maybe I'm just too critical of him. He did admit that he's very tired and wants to take a few days away from all this. Well, maybe I am too critical. Moi? Nah. . . .

*   *   *

Many times during the campaign I felt as though politics and private life was not a winning combination. The following entries address my frustrations with public life.

April 29

Sunday was Steve's birthday. A nice break from politics. Old friends and the children made it a good day for all, but I'd had to practically threaten the staff with their lives if they scheduled Steve for that day.

May 30

I have spent the last week or so with a house full of guests. Tom graduated from CU last Tuesday. It was terrific. Now we're one week away from the State Assembly. Let's hope Steve "graduates" into the primary. I've spent every spare moment on the phone calling the undecided delegates, and my mother is wondering if it is I who is running for public office! Obviously, this has not been the best trip for her. We have not been able to spend much quiet time together.

June 15

We've been married 28 years today. Neither of us has had the time to get a gift for the other! Oh well, it's not the gift but the thought that counts. Right? Now I know why people buy things well in advance and put the presents away for later!

August 13

Steve's folks have been visiting here since Thursday, along with his brother and his family. It's a family reunion, probably the last time we will all be together. Steve's father is in the final stages of cancer. It's going to be a very long, sad journey for him. I wish there was something I could do to ease the pain and uncertainty for him.

He came all this distance to be with everyone, and the damn phones, reporters, and schedules keep pulling Steve away. And the worst offense is that when Steve chooses to miss an event to be with his dad the article mentions only Steve's absence!

* * *

When we campaigned, our children were older, and it was important to me that they decide if and how much they wanted to participate. I vowed never to force them into attending any events or for that matter venturing out on their own. My aim was simply for them to enjoy as much of the process as possible. And if they were uncomfortable with being a campaigner, I honored their decision. Thus, two of our three children often distanced themselves from the campaign hoopla.

Our oldest child, though, seemed content surrogating at parades and large gatherings and speaking on occasion, as well.

May 31

Bill is having such a good time campaigning. This morning, however, he realized that people often forget he is not his father. There he was sitting on the back of a bright red convertible, waving to the crowds, with his father's poster hanging from the side door. During the procession someone called to him, "Hey, Steve." And when Bill turned to look at the person, he heard, "When did you grow the mustache?"

* * *

It was during the 18-month campaign that Tom graduated from college and later took employment in another state. However, while time permitted he also worked on his father's campaign, doing advance work.

July 10

Tom had quite a day. He went to all the events, setting up tables, putting out campaign brochures, hanging posters and banners. He did all this before Steve arrived. Then he had to dismantle everything after Steve spoke and go on to the next event, doing the same things all over again. Today, though, Steve was late getting to one place and the reporters were restless, putting Tom on the spot. In fact, one reporter even said, "You hear your father's speech all the time. Why don't you go ahead and give the speech for him?"

* * *

Our daughter, Ann, graduated from high school just weeks after her older brother's college graduation. Unfortunately, the logistical problems we encountered, with her graduation and the State Assembly occurring on the same day, added more stress to our entire family. There were, however, humorous moments to offset the stress.

March 2

Ann's graduation is scheduled for the same day and time as the State Assembly. Well, campaign or no campaign, I'm not going to miss her graduation, and neither is she.

June 7

What a day! I still can't believe we made it to both
events—Ann, Dede, and I, that is—and we also have a
video cassette of the ceremonies for everyone to view later
on. I probably should watch it, too, because I can't remember very much of anything before that glorious helicopter ride up to Denver. Oh, yes, I remember Annabel
saying, "I'm so embarrassed." Well, now that I think of it,
I could have killed the pilot, too. But I'm getting ahead of
myself.

While the boys worked the delegates at the State Assembly with their father, we attended the graduation ceremonies. And everything was going along according to plan
until we heard a loud thundering noise overhead coming
in our direction. Well, one and all checked it out, with
Dede and me pretending we didn't know who or what it
was—just a helicopter flying by—and Ann wouldn't look
at us, wanting to fall through the floor of the stage, I'm
sure.

It seemed to take forever before the pilot located the
field he was to land in. And by then people were nodding
at us in recognition of what must be happening. The only
thing missing was some sky-writing spelling out "Vote
for Steve." Miraculously, though, at that precise moment
in the program, several bagpipers were playing tunes,
drowning out the sounds of the propellers as they were
shutting down. Now we only had to contend with the
time schedule.

Of course, the ceremonies lasted one hour longer than
scheduled, but the three of us raced to the helicopter
anyway, laughing at the craziness of it all. We never
imagined that we might still get to Denver in time for the
rally. The ride, low and fast, was wonderful. And the pilot
couldn't have been nicer or more understanding. Well, we

made it to Denver, and the State Assembly was also running one hour late, so we were just in time to join the others. But just barely.

In fact, the rallies were already underway when we arrived. And staff, with walkie talkies, assisted us as they communicated with some invisible person whose voice was saying, "Run faster." But we made it, and so did Steve. He's in a primary race now. I think I'll take a short nap. It may be the last one I get for a long time to come.

*   *   *

Yet another difficult period for the family was adjusting to the death of one of our family pets.

June 28

Took Ruffin to the vet today. He was put to sleep. The cancer returned just weeks after his last surgery, and he was experiencing tremendous discomfort. The final look from him was so sad. . . . I told him I would see him again, some day. Then I cried. . . . He really seems like such an old soul. . . . How I wish we had the time to grieve as a family.

July 28

On Saturday we had approximately 50 campaign workers here for an outdoor BBQ. I had Sunday off, but Steve went to the El Paso County Fair, Douglas County BBQ, and Arapahoe County social. He said it went well for him, although the rain was terrible. Somehow it stopped raining long enough for our party and then started again afterward. Maybe it's Ruffin looking after us from his great big dog house in the sky. . . .

NOTES

1. Republican National Committee, "The Candidate's Wife" (Washington, D.C.: Fontana Lithograph Inc., undated), 1–8.

2. George Hackett, "Quayle's Closest Advisor," *Newsweek* 112 (24 October 1988): 23.

3. Barbara Gamarekin, "Hell Hath No Conflict Like the Political Wife," New York *Times,* 22 July 1987, Washington Talk.

4. Joan Conant and Eleanor Clift, "First Ladies in Waiting," *Newsweek* 110 (17 August 1987): 23.

5. Dave Larsen, "Two-Career Families," Los Angeles *Times,* 18 September 1987, sec. V.

6. Dorothy V. Lamm, *Second Banana* (Boulder, Colo.: Johnson Publishing Company, 1983), 14.

7. Conant and Clift, "First Ladies in Waiting," 23.

8. Republican National Committee, "The Candidate's Wife," 2.

9. "A New Breed Of Democratic Wives Looks for the Balance Between Liberation and Loyalty," *People,* 22 February 1988, 41.

10. Richard Scheinin, "Counting the Home Vote," *USA Weekend,* 6–8 November 1987, 5.

11. Marcia Chellis, *Living with the Kennedys: The Joan Kennedy Story* (New York: Simon & Schuster, 1985), 140.

Chapter Two

Rules of the Game

> If you're going to marry someone who's interested in politics, you bloody well should know what you're letting yourself in for.
>
> —*Charlotte Blacker*

Most of us view political life in the same glamourous light that shines on the world of entertainment. From all appearances, it is a star-studded life. Our politicians are seen on the evening news and in today's newspaper at yet another glitzy social function, enjoying the company of world leaders, movie stars, and even this year's popular professional athletes. Wherever politicians go, someone wants to take their picture, ask them questions, or be seen with them.

The politician, like any other celebrity, resides in a glass house, with every move and word recorded for public consumption. Camera crews appear at the politician's home, setting up their equipment for live action on the evening news programs. Usually the crew will capture the politician while working at his desk in the home's library or den. Whenever possible there is a roaring fire blazing in the background. Other times, reporters can be seen with their portable cameras resting on one shoulder, zooming in on the politician as he enters a building, hoping for some human interest story to present later. Both actors' and politicians' pictures can be found in magazines and in frames on people's desks and walls. No doubt about it, politicians are considered celebrities, and many people are very much in awe of them. Yet somehow the notion of politicians having star status just doesn't seem right. Most of us grew up assuming that people ran for political office because they wanted to serve their country.

Today, candidates hire well-known rock bands and other celebrities to entertain at their receptions, hoping to lure those undecided voters into their favor. And many times the person who stages the best party wins the voters' hearts. But do the candidates know that their choice in musical entertainment can sway or solidify a vote? They most certainly do, because we are a society that embraces the entertainment world and all the illusions that go along with it.

For example, on April 15, 1972, Barbra Streisand, performing in concert for the first time in six years, went on stage at the Los Angeles Forum. The event was a star-studded fund-raising effort for the presidential campaign of former Senator George McGovern, with Streisand and other celebrities serving as glamourous bait. The ushers included such well-known names as Warren Beatty, Sally Kellerman, Jack Nicholson, Goldie Hawn, Jon Voight, and Burt Lancaster. And the evening's receipts amounted to more than $300,000! Although this amount is hardly enough to wholly finance a presidential campaign, it's a good beginning. Too, regardless of George McGovern's loss, he did share the limelight for a while.

Yes, there are many actors in the political arena. We've all seen politicians who could win awards for presenting themselves in the brightest light of the entertainment world, where looking good is where it's at. And politics is now defined as much, if not more, by the beauty contest as it is by the issues. Today we're led to believe a candidate cannot expect to win an election if his tie clashes with his hairstyle! So if a politician's looks are dated, then I guess we are to assume that his views are, too.

It is a sad testimonial, indeed, that many of our politicians share this preoccupation with personal appearances. As Arizona's former Senator Barry M. Goldwater noted in his memoirs, *Goldwater,* "A senator does not live or die on his legislative effectiveness, as in the old days. Appearances—media attention, staff-generated bills, and professional packaging like some mouthwash—often replace legislative tenacity."[1] While we can surely empathize with a newcomer's short-lived labor over his personal appearance, can we excuse a seasoned player who buys into the beauty image? Perfectly groomed people make me wary, and I can't help but question the value system of a person who obviously has spent hours combing every hair on his head into place and coordinating his wardrobe until he is perfectly groomed and attired.

While so much emphasis is placed on superficialities, vital political issues and the true character of the political family often go unrecognized. I am reminded of Pat Nixon, who so skillfully concealed her true feelings from the public. Her public profile was of the cool and serene first lady, with never a hair or an emotion out of place. Granted, she had no desire to bask in the public spotlight; however, she seemed compelled to give us what we expected of her. It was only after President Nixon resigned that we learned of her personal agonies and thoughts related to political life.

Politicians' reticence about addressing certain issues should come as no surprise, for the political world has known for a long time that strongly worded opinions often lose votes, as illustrated by the landslide defeat of

Barry Goldwater in his 1964 race for the presidency. And while the politician's compulsion to project himself in the most positive light is understandable, the unceasing attention given to his appearance in place of substantive issues surely reflects terribly on our expectations of politicians. I wonder if we, the image-hungry public, haven't turned our politicians into 8 by 10 living glossies that reflect nothing about their true character.

Because of our society's infatuation with the glitter and imagery of the entertainment world, it should not surprise us that our political candidates seem more concerned with style than substance. Politicians and their wives understand perfectly the need to appeal to voters on many levels. For example, Jackie Kennedy was deftly thrust before the public as America's answer to royalty. She and her designer clothes set the style for American women. Accounts of her summers at the Kennedy compound on Cape Cod, including photographs of her frolicking with the children on the beach, whetted our appetite, and we craved more and more publicity about America's royal family. And when Jackie Kennedy stole the public's heart, she also became America's top cover girl.

If voters seem preoccupied with matters of style, then it stands to reason that so will anyone who hopes to get elected to public office. The expressed priorities of any politician in our democratic society will nearly always mirror the perceived priorities of the voting public, however distorted they might be. Even those politicians with the best intentions seem compelled to embrace the beauty image as they become accustomed to an environment that rewards one's appearance before one's performance. When political preferences are determined, issues seem to take a back seat to our, and in many cases, the candidate's, consuming preoccupation with physical appearances. He'll do what it takes to position himself in the spotlight.

Haven't we all observed politicians who cultive relationships with the media to assure that the morning newspapers always carry pictures of them attending all the right
events? So it seems politicians accept the rules of the game
that we have established, with some politicians portraying
the image better than others. But our politicians are not
alone. They are encouraged now by a whole new breed of
specialist: the image-maker.

Image consultants seem to understand our star-hungry
view of politicians, and thus strive diligently to produce
the illusion of politician as star to meet our absurd de-
mand. They also know how to transform a political hopeful into "somebody"—fast. "Here, try on these glasses.
Don't even wear those shoes with that suit. No bow ties,
please. And smile. Ah, that's better. You look wonderful.
You can't lose. That'll be a lot of money, please. Thank
you." And when we impose and embrace illusions, further
and further do the important issues recede. Gary Hart, for
example, has come a long way from his days at the Yale
Seminary. The constant comparisons between him and the
Kennedy brothers suggest that Hart's transformation,
from his hair style to his body language, was no accident.

If intelligence and a keen understanding of the issues
were the keys to being elected to public office, then more
than likely an Albert Einstein could have won a political
race. However, it is common knowledge among politicians
that voters make decisions about candidates by gut reactions. Consequently, judging by Einstein's physical appearance, I doubt if voters would have given him the time
of day. Why, he would have had to have his hair styled, his
colors done, and to join a health club! "Now, about your
eyeglasses, Al. . . . There, that should do it."

Many candidates who approach politics as a beauty
contest don't see their posturing as a means to a more
noble end. To many of them, it *is* the end. Too often, if a

candidate succeeds in convincing his constituents that his image is better than that of his opponent, he believes his own press. He is even flattered to have won approval for his appearance, rather than for his opinions and intentions. And we, starry-eyed public, have elected an actor.

Thus, many leaders and political hopefuls approach a campaign as they would an audition for the leading role in a Hollywood production. They seem to thrive in this duplicitous environment where they can dodge the difficult and controversial issues. We see politicians play on the public attention and represent themselves as celebrities instead of leaders. They pitch horseshoes at county fairs, kiss babies, give speeches that promise us there is a pot of gold at the end of the rainbow, and then they ride off into the sunset with their fashion-conscious, smiling wives. And they do all this to appease our insatiable appetites. But, of course, they cannot merely walk off the set at day's end when the economy is depressed and people are homeless, hungry, abused, or mentally ill.

Only recently have we opened the door of politics to actors and other celebrities. Ronald Reagan, Clint Eastwood, and Sonny Bono have all moved their act from the stage to the political arena. This is not to say that they are not viable candidates, but rather that the public now demands more glamour from its politicians. Could Shakespeare's wisdom, I wonder, have been directly intended for the political realm when the play's character Jaques stated: "All the world's a stage." Precisely because we are giving value to all the wrong things, we, the public, have created a massive muddle.

Once our politicians enter this world of entertainment, they have our permission to be outrageous. Why, we encourage it. Remember the escapades of the 38-year-old stripper, Fanne Foxe, and 65-year-old Congressman Wilbur Mills, including his appearance with her on stage at the Boston Burlesque Theater? And the scandal involving veteran Congressman Wayne Hays and the former Miss Virginia, Elizabeth Rae, who when questioned about her duties as the congressman's secretary said she couldn't type or file?

In today's setting, where reputations rest more on style than substance, there is, however, one major drawback to being a political celebrity. The players are well aware that while the public craves tales of celebrities' escapades, an entertainer's reputation and popularity can actually benefit from dubious conduct, but a politician's career can be jeopardized or even ruined by hints of indiscretion. Remember Teddy Kennedy's experience at Chappaquiddick? Or Gary Hart's clandestine romantic cruise to Bimini with Donna Rice? Both of these occurrences raised questions about the politician's judgment and morals, and the news publications filled their pages with the details, ad nauseum.

Considerations of personal character should, of course, influence our decisions to elect public officials. We need at least some degree of assurance that our leaders aspire to the noble ideals they represent. Still, if we expect our politicians to be entertainers, and then intentionally bestow upon them star status, is it any wonder that some of them become fodder for the scandal sheets?

Yes, we have created a system that is not reality-based but one that speaks to illusions. What we are left with is the equivalent of a theatrical production, a political environment that mirrors the entertainment world. For not only do the image-makers deliver what we want when they transform politicians into stars, but many politicians are doing their part as well when they present themselves solely through the bright light of celebrity.

And now with the illusion, illusionist, and star players on stage, the news media are there to do their job, too.

Their efforts to feed the public's cravings, however, take a different tack. The media often sensationalize the news, toppling an illustrious politician in the process in order to capture the readers' attention. They perpetuate the image, adding fuel to our illusions by covering black-tie events in our nation's capital which after all are purely for our starry-eyed benefit. This is what we want. And reporters, like the image-makers and many of our politicians, know how to oblige.

Now it is important to remember that reporters are no different from other people trying to advance themselves professionally. However, the news media do have a responsibility not only to themselves but to the public, as well, to be objective. According to the code of ethics adopted by the 1973 national convention of professional journalists, truth and objectivity in reporting, in fact, are the two cardinal goals for worthy newspeople.[2] Yet I am reminded of an article written by Jeff Greenfield, political commentator for Universal Press Syndicate, who denounced many journalists for taking liberty with the facts. Greenfield calls it "sloppiness" when a reporter makes assumptions and gets the facts wrong rather than verifying them first. "More consequential are those mistakes that flow from an unwillingness to let a hot story evaporate in a cloud of uncertainty," Greenfield adds.[3]

According to Marc E. Miller, author of *Politicians and Their Spouses' Careers,* "There are simply more journalists in Washington than almost anywhere else, watching and waiting for something juicy to fill their time and space."[4] This widely accepted approach to "news gathering" is rather appalling when judged by the directives of the journalists' code of ethics: "Journalists at all times will show respect for the dignity, privacy, rights, and well-being of people encountered in the course of gathering and presenting the news."[5] Perhaps the code of ethics should be dusted off and reviewed by journalists at their next convention.

Reporters' lack of objectivity and questionable news-gathering methods are common complaints among many congressional wives. "We have to be very careful of what we say. Tomorrow we could see our words in the newspapers. And I have," said one political wife. Another woman related an episode that occurred early in her husband's political career when she was inexperienced in talking to the press. Unaware that everything said to a reporter is quotable, she became quite relaxed during an interview, feeling as though she were talking to a friend. When asked about a controversial issue, she responded candidly with her own opinion, which was somewhat different from that of her spouse. The headline in the morning newspaper declared that the politician and his wife were squabbling.

Actually, few political wives talked very charitably about the current breed of political reporters who "invent," "print partial comments," and "are so uninformed," suggesting that the problem is a national rather than a regional concern. Wives from all parts of the country made similar comments about the press. "I was so angry at the end, I wouldn't talk to the press. I thought I'd say the wrong thing." "The press will print lies in the paper, and then people don't know who to believe." One political wife responded, "My husband put emphasis on nurturing relationships with the press because he saw what the press can do to people."

A frustration of political wives concerns selective reporting. In many instances its effect can damage reputations and careers. For example, rumors start to fly when a newspaper reports that a politician or his wife attended a function alone, when in fact the absent spouse was out of town tending a sick relative. Other times, the press will print an article attacking a member of Congress for miss-

ing an important vote when the truth of the matter is that
the politician was attending a funeral. In each instance no
effort is made to report the whole story.

Sadly, many reporters do not simply report the news—
they sensationalize it. And sensationalism is achieved instantly, with the stroke of a pen or with the flash of a
camera. One needs only to glance at news publications or
turn on the TV to witness sensationalized news. For
example, when Elizabeth Dole resigned her position as
Secretary of Transportation to campaign with her husband, Senator Robert Dole, Peter Jennings opened the
ABC evening news program with: "One of the most
important women in government has given up her job for
a man." Another time, a *Newsweek* magazine cover displayed Gary Hart's photo, his face reflecting enormous
rage. In the lower-right corner, Donna Rice is shown
gazing up at him despondently. The caption read: "Sex,
Politics and the Press. Gary Hart Self-Destructs."

While I find this technique used by the media rather
irksome, I am reminded that many people do, in fact,
respond to and are enthralled by sensational reporting
styles. A congressional wife, requesting anonymity, confessed to me that following the Gary Hart scandal she
asked her husband "to drive me by the Hart townhouse. I
wanted to see it. As we approached the house, there was a
waiting line of cars. In fact, there was so much traffic they
could have sold tickets!"

Another reason for the news media's poor image may
well be its one-dimensional approach to reporting, in
which the public is permitted to see only what the news
media wants it to see. False images are created for the
purpose of selling newspapers or achieving higher ratings.
For example, saying that the politician is a "wimp" suggests he is not a leader but a loser, a milk-toast type who
is incapable of taking charge of himself, let alone the

country. Regardless of the validity of such observations, by addressing an issue or evaluating a political candidate through a singular dimension, the public is deprived of the total picture. If the end justifies the means, then the media have done their job, capturing the reader's attention with nothing more than baseless bravado.

Still another reason for the press's bad reviews is its unrelenting investigative efforts. Reporters are masters at rooting out damaging details about one or another of our politicians, with Gary Hart and Joe Biden being national examples of how the press's scrutiny can affect politicians' careers. Reporters do not go at this haphazardly. They confront daily, sending messages to the public that cannot be ignored. In both cases, the politician's run for the presidency was thwarted.

In other instances, while a career is not destroyed, the press's relentless investigations damage the politician's reputation, causing an enormous amount of embarrassment for himself and his family. For example, on November 4, 1979, CBS news commentator Roger Mudd interviewed presidential candidate Ted Kennedy. At one point in the nationally televised program, Mudd asked Kennedy to respond to some unanswered questions about the events that had taken place at Chappaquiddick in 1969. Kennedy, who seemed unprepared and uneasy, evaded every question, unable to complete a single sentence. While Ted Kennedy may never be a presidential candidate because of the questions left unanswered in that disastrous interview, he still seems secure in his position as senator of Massachusetts. As the wife of a freshman congressman implied about the press's scrutiny, politicians can survive embarrassment but not character assassination.

I am reminded of one particular interview in which a former candidate presented a rather dramatic illustration of his experience with the press's investigative work. He expounded on the problems his wife had experienced in dealing with the press digging into their past. Oddly enough, he could not understand why she was so troubled by it. "They accused me of tax evasion, having girlfriends and bigamy." When I asked him if the press was accurate about his being a bigamist, he replied: "Well, my former marriage was such a long time ago I just forgot about it. But I told her there was nothing more they could do. So I don't know why she was so upset."

The reporter's job is to deliver "the goods," stories that are sufficiently enticing to the reader. After all, a newspaper boosts its sales by capturing the public's attention. Therefore, unless those political reporters write what the public wants to read, they may find themselves searching for work at yet another news agency. But of course there are just so many campaigns and so many political reporters, all trying to follow the rules of the game by delivering some form of acceptable entertainment for the public.

Granted, it's difficult for reporters who are covering the same candidates day after day to say things differently. However, I recall one first lady having this to say about a certain reporter's constant negative coverage of her husband: "He just waits for a dull day and drags up something old." I also learned firsthand, from a newspaper columnist, that when no new information about a candidate is available, reporters will "find something negative to say about him." And I thought a reporter's job was to report the news. How foolish of me!

It appears that in their frantic attempts to appeal to the ultimate god, the public, the press and the candidates find they need each other. I've often wondered if reporters' investigative articles aren't, in part, an attempt to influence candidates to pick up on the scurrilous data so the politicians can go on addressing or attacking it themselves. This mutually manipulative relationship was succinctly described by *Rocky Mountain News* columnist Gene Amole: "In this cannibalistic society, the media feed off the politicians and the politicians feed off the media. We need each other. We need Hart to put on page 4, and Hart needs us to get on page 4. It's that simple."[6] But more and more it seems the press is focusing its sights only on the negative aspects of the news.

Positive press simply attracts fewer readers. Why else would politicians and reporters give so much attention to it? Negativity has become a tradition, a way of life, a part of the game, something that goes with the territory. And along with the public's acceptance of this negative and sensational reporting style, there is a certain amount of anticipation. In the public light of politics, it seems that anything is fair game.

Consequently, those who decide to run for political office must be prepared to sacrifice their private lives to the diggings of both their opponents and the press. In fact, private life and politics just don't mix. As Mary Andrews, wife of former Senator Mark Andrews, says: "You cannot expect to have a private life in politics when everyone is looking over your shoulder." Or looking into your past?

Many candidates, regrettably, use the press to launch public attacks against their opponents. Of course the press eagerly responds, and the battle is on—attack and counterattack. If the politicians are willing, each can manipulate his press contacts to achieve the desired result—increased publicity for himself and the character assassination of the opponent. One first lady, for example, talked about the newspaper smear campaign her family had to endure. The opponent was accused of being a homosexual, while her husband was accused of being a womanizer and of having a mistress. When I queried her on how she and her children had dealt with the situation, she responded matter of factly: "Well, it's not so bad. It would be worse being accused of homosexuality."

The remarks of George Bush's political consultant, Roger Ailes, on election night 1988 seem to capture the mood of all this political negativity by both the press and the candidates in recent elections. He strongly suggested to Mike Wallace on CBS television that the media are interested in only four things—polls, pictures, attacks, and mistakes. Issue papers, he went on to comment, are not covered by the media because they don't fit into any of those four categories. Mr. Ailes suggested that the only way the candidate can capture the press's attention is to be as sensational or negative as the news media are when they attempt to capture the public's attention. His comments seem to pose a question: Is the politician to blame if he resorts to attacking his opponent to win votes?

Although political wives do not engage in smear tactics against each other, they, too, are open to the press's scrutiny, especially those who have moved out of their husbands' shadows. Former first ladies Nancy Reagan and Rosalynn Carter can attest to that. However, most of the women with whom I spoke agreed that their husbands are usually the prime target for criticism. Political wives, though, must contend with condescending attitudes about their abilities and their value to the political system. On July 27, 1987, at Drake University, all but one of the wives of the Democratic presidential hopefuls met on stage for a forum organized exclusively for them. A great number of the news media attended, covering the event as they would had it been organized for the presidential candidates. After learning which political wife could best deliver humor and that Jackie Jackson, wife of the Reverend Jesse Jackson, had a schedule conflict, the chairman of the Polk County Democrats summed up both the event and the political wives' ability to significantly influence voters: "I don't think it makes a difference one way or the other."[7]

When the inevitable criticism of the politician does

come, it can be hard for the political wife to handle. In fact, many wives admit they take personally any criticism of their husband. So during campaigns those women ignore the newspapers because "criticism is devastating." Caroline McMillan, wife of Congressman J. Alex McMillan, has this to say about the criticism of her husband: "I try to deal with it intellectually. Emotionally, though, it never stops hurting." But veteran political wife Joanne Kemp remarked: "Jack was a professional quarterback and criticized often, so I'm used to it." And Marilyn Quayle responded, "I don't take public criticism personally. I understand the need for the game."

"The game," of course, continues as long as the public refrains from expressing displeasure with the negative reporting styles and the tedious sensationalized stories about politicians. Silence is interpreted as acceptance. When we fail to question reporters' methods and products or to hold ourselves or others responsible for accepting the political theatrics, we, in effect, are asking for more of the same. I am not suggesting that the public has no right to be informed about a candidate's shady dealings, because a candidate's private life often reveals much about his potential performance. But I do believe there is a point at which reporters continue beating a dead horse, so to speak, when they can and should stop reporting the same old news the same old way.

Long ago, politics was different, with the media assuming a lower profile. Politics in those days was conducted in back rooms, smoke-filled rooms I think the story goes. The party leaders selected the cast of politicians before the candidates announced their intent to seek political office. And while this process seems rather undemocratic, more often politicians were selected for their merits as leaders rather than for their looks or charismatic style. Peter F. Drucker, Clark professor of social sciences at the Clare-

mont Graduate School, remarks that charisma isn't even a
necessary requirement for being an effective leader. Of
former presidents Eisenhower and Truman, Drucker says
they were "singularly effective leaders yet [neither] pos-
sessed any more charisma than a dead mackerel."[8]

I recall one political wife, married to a former journalist,
who remarked that not only our political process, but the
news media as well, has changed from what it was thirty
years ago. With remarks intended for the new breed of
investigative reporter, she said: "Today, whatever you say,
reporters turn it around. They write what they want, not
what you say. My husband was not taught that kind of
journalism in his school." Many political wives in frequent
contact with the press complain that today's reporters take
a tiny bit of truth and build a story around it. Then, "they
hide behind the First Amendment," said a veteran Native
American political wife. One former senator's wife went
so far as to say: "Reporters, today, are not friendly. Those
under 25 are interested in scandal rather than the needs of
the state. The bigger problem is the effect of such reporting on the American public."

Because today's news media are so oriented toward
interrogative tactics and uncovering the sordid and sensational, we are faced with an interesting and new circumstance—a role reversal. Now the voters make their decisions only after the press has done the screening for them.
Apparently, we prefer this arrangement. We look to the
media for guidance when trying to determine which candidate we should support and even expect the media to do
the investigative work. In turn, reporters compete with
each other for our confidence. And as a result, the news
media assume our rightful role in the decision-making
process. For all intents and purposes, they are the alternate
electorate for our cast of candidates. And by elevating the
news media to this stature, we have become passive spec-

tators at election time, choosing our leaders by what we are "fed" on television and in our news publications.

No doubt about it, those in the media have tremendous influence over our lives. Quite often they define what "the" issues are and determine who receives publicity and whether it be positive or negative. And how many times have we heard a politician's speech on television, then gazed at the screen in disbelief as some news anchor told us what the speaker *really* said.

As the media have gained more and more power and the public has become more and more obsessed with celebrities, the worlds of politics, entertainment, and communications have merged. Today, news programs feature politicians as well as stars of stage, screen, and the sports world. The "hard news" programs have all but vanished, having been replaced by "shows" which devote increasingly lengthy segments to personality profiles and interviews. And as greater numbers of entertainers are entering politics, more and more news anchors and correspondents are becoming "stars." The public is so familiar with the details of these media celebrities' lives that many feel they know them. We have learned, from watching television and reading the newspapers that Diane Sawyer is married to director Mike Nichols and what they eat for breakfast. We know where Connie Chung buys her clothes and what she pays for them. Reporters reveal when and where Barbara Walters had her face "done" and where Tom Brokaw spends his vacations.

John Kolbe, a Phoenix, Arizona newspaper columnist, remarked that during Evan Mecham's brief tenure as governor of Arizona, he broke "the cardinal rule of politicians: You can't fight people who buy ink by the barrel."[9] Political wives, too, view the news media as being very powerful because "you can't control the press" and "if you criticize them, they treat you less favorably." One wife stated that she doesn't like "having to be so dependent on them and what they think," because their views, whether biased or not, reach the public's ear and influence public opinion.

Barbara Bush had this to say about power and the press: "It's hard not to define power as reporters do. The common perception of power is people running around seeking it." Indeed, politics is a game of power struggles—with the candidates battling their opponents, politicians vying for press coverage, and reporters competing against each other for the scoop on a politician. It all boils down to the quest for power.

The theme of political power—who has it, wants it, seeks it—pervades the political arena. If you walk the halls of the Capitol Building in Washington, D.C., you can, on any day, hear numerous people referring to the power lunch or power meeting that they recently attended. In the Senate and House dining rooms, you can detect the workings of power in the air. The House dining room is action-packed. Heads, hands, and jaws are in constant motion. Eyes move across the room and pause momentarily at the door as a group of politicos enter. Politicians position themselves at particular tables that allow them to consume their meals while conversing with a peer at another table and to move about easily from one table to another. One group of congressmen always receives the most attention, leaving no doubt in anyone's mind that they are regarded by their colleagues as powerful.

Conversely, the Senate dining room is large and quiet, with some private rooms leading off the somberly elegant main hall. The walls are covered with history. During one of my interviews in the Senate dining room, I overheard a senator's wife lightheartedly telling the staff officer that she and her husband had moved up in the political world (her husband had previously been a congressman). After she departed, the staff was given explicit instructions to "remember Mrs. ——. Her husband is a new senator." Obviously, the political wife's remarks reflected her belief that a senator possesses more power than a congressman. The staff officer's remarks suggested that some of the power obtained by her husband in his newly acquired position had somehow been bestowed upon his wife. In obvious disgust, one congressional spouse commented, "Some women are so impressed with their husband's position and themselves, I could kick them into the Potomac."

Kathy Carruthers, New Mexico's first lady, talks about power the way the majority of political wives do. She says: "Power is how much access you have and the ability to influence. It's a position, and money, too. Money provides influence." Influence. Position. Money. And political power appears to combine the basic elements of position and wealth with the ever-important power of persuasion, playing its crucial role in the governing of our country at all levels.

Moreover, there are political wives who believe power is something one can seek or acquire and then measure by the political position one holds. Renowned author and Harvard University Professor of Economics John Kenneth Galbraith says that John F. Kennedy was of a similar mind. He quotes Kennedy as saying, "I run for president because that is where the action is."[10] Mr. Galbraith suggests that Kennedy's use of the word "action" meant "power" to him. Most of the political wives interviewed do consider power to be one of the perks of political office and believe that the higher up one goes, the more power one has. Lynn Waihee, Hawaii's first lady, even stated, "Just the office itself gives the person power." I am reminded of one congressional wife, though, who seemed stumped by the question of what power means to her. She said: "Oh, my,

no one ever asked me that before." After gaining composure, however, she responded with, "Probably one's perception of power is greater than the reality."

Frequently, as a consequence of seeking political power,
the politician believes himself powerful simply because of
the position he holds. And that can be dangerous. Pam
Herger, wife of California's Congressman Wally Herger,
says: "I don't have a lot of respect for people who abuse
power. It is not something to be abused. And some people,
if given a little power, tend to use it without restraint."
Perhaps she was referring to the common practice among
many committee chairpersons of killing bills by delaying
action on them.

The wife of Colorado's Senator William Armstrong,
Ellen, had this to say about those people who think they
are powerful: "There are so many people back there,
congressional people, who believe they are powerful because of their position, and they act that way. I'm not
impressed with people who think they have it. Bill is the
least egocentric political person I know."

The power attributed to those who hold political office
is so appealing that many politicians believe it justifies the
rigors of campaigning. Oftentimes, the public's attention,
adoration, and acclaim are hard to relinquish. For example, Ronald Reagan, just weeks after stepping down from
the presidency, announced that he was ready to go on the
speaking circuit.

In politics, you are your title. For example, "Who are
you?" is often responded to with "Congressman" or
"Senator," rather than with a person's first and last name.
Why, many of us even refer to a congressman as Mr.
Congressman. One political wife stated that she thoroughly enjoys being called "Mrs. Congressman" by her
husband's constituents because it makes *her* feel powerful.

If the politician's sense of self is defined referentially by his acquisition of political power, his wife's identity is even more tangled in a web of external influences. But her connection to "power" is indirect, the consequence of her husband's position. And when she allows her identity to be defined by his position, the result often is self-destructive behavior and feelings of inadequacy, as if her hands are tied. Many of the women with whom I talked articulated the sacrifices they made to an unappreciative political system. In essence, they implied: "Look at all the work I put into this campaign, and they still don't know my name."

After my interviews with political wives were well underway, I had an opportunity to interview several Native American first ladies. What resulted from my discussions with these women was a new definition of power. My interview with Virginia Lewis, first lady of the Zunis, captured the Native Americans' view. My daughter Annabel accompanied me on this trip to the Southwest, giving each of us many enjoyable memories. One late night episode, though, was at my expense.

We arrived early so that we could observe the Zuni lifestyle and enjoy the natural environment. Since the nearest airport is a one-hour drive away from the Zuni reservation, our plane was met in Gallup, New Mexico by two of Governor Lewis's staff members. First, we were driven to our quarters on the governor's compound—an adobe dwelling with no running water. Then dinner at the local cafe in the town of Zuni, where we listened to concerns about the Zuni nation. We retired early in order to be fresh for the morning interview. However, at 3 a.m., Ann caught me wandering around the compound looking for the "bathroom." (Fortunately, the moon was full and the dogs were friendly.)

In the morning, Virginia Lewis welcomed us to her modest trailer home, then quickly ushered her grandchildren out to buy donuts for all of us—"for the special occasion." After the interview was well underway, I asked her if we could talk about power, and she responded, "Ah, power. Yes." After a pause, she added: "That can only come from within, Joyce. Personally we are all powerful, no matter who we are."

It wasn't until I had pored over my notes that I realized the very interesting contrast between the Native American women and all of the other women interviewed regarding their responses on the subject of power. Indeed, their differing opinions said a lot about both the women and their cultures. And based on each of the political wives' responses, there was no discernible way to detect whether a woman was a Democrat, Republican, or Native American before she answered the query on power.

The Native American women defined power as a state of being that emanates from within, rather than an external circumstance such as holding political office. "By feeling it, you recognize it," offered one Native American first lady. And because these women view power as something that stems from their inner resources, they view themselves as the sole keeper of their power.

The other congressional and gubernatorial spouses linked power to politics, defining it as something referential and external, the brass ring on the merry-go-round. Of course, power, when viewed from this perspective, generally excludes women. They do not exist in its definition, except as recipients through someone or something outside of themselves. This perspective also brings illusion into the equation. For if the candidate is able to manipulate the media and his constituents into believing that he is powerful, then he is. Politicians who make it to the top of the heap attain power because they're masters of manipulation, whether Reagan, Kennedy, or Hart. Furthermore, their wives also are viewed as having power because of their husbands' position.

In *How the Good Guys Finally Won,* Jimmy Breslin states that the person who has power is the one who can manipulate the blue smoke and mirrors—the blue smoke that distorts reality, the mirrors that reflect images of the distorted reality. According to Breslin, Tip O'Neill's success in politics can be directly attributed to his ability to manipulate and his understanding of the necessity to do so. "Tip O'Neill at all times has one great political weapon at his disposal. He understands so well that all political power is primarily an illusion. If people think you have power, then you have power. If people think you have no power, then you have no power."[11]

Power as an illusion relates to our American culture's orientation to external influences. For example, wealth and position are symbols of success in our society, and a great number of individuals are vigorously striving to achieve them. Those who have wealth or stature are perceived as being powerful. And we have only to look at what others have labeled "yuppies" to realize the validity of that.

Granted, we all project an image—in the way we dress and the things we say. It allows us to operate socially within a certain frame of reference that we, for whatever reasons, prefer. However, so many of us, regrettably, feel compelled to impress others with our wealth and stature by striving for and then displaying our material goods— the cars we drive, the manses in which we reside, and the finery we wear. When we set our sights on wealth and position as means to achieve political power, the power becomes the reward instead of the instrument—the crystal instead of the sand.

Native American women define their world in a much different way than other political wives. Position and image are tantamount to success for nearly all political wives, but not the Native American women, who don't even argue from the same definitions. Illusions, and particularly political power, have no meaning to Native American political wives, for their beliefs and values are formed from within themselves. Similarly, while most political wives may look at beauty as an orderly garden, a defined area with flowers in their proper place, the Native American looks at beauty as the whole universe. Where we attempt to create a beautiful setting from barren land, the desert is their beauty. Indeed, beauty for the Native American political wife is not something that plays to illusions or is humanly structured or organized. It is nature. It is reality—not an illusion.

*   *   *

During the course of my husband's campaign, I discovered how similar the entertainment world and the political world are when we were invited to attend a celebrity tennis tournament in Aspen, Colorado. The host represented that we would experience a very non-competitive, relaxing weekend. A "hit and giggles weekend," he said. We did. We also saw the movie stars being followed by cameras and awestruck fans. And I came away with a new understanding of star-status politicians. The following journal entries reflect my feelings.

February 23

Went to Denver Saturday night to "mingle" with Vice President Bush and Mrs. Bush. The cocktail party was small—30 people. Visited with the Bushes, who are real in this world of illusion. Barbara is warm and gracious.

The dinner was just a little intimate group of 900! All the candidates were there and were recognized at the beginning of the evening. Applause. Applause.

One candidate's wife was wearing a rhinestone ankle bracelet *over* her black hose. How's that for attention getting? What a hoot! Wonder if anyone else noticed.

What a way to live. But I must admit it's a hell of a lot better than the cocktail circuit—that is, of course, if those are our two choices. . . .

April 14

Today Steve met an image consultant. She told him she was working on Roy Romer, the Democratic candidate for governor, and would be happy to do the same for Steve (for a fee, of course). Fun, fun, fun. Steve said thank you, but no thanks.

April 17

I have a curiosity about external factors that contribute to this world of entertainment, which is comprised of illusions and images. Is it the politician who responds to the public's quest for a star, or is it the public who responds to the politician's quest for stardom? Or is the press responsible? Do we believe that elevating someone to star status will produce more dedicated public service from our politicians? Do the politicians believe that placement on a pedestal will condone any behavior and earn them power through acquisition?

May 22

I can't believe the theatrics we've been exposed to. I wonder who is authentic around us. Everything in politics seems to go back to projecting an image. One's image should be formed from the depth of one's character and the strength of one's convictions—not one's ability to act, for heaven's sake!

June 27

I think we create our own world, but I don't know what's happening right now. I remember thinking, when

I was a young girl, how wonderful it would be to be married to a celebrity. And here I sit married to an almost celebrity. We enjoy good health, our three children are on an independent course, doing what they want with their lives. We really have no major worries outside of his winning or losing a political race. Now, however, I have come to the conclusion that I don't want to spend my life just being a celebrity's wife. . . . Life in the limelight is not what it's cracked up to be.

July 7

Well, we attended another party tonight. But it is just another place to do our work. Work the crowd. You enter a room, usually with at least one other person who is good at remembering names (I am not) and proceed to shake every hand in the room, make conversation with the owners of those hands, and at least once during the idle chats call each person by his or her first name. Now that's entertainment. (I find it impossible to carry on a conversation when I'm concentrating so hard on trying to remember someone's name. No, politics is not intended for the likes of me!)

Anyway, the party. . . . Everything in the house was black and white with accents of the latest designer colors—in paintings, rugs, and pillows. Shiny enamel everywhere. Furniture made to scale. You name it, it was there. Everything seemed to be perfectly appointed, except the owner's wife. . . .

July 10

Politics is so much like the entertainment world. We make politicians bigger than life, forgetting that they're only human, with flaws and all, just like the rest of us.

July 26

Went to a BBQ at Vail, sponsored by the Colorado Broadcasters Association. Met some people from Washington, D.C. and had a good talk with a woman who is a close friend of Tip O'Neill's daughter. She told me that most candidates' wives are scared that they'll do or say something that might hurt the husband's image. But she said I seem relaxed and appear to "go with the flow." Interesting to be experienced that way. I am becoming more comfortable, though. Guess it shows.

September 2

The process of politics is like watching the sky ready itself for a thunderstorm. Instead of clouds, though, there are separate egos floating around, colliding with each other on a regular basis. Oops. Bam. Look out. Here comes another collision.

November 16

If there's anything that ties politics to the world of entertainment, it's that we are living in a winner-take-all environment, and the competition is fierce. Behind those smiles and friendly handshakes, it's every man for himself.

Big play by opponent to spread rumor that Senator Armstrong has committed to his candidacy. Seems that SV, WR, and SN tried some dirty pool and now some people have told Steve they liked him but couldn't go against Bill Armstrong. . . . So Steve called Bill to let him know the word on the street. Bill, of course, denied his supporting anyone in the gubernatorial race. He told Steve he'd know directly from Bill when he made a decision. . . . So Steve called PA, and PA called JR, who called everyone else to spread the truth. . . . Great game, huh?

But I ask you, does putting someone else down really elevate our own standing? We say we want strong leaders to govern our states, then we stab, jab, and distort at every turn along the way.

* * *

The following entries reveal the press's impact on this political wife. I must confess, despite my ranting I do respect our freedom of the press. Many reporters are quite responsible and care a great deal about our country's future. There are those in the news media who make well-intended contributions to the public's right to be informed. But others abuse their positions by intimidating and badgering their "subjects."

January 6

I don't feel ready for the press. As Patty said, whatever you say you will have to live with for the rest of the campaign.

January 13

Went out to dinner with JD and Steve. We discussed the new poll that came out in one of the newspapers that cited a veteran politician as the leader even though he hasn't even announced his candidacy! Could the "big city" press be trying to add more characters to the gubernatorial cast so they'll have more candidates to write about? Or am I giving them too much credit? I must admit I really prefer the reporters who aren't trying to make a "name" for themselves. But then again, you know where you stand with the "big city" types—Nowhere!

January 26

Guess my first interview with a newspaper reporter went well. Big color photo, big spread in Sunday paper.

Headline reads: "True Partner." I can't believe how lucky I am. The article reads a hell of a lot better than I thought it actually went. In fact, when it was over I couldn't even remember the questions or my answers.

One of the questions posed was, "With much emphasis put on appearances in politics, have you had to change your appearance since your husband's announcement?" My less than brilliant response did, at least, reflect how I feel about portraying an image. I said, "No, I try to be me at all times and so I dress the way I always do. That way people will recognize me (smile)."

January 29

Hit the front page of the newspaper! Big picture of Debbie (the girl at the Sheltered Workshop) and me dancing. Short story, too. So happy to have a clipping to keep that day in my memory.

January 30

Tuesday Steve had a difficult two-and-a-half-hour interview with the new reporter. Several people have concerns about him. He did a hatchet job on one of the senatorial candidates. Seems people think the reporter has an "if I destroy, I have power" mind-set. If their assessment of him is accurate, everyone had better be on their guard. . . . Ugh.

Wednesday I went to the Capitol with Steve for a press conference on higher education. It seemed to go well, although the press wasn't very thrilled about covering issues. I met the new reporter everyone is talking about. What a pompous young man!

February 4

Apparently the new reporter is calling people looking for sensational news about Steve's campaign. He's been tossing out phrases like "slick organization" and "machine" to them. If he only knew how disorganized this machine is. Oh well, if he wants to go down the wrong street, maybe he'll get lost, never to be heard from again. . . .

February 10

The long-awaited article appeared today. As usual, Steve and I disagreed about his press. He said the article was okay. I said not okay. And I was wrong, again. Most of the people who called, including staff, said it was good. Maybe they were referring to the old adage that it doesn't matter what you say, as long as your name is spelled right and kept before the public. Oh well, it doesn't really matter. I just don't understand this game.

February 12

Big picture and profile of candidate and spouse. The article noted that "although he says he will wait months to make an official candidacy announcement . . . his new career goal is to run for governor." They then quoted Steve: "Our decision won't be impacted by any moves made by any other candidates. . . . Our program is oriented toward issues and positions." No quote from the candidate's spouse, but these words, "His wife plans to continue her work with juvenile justice programs and setting up a rehabilitation-education center for battered women" (close but no cigar). Of course there was reference to the "prominent political consultant whose firm has represented such moderate Republicans as Gerald Ford and Nelson Rockefeller."

March 1

On the western slope again for a round of Lincoln Day dinners. Before we left town, saw Steve on a TV interview.

In response to the reporter's first question, he kept talking until time ran out and the reporter had no opportunity to ask another question!

March 23

News commentator came by in p.m. to conduct a live interview for the evening news. Came out well, but Steve gave him our unlisted telephone number instead of the listed one. Hopefully he'll lose it.

April 15

Interesting letter to the editor in one of the newspapers responding to the article on the supposed winner on caucus night. The letter writer said the newspaper article was slanted and biased and showed a distorted picture of what actually happened. Too bad he didn't mention that each candidate claimed himself to be the winner that night! Which is worse—the candidates slanting the polls in their favor or the press running a potentially damaging article that doesn't reflect the truth?

April 30

Another newspaper article, this one about all the candidates and surrogates who were detained in various places because of the spring snow. At least this report was accurate!

May 10

Continental breakfast today with supporters and the press. The question and answer period was the hardest of all. One reporter wouldn't stop asking questions or listen to the answers. But I think it was a power play directed at the other reporters. They, too, try to upstage each other.

May 14

Steve called to say his meeting with the editors and publisher of one of the Denver newspapers went well. I'll get the details when he gets home tonight.

Dan set up appointments for me. Steve told him to just schedule me with the press. Now I'm getting nervous. It's easy to sit here and write my little entries, but to actually go out on my own. . . . I guess there's no turning back.

May 30

Another two-week blur. Steve has had a couple of debates with all of the other candidates. Each of them, except Steve, is saying what the group wants to hear. In fact, one candidate changes his stand wherever he goes to suit the different factions! But the press never seems to pick up on this.

June 9

Too bad we couldn't capture this incident in a TV commercial. Ken came by with his sister to talk about the progress of the campaign. Then we all helped Barbie groom the dogs and cat. We looked like a short segment in a Three Stooges movie. We all worked for two hours trying to get the dogs to obey, and were as wet as the animals by the time it was over. To add to the confusion, the wind blew, it rained, and it hailed, accomplishing nothing except putting a lot of fear in the animals. The garage was filled with shampoo, water, and dog hair. Poor Stan (the cat) crawled under the car and clung to one of the tires until I finally pried him loose.

June 14

Talk about taking words out of context. . . . This whole experience has been a real eye-opener for me. It started on

June 12 when Steve lauded one city for its terrific planning (meaning that it was growing and people were finding it attractive to move there). Then, when the reporter stated that Governor Lamm thought the city was "ugly," Steve responded with, "If you want to see ugly, come with me and I'll show you ugly." Of course Steve was referring to the other city's depressed economy that was causing people to move out of the area, rather than to the city's physical appearance. Well, that was not what was reported. One paper extracted that particular response without including the comments leading up to and following it. Another headline, in their afternoon edition, read, "Who's Ugly?" And a third paper on June 13 suggested that the candidate's remarks had caused the campaign to turn ugly!

June 30

What a turnaround! Now, because of all the "ugly" publicity, the mayor of a struggling community on the western slope offered Steve a challenge, in jest, to travel to the mayor's town and call it ugly!

July 3

Press conference about the highway tax. Most of the TV coverage was good and the newspapers, too, although the press seemed fixated on showing Steve throw money into a garbage can rather than giving time to his reasons for being opposed to the tax. The good news is that Steve was endorsed by one of the "big city" newspapers that I am always finding fault with. Oh well, I'll just pretend that I'm Gilda Radner performing "Emily Litella" and mimic her words—"Never mind!"

August 6

It's Sunday and so much has happened since last I wrote that this will have to be a summary of two weeks.

We've been everywhere.

The press is all over us now. Today a TV camera person put a lens right in my face. I couldn't believe it. Thought about crossing my eyes but remembered that Patty said the media doesn't have much of a sense of humor, so I opted instead to do what most political wives do—I *smiled!* I don't know how Steve contends with public life all the time.

Last night about 40 of us covered all the gates at Mile High Stadium, before the Broncos game, to give out flyers for Steve. But we were outdone by one of the other candidates who'd arranged for a plane to fly over with a message written in the sky. . . . I have a message for him, too, but I don't think I want to write it in the sky. . . .

One TV station said that Steve was ahead in the polls.

Another TV station interviewed Steve.

My interview with the *Denver Post* was in the paper today, along with those of other potential and former first ladies.

August 10

You won't believe this one! What insanity! Where do reporters come up with these questions? Today a reporter asked me if my husband had ever discussed putting our money into his campaign. After thinking about all the quips I could respond with, I told him that we had discussed it and that I totally supported my husband's campaign efforts. The reporter muttered, "That isn't what my wife would say," to which I responded, "Your wife might think differently if she were married to Steve Schuck."

October 31

I have come to the realization that misrepresentation and sensationalism are not limited to politics. We attended

Barbara's funeral at the Colorado College Chapel. After twenty years of working together on community projects, she's gone. It's so incredible. Everywhere I looked there were reporters, and TV cameras. There was even a politician working the crowd! And those cameras moved right through the crowds, filming prominent people as they waited in the chapel line. You would have thought we were attending a social event, a gala. The reality, however, is that Barbara died violently at the hands of an unknown assailant. All of us who knew her are devastated. And neither family nor friends are allowed to grieve privately. Instead, the cameras roll on, portraying "Life" on the big screen. Is that really what people want?

To my way of thinking, we've lost perspective. The news media have a responsibility to the public. They have been charged with being objective. By not adhering to their responsibility, they are shortchanging us and wrongfully influencing our future generations.

What would happen if all of us started voicing our concerns about the media's irresponsibility? Would they stop sensationalizing? Would it discourage some of the less conscientious news media from taking liberties with the facts? Would reporters be forced to report more of the truth? I wonder. . . .

* * *

There were times when I would just record my thoughts about the press and the candidates. The following entries offer a glimpse into some of my musings.

February 6

I don't understand politics. Everyone tries to upstage the other, losing sight of all reason for being there. The political arena is looking more like a three-ring circus.

Hear ye, hear ye. Come see our special show. The candidates are on next, and you can watch them bump into each other as they attempt to shake your hand. The only thing missing is that brightly painted car in the center ring of the circus from which all the clowns emerge. Sometimes I wish we could go back to earlier times, when people cared about each other, worked together to solve problems, and admitted to being human. Still, maybe it wasn't any better in earlier days. Maybe it just seems that way.

May 7

Each time, and I know there will be many of them, that Steve is either misquoted or misunderstood, I feel so helpless.

I wonder if other spouses feel they are standing on the edge of a precipice . . . at times, not knowing if the earth is going to give way and send them careening down.

Perhaps that's what life is all about . . . the unknown and being able to cope with it.

Perhaps it's an attitude. . . . Is the cup half full or half empty? Have you fallen down or are you getting up?

Perhaps it's an opportunity to make changes . . . but can we?

*   *   *

Power became a topic of interest to me when I realized that many candidates and workers alike were attaching so much significance to it, usually confusing it with money and/or position. I sensed that many people assume their titles assure them of a personal identity, separating them from the rest of the crowd. The next set of journal entries reflects my feelings on this subject.

March 2

What is the significance of power? Why do people reach for things they consider powerful? What's so great about power, anyway? Is it not an illusion?

April 8

It's interesting to watch the power positioning. PM fell all over himself trying to help GG. MA kept telling stories to keep GG laughing. ER threw in comments to spice it up. FR tended to GG and thwarted PM's efforts. TP and JC just wanted to be there. MA chatted with GG about the old days. DM kept telling me what good friends they (DM and GG) are. Wish I had a film clip of it all. . . .

May 12

Along the way, one of the campaign workers has managed to alienate every staff person and to play a major role in upsetting the cohesiveness that existed before BJ entered the picture. Seems that BJ thinks she knows more about politics than the professionals—and BJ has never worked on a campaign before!

June 4

PA called to say that CN was telling everyone how important her job was and that RC was not doing a good job and should be replaced. PA said that CN thinks her job makes her a powerful force to deal with in the political realm. But RC and CN really do have problems, PA said, because they are now "legends in their own minds!"

July 2

Brought Ken back to the Springs with us. He wanted to talk to Steve about one of the campaign workers. Bottom line is that Ken says the worker is power hungry. Apparently the worker tried to malign Ken and did some pretty devious things to others, all to advance professionally. Advice to Steve: the worker will self-destruct, but it will take a few months.

July 11

Political power and a politician's image must be tied together. Because if the politician can convey the proper image, political power is his reward.

August 3

Poor Steve is having a difficult time. He had to dismiss one of the campaign workers for continually overstepping boundaries. I can't ever remember him letting someone go in all the years he's been in business. But the political world is different. It seems that not only politicians, but campaign workers, too, can be enthralled with power. It was the appropriate decision, though, to dismiss someone who thinks he has the power to unilaterally overrule the campaign manager. Power really can be destructive.

August 25

Maybe it doesn't matter what compels a person to do things, just that the desire is there. . . . Then again, maybe it does matter.

September 3

Jim came by to bring over some old *Saturday Evening Post* magazines. He said they may come in handy some day when I sit down to write my book. In the June 10, 1961 issue (for 15 cents, if you can believe it), Stewart Alsop writes about "The White House Insiders" and comments on President Kennedy's close advisors: "One reason for all this attention is that they already seem certain to become collectively one of Washington's great centers of power— and Washington is one place where power is even more respected than money. The power of the members of the White House staff is, of course, derived wholly from the

President. Cut off from Kennedy, these men would be so many hairless Samsons. Yet the powers of a President are vast, and President Kennedy, unlike his predecessor, revels in the exercise of power. The White House insiders are his chosen instruments in that exercise, and they are without exception tough, able, power-loving men." Alas, nothing really changes.

NOTES

1. Barry M. Goldwater with Jack Casserly, *Goldwater* (New York: Doubleday, 1988), 3–4.

2. The Society of Professional Journalists, Sigma Delta Chi, "Code of Ethics," 1973.

3. Jeff Greenfield, "A Journalism That Tolerates Error Gives a Flawed Picture of Reality," *Denver Post*, 14 March 1989, Denver and the West section.

4. Marc E. Miller, *Politicians and Their Spouses' Careers* (Washington, D.C.: Tilden Press, 1985), 17.

5. "Code of Ethics."

6. Gene Amole, "Pols Addicted to Spotlight," *Rocky Mountain News*, 5 January 1988, 6.

7. Lois Romano, "The Spouses' Representatives," Washington *Post*, 27 July 1987, sec. C.

8. Peter F. Drucker, "Leadership: More Doing Than Dash," *Wall Street Journal*, 6 January 1988, Eastern Edition, sec. 1.

9. "Maverick Governor Pushes States Rights," *Denver Post*, 3 May 1987, sec D.

10. John Kenneth Galbraith, *The Anatomy of Power* (Boston: Houghton Mifflin, 1983), 11.

11. Jimmy Breslin, *How the Good Guys Finally Won* (New York: The Viking Press, 1975), 33.

Chapter Three

All the People You Meet Along the Way

> We seldom stop to think how many peoples' lives are entwined with our own. It is a form of selfishness to imagine that every individual can operate on his own.
>
> —*Ivy Baker Priest*

As more and more of their time is consumed with campaigning, politicians and their spouses naturally encounter an ever-increasing cast of characters on the campaign trail. Their tried-and-true old friends aside, they now confront the challenge of recognizing the opportunists; choosing from a rainbow of consultants, including self-appointed advisors and experts; discouraging or encouraging the enterprising women, as the case may be; and even welcoming wonderful new friends along the way. Some people are sensitive to the politician's needs. Others are not. Some people help politicians because they believe in them. Others became involved in a campaign for the sole purpose of furthering their own careers. Once in a while a blackmailer may surface. And, as I noted in my journal upon realizing the difficulty of determining the motivations of all the players, "even if the campaign pace doesn't wear you down, you will feel as though you're being nibbled to death by a duck."

But feeling as though one is being nibbled to death by a duck "goes with the territory," as those in the know say. And the condition has no cure as long as one remains a politician or a political spouse, because it seems that everyone wants to advise the politician. The problem really is not so much that people become self-appointed advisors and are always telling the politician what to do, but rather that all the advice, when taken as a whole, tends to be contradictory.

Sometimes the most well meaning people, whom I affectionately call the "gottabees," are the worst offenders. However, regardless of which political "experts" are making the contribution, it seems people are always there to tell the politician about their problems or to offer their advice about the politician's problems. Friends who wish the candidate well will call at all hours of the night, with their part of the conversation usually including some friendly advice. During these late-night chats, sometimes the caller will say, "You gottabee" on time, wear white shirts with those suits, and smile when you're on camera. Or the politician, during a totally unrelated talk with another well-wisher, may be advised with these words: "You gottabee smart and stop wearing those suits with white shirts, and your smile is too big when you're on camera." In closing, these friends will add, "For heaven's sake get some sleep; you look terrible." And after each bit of friendly advice, politicians and their spouses think, "nibble, nibble."

Other friendly advice arrives by mail. During one interview, a former political wife commented to me that a campaign worker wrote to her husband urging him to be cautious of certain people who were "pretending" to be his friends. Included in the letter were detailed examples of how those people had taken advantage of the politician. At first, the political wife's remarks seemed to suggest that politicians are very naive when it comes to determining another person's intentions. Further into our conversation, however, she implied that such warnings are given, in most instances, because workers and staff alike become very attached to their candidate and his candidacy, and they try to protect him from the ever-present sycophants. Sometimes workers and staff want him to win more than he wants to win. And because they don't want to see their candidate make a grave mistake, they tell him what to wear, how to comb his hair, which individuals to befriend, and what to say, bringing me back to that old refrain of "nibble, nibble."

But most politicians, at least the ones I encounter, do enjoy the people, the challenge, and the attention. The politician also enjoys the staff's pride in his candidacy, even when they tell him what to do. "He's outgoing and aggressive. I would rather see and do things from behind the scenes," remarked one former political wife. Then, with a twinkle in her eye, she added, "I call him a salt shaker. Salt shakers always like to be right in the center of the table." Precisely because he likes to be and in fact is the focus of attention, one first lady said, "the staff, and everyone, wants to be close to the governor. They build walls to cut me out."

As a direct result of her husband's entry into politics, the political wife is surrounded by both the well intended and the not so well intended. And if she were not also confronted with the loss of many of her old friends' company, she might not be so alarmed by the staff's devotion to the politician. Regardless, the political wife has little time for friends or non-political socializing.

Part of the reason for feeling cut off or isolated can be attributed to the fact that few of the political wife's old friends understand her intense involvement in politics. "They see the glamour and fun part instead," remarked a freshman congressman's spouse. Regrettably, for the wife of a politician, people assume she is different once she boards the political train. Often they treat her involvement in politics reverently, and begin to regard her as a celebrity. "Friends call now and then apologize for invading my privacy," says a veteran first lady. As a result of this "special" treatment, she is alone, and not because she necessarily chooses to be.

Contrary to public opinion, the great majority of politicians and their spouses do not spend their spare time hosting or attending dinners and parties for their newfound friends. When George Bush was vice president, Barbara Bush remarked, "We have little social life after work. We don't get involved in 'political life.' We're involved in politics and the country." And many of the congressional wives whom I interviewed concurred. The truth of the matter is that the House sessions go long into the night, leaving the wife to fend for herself a good deal of the time.

Yet another reason for the wife's isolation is the political world's confusion between office and home. Webster defines "home" as the place where a person lives, one's dwelling place. In the political world, the politician's office often fits this definition, since some congressional officeholders, in fact, reside at the office when not commuting back to their home state. The same situation occurs at the political candidate's campaign headquarters. After all, the office, whether it be in Washington, D.C., in one of the fifty states, or at campaign headquarters, represents a life line to the politician.

Without question, the politician's office operates like an intricate machine, with the group dynamics mirroring the politician's present public standing. When I arrived early

for interviews with political wives scheduled at the politicians' offices, I would sit quietly, observing everyone at
work. If the politician had won the election, his staff
reflected the excitement of the victory, with each person
taking a turn in the center of things, directing and orchestrating the day's schedule. It seemed the more commotion
there was the better everyone liked it. The constant action
pumped them up as the telephones rang in unison with
the second hand on the clock. The adrenalin was flowing.
On the other hand, when the politician had been defeated
at the polls, his staff reflected the loss. There was no
commotion, just the harsh reality of cardboard boxes and
a great deal of work to be accomplished before the new
politician moved in.

Regardless of whether the politician has been elected,
defeated, or reelected, workers and staff toil long into the
night at the politician's office or campaign headquarters,
leading me to wonder if political workers have any life
outside of politics. They seem to love the intrigue, the
drama, and the social aspects of politics. In a campaign
year, however, the pace increases to a frenetic level, as the
staff focuses all efforts on executing the plan to elect or re-
elect their candidate. Indeed, the staff's commitment and
long hours of labor play a big part in getting the politician
elected, and they give their all to make that happen. In the
process they form close ties with each other and with the
politician that might not occur under a different set of
circumstances. Understandably, as a result of this interde-
pendence, the politician's wife often feels cut off from her
husband if she is not an integral part of "the team" that
works together day and night in an effort to bring to light
their formula for success.

If she takes on a major position in the campaign, the
wife adds new responsibilities to her already full schedule.
But regardless of whether or not she is in a clearly defined

position, the campaign becomes her vocation. Granted, she is the candidate's spouse and should be a part of the campaign, but now she is one of the most important workers on the campaign, too. And just as her friends now view her differently, the staff may also tend to set her apart.

During a campaign, the staff rely upon each other for support, advice, and encouragement. They have their meals together, arrive and depart together, and travel the state together for the candidate. Like siblings, they argue, but all is forgotten the next day. I observed staff members taking a break around dinner time only to be back at work within the hour. Their days are just as long as the candidate's. And because politicians and their spouses focus almost entirely on the campaign, their world is comprised primarily of those who make the organization run.

For the political wife who must interface with many of the campaign staff, her role entails more than meets the eye. Individuals in some positions, such as campaign manager, require frequent communication with the candidate's spouse. The campaign manager oversees all operations of the campaign and works directly with the staff and coordinators. This individual, prior to the campaign's existence, will have met with the candidate and his wife to set the ground rules for the campaign. Before that meeting concluded, the manager needs to have formed a clear picture of how much or how little the spouse would agree to take on. The wife may choose to make the final selection of campaign photos as well as determine when the candidate is not to be scheduled. One political wife, in fact, said that Wednesday and Sunday afternoons were absolutely unavailable to the campaign and would not agree to having events scheduled during those times for either the candidate or herself.

The ultimate goal in any campaign is to win fifty

percent of the votes plus one, and campaign managers are responsible for soliciting the input necessary to achieve that goal and to steer the campaign on its course. In addition, they usually run interference for the candidate and sometimes for his spouse as well—a critical role, as everyone loves to have direct access to the political couple. This individual also keeps the candidate from getting caught up in the middle of the day-to-day arguments and turf battles that can develop among staff members. The interference run by the campaign manager prevents turmoil from breaking out at campaign headquarters; otherwise, staff members would be running directly to the candidate with their questions and grievances. If the manager does the job well, the workers, as well as the public, will adore the candidate rather than view him as the mere human he is, with flaws and all. Ah, maybe that's how all those illusions about politicians began!

Another staff member who has direct contact with the candidate's spouse is the organization director. Usually, this person is responsible for building the grass roots organization and encouraging and motivating the field workers to recruit district, county, and precinct workers. Most of the time the organization director is glued to the telephone, talking to the field people and keeping track of which way the voters are leaning in order to determine the candidate's position. Generally, this individual keeps the political wife posted on the numbers and the trouble spots. Many times, for example, the director will alert the campaign manager that the candidate's spouse is needed to attend an event or make an unscheduled appearance in a particular community. In many cases, that is all that's necessary to get the campaign back on track.

Press secretaries represent the voice of the campaign and thus must have the confidence of both the candidate and the spouse. While they do not shape the message of the candidate, they act as a conduit to the press, both responding to press queries and generating press stories about the candidate. It certainly helps the candidate if this person is on friendly terms with the press corps because, as we all know, the number of votes the candidate captures is dependent upon the amount of positive press coverage he receives. Many times, the campaign's press secretary will accompany the political wife to her appointments with the press. One political wife remarked that if it hadn't been for the press secretary's cues and interjections, she might never have survived her first newspaper interview.

The scheduler is often the most unappreciated of the campaign staff. This individual schedules every meeting and event in the candidate's day, attempting always to make the best possible use of the candidate's time. Being very cognizant of the importance of political strategy, schedulers also serve as diplomats, continually selecting from an unlimited number of possibilities those activities that will increase the candidate's chances of carrying the election while dealing directly with those whose requests must be refused. Thus, they not only respond to requests but also must be creative and flexible enough to change the candidate's schedule from one day to the next to capitalize on the most promising opportunities.

And of course with most days consisting of 16- to 18-hour schedules, there are always conflicts—conflicts with callers who are trying to schedule the candidate at their events, conflicts with times and logistics, and conflicts with the candidate's personal preferences. "You've scheduled me *where? There?* Do you know how long it takes to get there? No way." Without question, conflicts also arise with the political wife. For example, when she feels that her husband is being over-scheduled to the point that his efforts are unproductive, the political wife confronts the scheduler with her concerns. Emily Malino, wife of New

York Congressman James Scheuer, was quoted as saying, "Staff members want all of your husband. They'll schedule on weekends, birthdays and anniversaries."[1] Moreover, when the political wife is dissatisfied with how her own time has been scheduled, she and the scheduler must work things out.

Not all of the staff have continual contact with the political wife. For example, the finance chairperson essentially executes the financial plan and is in charge of the campaign's fund-raising efforts. The research director is responsible for obtaining and compiling a wide range of statistics and background information to use in preparing speeches and issue papers and, yes, for bringing before the public all the negatives about the candidate's opponent— whether it be a poor voting record, past or present love affairs, or legal entanglements. Extensive research is also conducted on the candidate himself in order to strategize how best to squelch any negative press. Finally, there's the campaign chairperson, an honorary position held by a prominent individual who can lend credibility to the campaign.

Most campaigns also benefit from the services of a steering committee, usually comprised of six or seven people who act as a sounding board and give critical advice to the candidate. This group generally has excellent political instincts and can sense when the campaign is on the wrong course. When the staff or candidate overreacts to negative press coverage or some other threatening situation, or staff begin to express concerns, one to another, on and on until an issue is totally overblown (referred to as the "echo chamber"), it often is the steering committee that steps in with objective analysis and advice.

When the political stakes are high, the politician usually enlists the services of national consultants who have years of experience in reading the pulse of the public. Usually, these consultants are expert political strategists who are masters at planning the overall strategy of the campaign, especially as it relates to the mass media, leaving the details to be carried out by the campaign staff. A major responsibility of the consultant is orchestrating TV and radio spots that present the politician in the best possible light while, in most cases, denigrating the reputation of his opponent.

The national media consultant is also a wordsmith, having an uncanny ability to influence through carefully crafted phrases and a knack of discerning what will and won't go over with the public. Sometimes these powerful political masterminds are able to convince their less-discerning clients not to utter a word that hasn't been written for them and/or rehearsed. Perhaps Arizona's former Governor Evan Mecham should have hired such a consultant. National consultants come attached to high price tags. They serve as writers, designers, and directors of the spots, and for this they charge the campaign a "creative" fee, a commission, and sometimes a retainer as well.

During my interviews, I met two political wives whose husbands had enlisted the services of the same national media consultant. Both wives were given the same three rules to follow: "Do not discuss the political issues. Talk about what you have done and would do as the political wife. Talk about the family." Sound familiar? In addition, each woman said her husband's political consultant was responsible for creating all the TV and radio commercials and then selecting those that the candidate would use throughout his campaign. The script for such commercials, which includes the portrayal of the smiling candidate and his family, is carefully designed to attract both the public's attention and the vote. The most persuasive and provocatively packaged message nearly always results in a victory.

A recent example, a TV spot referred to as "the revolving door" produced for the George Bush presidential campaign, showed convicted criminals entering and leaving a prison compound through a turnstile-type gate. Roger Ailes, media consultant to the Bush for President campaign, is credited with (and sometimes condemned for) the damning portrait of a Governor Dukakis who was soft on crime and criminals. The commercial apparently was quite effective at reminding voters that the governor's prison furlough program had enabled prisoner Willie Horton to commit murder and rape during one of his weekend furloughs. A second, even more controversial spot, referred to as the "Willie Horton" ad, was created by Larry McCarthy and produced by the independent Americans for Bush Committee. Though not endorsed by the Bush campaign, the ad noted that Governor Dukakis vetoed the law denying murderers furlough and closed with a mug shot of Willie Horton; and it succeeded in convincing the public that Dukakis's policies had failed and helped to propel Vice President George Bush into the winner's circle.

Barry Goldwater suggests that this type of TV commercial began when he was running for president in 1964: "It was the beginning of what I call 'electronic dirt.' Moyers and the New York firm will long be remembered for helping to launch this ugly development in our political history." In his memoirs, Goldwater describes the well-known TV commercial that helped to destroy his own presidential candidacy. That commercial, commonly referred to as "the bomb ad," apparently was ordered by Bill Moyers, President Johnson's White House press secretary, and produced by the Doyle Dane Bernback advertising firm in New York City.

The strategy behind "the bomb ad" was to convince the public that Senator Goldwater was a warmonger, and that if they voted for him the world would be destroyed.

Although the one-minute commercial appeared only once on national TV, the results were devastating to the Goldwater campaign. "It showed a little girl in a sunny field of daisies. She begins plucking petals from a daisy. As she plucks the flower, a male voice in the background starts a countdown . . . ten . . . nine . . . eight . . . becoming constantly stronger. The screen suddenly explodes and the child disappears in a mushroom cloud. The voice concludes by urging voters to elect President Johnson. . . ."[2] Yes, media consultants play for high stakes, and they can make or break a campaign.

The necessity of obtaining endorsements from the politically powerful brings the candidate and his wife into contact with individuals who share the same visions as well as those who view their own position and clout as prizes to be auctioned off to the highest bidder. There are those who inform the candidate in private that they want to support his campaign efforts, yet when the time comes to publicly announce their commitment (and the key here is "going public") they always have a seemingly plausible reason for withholding their endorsement. I recall one political wife who saw the humor in these people. She related a story about a silent supporter who told her husband he couldn't commit to his candidacy "today," but that if so and so did not enter the race he'd surely be there for the candidate. Apparently, that conversation occurred several times over a period of months, with the so and so's name changing each time they talked.

Of course, those who refuse to commit immediately and publicly are assured of receiving a great deal of attention, not only from each of the candidates but from their staff members as well. Keeping everyone off balance ("Will he say yea or nay?") brings these folks some sense of power. "I must be important. They keep calling me, trying to get my support." Consequently, the game is played out as long as possible—with the sought-after prolonging the process before signing up or prolonging it just long enough that they don't have to sign up. For example, a former congressman from a northern state had an especially difficult time obtaining open support when he was running for the Senate seat against a well-known incumbent. Though the congressman was assured of support by many well-known individuals, nearly all remained "silent supporters" to the end. "You can't take on a national hero," said his wife, realizing only too well how important it is for a candidate to be publicly endorsed by "big names."

In every campaign, regrettably, there are those who work for or publicly support a candidate solely to serve their own interests. In many cases, these individuals want to be able to tell their friends that they're chummy with a politician. They relish using the politician's name in conversations, and they do just that as often as possible. To achieve this status, however, one must wait until all the candidates' positions are clear and then quickly jump on the winning bandwagon.

Another breed of "supporter" strives not only to become acquainted with a politician but to gain access to him. Often this requires that the individual contribute large sums of money to the candidate's campaign. Of course ensuring access to the winner sometimes requires that several candidates be backed. Then, by covering all the bases, an individual increases the chances of having access to the politician and as an added benefit may gain recognition for being one who can pick a winner every time. The ability to pick winners, after all, is often revered as a sign of good judgment. That is, "By gosh, Fred picked the party's nomination again. We should listen to him." Later, in the general election, these self-serving individuals also contribute financially to both the Republican and the Democrat, continuing the effort right up to the finish line.

So it seems there is a dark side to the political world, and it attracts many hollow, Machiavellian people who can skillfully exploit a relationship. And political wives, like their husbands, are enormously vulnerable to a host of opportunists, which now that I think about it is good reason for most political wives' guardedness and caution. In order to enjoy true friendships, political wives must sort out those people who are, were, or aren't her friends. And always, they must determine if a person is interested in getting to know them or in using them to get to their husbands. "I never told my neighbors what Mike did, but they'd find out," says a former political wife. "I was always surprised by the people who wanted to know me just because of his position," she added.

During one interview, another political wife told me about a new "friend" of hers who had worked on her husband's campaign. It seems the woman had rarely communicated with the politician during the campaign since she was officed in a different city, but following the election she requested a glowing reference from the politician and additional assistance in obtaining employment. It wasn't until much later that the wife learned her newfound friend was in search of a job before joining the campaign effort and in fact developed a relationship with the wife to gain favor with the politician, and ultimately a well-paid position. The wife's new friend apparently thought there was nothing unusual about her request or her reason for initiating the friendship in the first place. After all, how could the politician refuse? She was one of his wife's dear friends. Other political wives, not surprised by this example, echoed, "The higher up you go in politics, the harder it is to find real friends."

Some new acquaintances, in the guise of friendship,

place a political wife on a pedestal and pay homage to her in order to gain entrance to a more powerful world. The unassuming wife who gladly embraces the flattery, attention, and companionship often is eager to invite her new friend to attend well-publicized events with her when her politician husband is unavailable. But when she is no longer "useful," she is abandoned by her new friend, and the inevitable fall from the pedestal is always painful. One former political wife revealed that when her husband's loss at the polls was followed immediately by the sudden termination of a friendship, she felt used and unsure of her own judgment, and found it difficult to trust people.

Yes, there are many who exploit relationships with politicians and their spouses—generally to further their own ambitions. Oddly, though, the politicians themselves play the same game to enhance and protect the image they've so carefully crafted. Many go to great lengths to become known as the friend to someone more influential. One interview with a political wife revealed that political couples often arrange to be out of town when dinners are held at the White House, giving the impression to others that they are too busy to attend or have previously committed to another engagement when in fact an invitation was never received.

Some people have no agendas apart from friendship. They are the committed people who believe in the candidate, working for and supporting his goals. And these people come in all shapes and forms, from the volunteer who is a door-to-door precinct walker, to the county chairperson, to another candidate's wife. Thus, many political wives have discovered new friends right at campaign headquarters. One former political wife talked of traveling the state with various staff members and coming away from one such trip with a "new best friend." Another political wife related the story of her friendship with a woman who worked for the candidate in another part of their state. Although their contact was fleeting during the campaign, when the campaign was over their friendship continued to flourish.

Often when a political wife travels the state, the other candidates' wives are also there representing their husbands. As they prepare to go "on stage," it is not uncommon for the political wives to help and support each other. Sometimes, in order to conserve finances, the wives of various candidates may even drive together to different events. Under these circumstances, it is easy to understand that each woman is acutely aware of the other person's apprehensions, and, frequently, close friendships are formed with another candidate's wife.

Then again, there are some people who want to establish very close friendships only with the politician. For example, public figures, often regarded as "stars," are continually confronted by designing women. And it's no secret that some politicians spend more time with their girlfriends than they do with their wives and children. It is also true that not all designing or enterprising women become girlfriends. Some are more flirtatious than serious. Regardless, the political world has more than its share of enterprising women. In fact, politics acts as a magnet for these upwardly mobile women who strive to get close to the candidate—some closer than others. Sometimes, these women join the campaign organization in paid positions that provide direct access to the politician. And on occasion they travel with the candidate because there never seems to be enough time to discuss the many campaign problems at headquarters or on the telephone.

One political wife related an incident that illustrates the turf battles that often occur between wife and designing woman. The political wife had rearranged her schedule at the last minute, making it possible for her to travel with her husband. When she arrived at the airport where her husband and his staff had gathered, the enterprising woman, totally surprised by the change in plans, greeted her with: "Oh, hello, what are *you* doing here? Well, I mean I didn't know you were planning to go with us. Well, I mean. . . ."

The women with hidden agendas, I learned from the interviews, use different methods to attain their goal. For example, some women choose to send books, cute little stuffed animals, or letters marked "personal" to the candidate. The general rule seems to be "never send anything to the politician's home," although one political wife commented that sometimes gifts containing no name or address arrived at her home. She, of course, would open the unmarked packages immediately and "have a great time giving my husband a hard time about it."

The few political wives who were willing to be candid about the subject of infidelity concurred that when the "other woman" is confronted by the political wife, she usually responds with silence, and then indignation. Though these women are seldom subtle, they seem truly surprised that the wife could guess their intentions. Was the husband foolish enough to tell his wife about her or is the wife psychic? In most cases, it seems, the other woman eventually distances herself from the politician, sometimes moving on as far away as another, more promising camp. However, one political wife was known to include the "other woman" in family gatherings, commenting that it might possibly discourage the relationship from becoming intimate. Another political wife was quoted in *Time* as recommending that wives work in their husbands' offices as marriage insurance. "With adoring staff all around, your husband might not want to come home to reality."[3]

Over the years much has been said about politicians' infidelity. And while it was rare, in the past, to ever see anything in print during the politician's tenure, the news was always disseminated anyway. After all, a well-known person's acts of indiscretion make good conversation at social gatherings. It is now widely accepted as fact that President John Kennedy had a number of liaisons with women at the White House. Actresses Angie Dickinson and Marilyn Monroe were two of the better-known women thought to be romantically involved with him. Presidents Roosevelt, Johnson, and Eisenhower apparently had long-standing romances with other women either before or while governing our country. Yet, no matter how flagrant the affairs were at that time, they never became a campaign issue for the politicians.

Though many of our political leaders have had reputations as womanizers, until the 1988 elections, the press either overlooked the behavior as irrelevant to the person's ability to lead or else respected the privacy of the candidate. The result, in both cases, was that the politician's philandering was never recorded in print. Thus, one has to assume that as press coverage of politicians has become more intensified in recent years, the public has been awakened into clarifying its expectations regarding the character and morals of its political leaders.

The turning point may have occurred in 1987 when, amid widely circulated rumors of his philandering, presidential hopeful Gary Hart challenged the press to follow him. They did, and the subsequent headlines convinced the majority of Americans that Gary Hart's poor judgment made him an unacceptable candidate for the presidency. The sharks went in for the kill, relentless in their interrogation. Antagonism between politician and the media was never greater than when a reporter asked Hart in public if he was an adulterer, surely the first time a presidential candidate had ever been asked such a question. However, Hart's earlier reported indiscretions, during the years that he was a U.S. senator, seemed to have resulted in a minimum of press coverage and virtually no public condemnation.

The feminist voice has influenced our views on politicians' infidelity. Many women now believe that such behavior says much more about a man's view of humanity than does his rhetoric. And they reject the sexist argument that condones men's extramarital affairs on the basis that women possess little or no personal value other than to please a man.

The real issue facing our society, of course, is that if we elect politicians who go to great lengths to transform their looks, to say what we want to hear, and then go on to conduct their private lives like children let loose in a candy store, we are validating their duplicity and in fact encouraging it. The result is that we serve their purposes, rather than they serving ours. Though the public seems to abhor the press's high-handed and occasionally unscrupulous investigative tactics, the consensus is that the manner in which individuals conduct their private lives is a good indication of how they will manage their responsibilities as public figures.

In *Laughing All the Way,* author Barbara Howar sees the issue of infidelity among politicians this way: "Political power, like wealth, gives an otherwise ordinary man the sexual attractiveness generally reserved for movie stars, athletes, and playboys. The younger the man with power, the more exposed he is to temptations and the more vulnerable is his career if he is discovered. A Ted Kennedy had more to lose at Chappaquiddick than did Louisiana Senator Russell Long, who divorced to marry his longtime companion."[4] And while Howar's description suggests that the political environment kindles infidelity, the public seems unwilling to excuse such behavior in its leaders.

Yet it is no secret that adultery has been the companion

of politics since the beginning of time. In fact, *Fail From Grace* author Shelley Ross says, "As a journalist who has reported scandals for the past twelve years, I believe sex, scandal, and corruption in the political system are as American as apple pie."[5]

* * *

The following journal entries offer a glimpse of the people who inhabit the political world. There is a certain closeness that develops between people, a closeness not unlike a familial bond, when they are thrust into the same environment for a short, intense period of time. I recall a particular day when headquarters seemed in total disarray.

March 4

Tempers are hot. Lots of dissatisfaction. At the insistence of some of the staff, a meeting was called, in Steve's absence, to resolve the difficulties, and I was asked to attend. We got things worked out, but I was asked not to tell Steve about the meeting. I have agreed. Instantly, however, I realize that I've reverted back to the role of wife and mother, peacemaker, nurturer, helpmate, and protector because he is busy enough without having to worry about any dissatisfaction on the home front.

July 17

Steve was late again for a scheduled event. This time he blamed his tardiness on poor scheduling. Actually, he loves talking with people, and it wouldn't make a speck of difference if he were allocated two days at each event; he'd still be late getting to his next meeting.

November 11

The campaign seems to be progressing well—that is, if you listen to the people on our side. . . . Talked to Patty today and learned that BC may drop out of the race. But Patty fears that MT will enter the race if BC's campaign folds. So she suggested that Steve call BC's workers to get them lined up for his campaign.

*   *   *

Because I had little experience in the political world prior to Steve's bid for the party's nomination, I called upon my instincts to guide me. In the past, for the most part, I'd been good at recognizing who was authentic and who wasn't. But to be successful at this, one must listen carefully to a person's unspoken words.

March 7

The problem I'm having right now is reconciling my disappointment with some of the duplicitous people. While it's no secret that duplicity exists, its prevalence in the political world is disturbing. And it isn't so much my disappointment with duplicity as it is my disappointment with what that duplicity reveals about the political world.

April 2

Tuesday Mindy picked me up to drive to the luncheon. Met a lot of people, gave my speech, received good reviews, and had pictures taken by CC, who apparently is a turncoat. Nancy told me we really are better off having CC work for another candidate and that no one takes him seriously, anyway. So that takes care of him!

July 9

Ken stayed for dinner. Lots of talk about RC hearing that BJ wants her job. Now, how did that get started?

July 16

Steve said FO called to tell him about the slander one supposed supporter is spreading about him. It seems that the "supporter" is telling everyone that the reason Steve does not drink is because he's a recovering alcoholic! I can't believe people don't have better things to do with their lives than to fabricate stories about others.

August 14

Now I think I've heard everything! For the past two weeks PB, a new acquaintance, has been making offers to take me to different human service projects around the state so I can see what is being done firsthand. Sounded good. And for longer than that PB has been telling me what a great first lady I'd be, which should have been my first clue to question his honesty. In addition, PB convinced a number of people that he knows how to win elections. To think that I might never have paid attention if his greed hadn't entered in so early! Today there was a proposal from PB: $100,000 to consult!!! Give me a break. . . . Politics. People.

February 5

There has always been something about her, I don't know what, that makes me uncomfortable. My visits and phone conversations with her suggest that she is impressed by position and money, which I guess is where we fit in. Everyone she mentioned had a label attached to them—rich people, party people, important people. Now I learn that she wants a paid position in Steve's campaign. I guess that explains why she preferred dealing directly with the candidate rather than with the candidate's wife. The bottom line is that there are times when you have doubts

about everything and everyone, and this time it's: Whatever happened to the dedicated volunteer?

May 20

Met a couple who wanted us to know who they were.
Even Fortunoff would have been embarrassed by their
appearance. But, then again, Mrs. Z doesn't have to worry
about locking her doors when she leaves home—she wears
all her jewelry when she goes out! What a hoot! I wonder
if they were trying to tell us to "court" them for their
money and votes.

February 10

Today, WG told Steve he's also supporting another
candidate. It's becoming alarmingly clear that Steve's campaign will have to be a grass roots effort. Not only do we
not have the "big name" people; we don't have the
"money" people either. (I wonder if Hot Lips will go to
the other side, too?)

February 11

Met with Mindy and John. Learned that FL and HL are
spreading rumors already. Steve must be making headway!

March 23

Funny how some people want to jump on the bandwagon when they think they've got a winner! So many
people who recently were just too busy now want an
audience with Steve.

* * *

*I had heard candidates and incumbents say you have to voice
what the public wants to hear if you are going to get elected or*

reelected. And even though duplicity seems to be prevalent in many political candidates' repertoires, we rejected the notion that honesty spells defeat. An honest politician?

April 1

Steve is still arguing with some of the campaign staff about the importance of being authentic and having the public accept him because of his candidness. So, in an effort to present the honest politician to the public, Steve has hired a political consultant to work with the campaign. I hope he knows what he's doing. . . . Which he?—both the politician and the consultant!

January 13

JD arrived. Went out to dinner and discussed the new poll that came out. JD isn't very pleased with the press that is or isn't getting out. He plans to generate some publicity for Steve.

February 5

JD played the first draft of the video for us. I'm not pleased with it. Steve looks stiff, the family posed.

July 26

Today I'm on my way to meet JD to work on editing the film for the TV commercials. Don't think he's at all happy with my involvement. Patty and Jerry are also going along.

April 30

JD's mother died today. It is also his wife's birthday. . . . Reminds all of us that people have lives apart from the campaign and they're not just "positions."

* * *

Once in a while a political spouse is confronted with persons who can be considered "unstable." Despite the fact that she recognizes the acts as irrational, the encounters are very unsettling. The following set of journal entries illustrates the point.

February 4

The calls keep coming at all hours of the day and night, but only when Steve's away. The caller says he's "a friend" who wants me to know "the truth" about my husband. "He's not always campaigning like he says he is," etc. And then he says he's going to kill Steve. The police have traced the calls to a number of pay phones.

February 12

I called the police today to check on the person who appeared at the door this afternoon. This character informed me that since Steve's soul has been saved, he has been assigned to Steve to help him. The police will try to determine if there's any connection between this person and the bizarre phone calls we've been getting lately. When I'm all alone in the house, these things make me uneasy.

* * *

While I am sure that all the candidates and their families have similar problems, I recall the ordeal we experienced during the filming of the campaign's commercials (TV spots). Coordinating schedules for a candidate and spouse are difficult enough, but our three grown children also were required to be present for a portion of the time. As luck would have it, the filming was scheduled when our daughter was away on a school excursion, one son was back in college, and our other son was to represent his father at a political event. However, the good news was that our cat and two dogs were still living at home, so scheduling them was not going to be a problem!

July 21

We were told that the filming session would take three days; however, the children needed to be available only on the first day. Well, we rounded up the children, got everyone home on the right date, dressed according to specification, and filmed the same scene over and over for three hours until we got it right. We did all of this for a fifteen-second spot on TV! The rest of the day was spent filming the candidate as he conducted business in the business world, worked out in the fitness world, and campaigned in the political world. How worldly is my candidate.

July 22

Second day in a city on the western slope of Colorado filming additional TV spots. JD met us at the airport with the film crew. It was a nasty day, with no signs of potential cooperation from Mother Nature. So, in wind and drizzle they tried to get a shot of Steve and me in different settings. The first shot was to feature us as we were deplaning. What a riot! They shot the same scene over three times, and I ruined it each time. My hair covered my face like a sheet as the rain and wind did their thing. Poor JD. He was looking for an artistic happening but instead was left with plain ole unadorned me.

Next was Danny's print shop, our temporary headquarters between events, where Steve was doused in make-up for TV. Then off we went to a press conference at our phone bank location to promote its opening. The consultant kept telling me to get into the TV spot. "Be creative. Do something." Fortunately, two friends arrived just before I was about to strap on my ballet slippers for my version of "Swan Lake" and whisked me off for a few hours. We visited senior centers and a retirement home. As I was speaking to one group, an older woman seemed to be smiling at me, shaking her head in agreement. I remember thinking I must have been saying all the right things because she seemed so enthusiastic. After my talk, I walked over to her table to chat. As I approached her she said, "Honey, you'll have to speak up. I can't hear a word."

Later, there was a two-and-a-half-hour take in a local cafe for some spontaneous dialoguing with a group of people. Another fifteen-second spot. That was rounded out with a town meeting. Home at midnight. Eighteen-hour day. How do the media experts do this all day long with all the different candidates?

July 23

Today the make-up person told me how pleased he was with the shoot. "We got a great shot of you smiling at Steve as he was speaking." After thanking him, I suggested he might also do some filming at our home. Not waiting for his response, I quickly added, "And, if you're agreeable to my suggestion, you would be able to get another terrific shot of me. This time, though, I would take off my shoes and cook!"

And then we drove up to Denver for more filming on this our third and last day. A precinct walk—the candidate at the Capitol and at the downtown mall greeting strangers. Sometime during all this, David and I had some fun when a supporter in a T-shirt came up to us wanting to know if we'd vote for Steve. When we told him we were undecided, he took the bait. He went on for ten minutes trying to elicit our support, only to have someone call out to me that I was needed for more filming. The poor man was so embarrassed, but I thanked him for being such a good sport and adding some fun to our day.

* * *

When you begin a campaign effort you surround yourself with loyal people. Later on, you need people who are capable of planning, marketing the candidate, organizing, and coordinating. Regrettably, those needs are not necessarily met by those same loyal people. The following entries relate to some of the staff positions that are a part of any campaign.

February 9

Gloria is stepping down from her long-held position as county chair to work full time for Steve as his state coordinator. I think it is a very emotional time for her, but she is enthusiastic about the future. She's vivacious, comfortable in the company of both men and women, likes her husband, doesn't like confrontations, and wants Steve to win.

February 11

Steve is taking the scheduler out with him today so she can see firsthand how her scheduling of him really works. Don't think there's much anyone can do about the complexities of scheduling the candidate, but it would be fun to watch the two of them defend their roles. It's a good thing Sally is a strong woman!

April 30

Monday, we flew into Grand Junction for some press stops, a delegate and alternate event, and the central committee meeting in the evening. Diane and Danny, who are

Steve's county coordinators there, set everything up. And they did a fantastic job!

May 9

Met with Frannie on Thursday to go over the delegate counts. She estimated that Steve has a 27% hard count going into the Assembly. That, however, is not enough for top line on the ballot. Next, she gave me the "bad" news. . . . Steve drew second slot to speak at the Assembly—between two very polished speakers. I asked her if she had any "good" news to tell me. . . .

September 29

Dan is the campaign manager. He said that he can start within two weeks. He is truly in for a difficult few days until he earns everyone's respect. He allowed that his job, as in every campaign, is to stroke, encourage, and direct the staff. And if he does that things should work out well. In addition, he said part of his job is to run interference for the candidate. Sounds good. Hope he can accomplish that, too.

December 12

The brochure is out, and the pictures are awful! In fact three friends called and asked "How could you have let them select those shots?" Well, I didn't. I called Dan and told him we seem to have a problem and need to make some decisions about any future photo selections. Then I learned that *he* selected the photos. After I removed my foot from my big mouth, we decided that I will make the final approval on all the family photos.

I hope he wasn't insulted, but I don't intend to become

passive simply because my husband is a political candidate.
Oh well, maybe Dan wasn't insulted. . . .

December 13

Steve is going to meet with Dan for two hours to go
over yesterday's photo session. Steve said he would bring
home the photos for my approval. It'll be interesting to
hear if Dan says anything to Steve about our conversation.

* * *

*The continual advice from friends and supporters has a way of
wearing you down. The next few selected entries give some
indication of that for both candidate and spouse.*

December 15

Spent the afternoon at headquarters hosting a holiday
party for staff and volunteer workers. The "policewoman"
was there giving everyone a hard time. It's as if she carries
a tape recorder around with her, then brings things up to
you later on to remind you of what you said. With
supporters like her . . . nibble, nibble.

July 17

Heard from BG today. Get this—she said we shouldn't
go to the dinner on Friday night because it'll just be for a
group of homosexuals. She said the invitations were sent
to women to honor women. Come on, give me a break.
Nibble, nibble.

September 2

AC told Steve he needs two hours of his time to go over
what he's been hearing and to offer his advice! Nibble,
nibble.

* * *

Sometimes Steve and I talked about the ploys used by the women with hidden agendas, which interestingly enough he recognized only in other political campaigns. After observing some of these women, I registered a profile in my journal, because what is a political campaign without its enterprising and designing women?

June 9

She's attractive in a non–threatening way. She wears the latest styles and applies lipstick in layers. She's a "social" athlete and enjoys the same sports as the politician. She has small children and breasts. She's divorced. She has no aura of mystery about her. She would love to help the candidate find another place to live while he's campaigning, for those nights when he's too tired to drive all the way home. In fact, there's an apartment adjacent to hers that would be perfect for his needs. Whose needs, Hot Lips? The media consultant tells me that in every campaign, there are people "who want the candidate's body."

* * *

Friendship is founded on mutual trust. Without trust there can be no friendship. Friends share, support, encourage, advise, care, and cheer with and for each other. Our reward is knowing that our friends will always be our friends. We don't have to communicate daily, or even on a regular basis, for that matter, to know who our friends are.

I had an opportunity to test my friendship theory during the campaign when I visited with a few of my childhood friends whom I hadn't seen since our college days.

October 5

Our luncheon for four satisfied my curiosity about the direction our lives have taken. Two of my friends are divorced. One has remarried and the other lost a son by suicide. The third friend was looking at the marriage of her son to a woman fifteen years his senior. Two hours later, after much talking, laughing, and some tears, Linda and I decided to meet for dinner.

October 6

We went to dinner at 8:30. At 2:30 in the morning, we were still talking. At one point we both realized we had just picked up where we left off all those years ago. Our tastes are quite similar, our memories are the same, and our parents are experiencing the same difficulties. We talked about women, politics, art, psychology, our children, and our sisters. We even reminisced about Lizzie's great fudge—a sure picker-upper on dreary days. A lot has happened since our girlhood days of fantasies and fairy tales. It is a delight to know that today we are still there for each other.

*   *   *

As the campaign progressed, I met a number of people who brightened many a dark day. The next set of journal entries brings those people into focus again.

September 9

What fun it was to meet Rosa. Her light sarcasm reminds me of my mother when she says she would like to work for Steve for "not even a tomato."

February 4

Snowbound in Rifle, Colorado. But Irene's sandwiches to go, after the event tonight at her home, were terrific!

March 1

Ann, an ardent supporter, saved our day! She prepared the most wonderful pastries for us. What a character! She kept calling me Joycey and telling us that Steve was going to win.

May 12

I can't believe I did it. When I realized I'd forgotten to pack a slip with my change of clothes, Karen took hers off and handed it to me.

* * *

And after the campaign, as I was paying for groceries in the market, there was another, more subtle day-brightener.

August 16

While he was packaging the groceries, the checkout person said, ever so softly, "I don't know why anyone would want to move to Denver." Instantly, we exchanged glances, our eyes expressing our thoughts: "I'm glad you're back," and "Thank you very much."

NOTES

1. Margaret Carlson, "I'm Nobody, Who Are You?" *Time* 133 No. 19 (8 May 1989): 29.
2. Barry M. Goldwater with Jack Casserly, *Goldwater* (New York: Doubleday, 1988), 198.
3. Margaret Carlson, "I'm Nobody, Who Are You?" 29.
4. Barbara Howar, *Laughing All the Way* (New York: Stein and Day, 1973), 105.
5. Shelley Ross, *Fall From Grace: Sex, Scandal, and Corruption in American Politics from 1702 to the Present* (New York: Ballantine Books, 1988), xxi.

Chapter Four

From White Gloves to Bare Hands

> Girls are the spectators and the cheerleaders. . . .
> Perfect preparation for the adult role of woman—to
> stand decoratively on the sidelines of history and
> cheer on the men who make the decisions.
>
> —*Kathryn Clarenbach*

Until recently, most women have perceived their world in a black or white light, opting between being a career person or being a housewife, with few of them able to successfully combine the two. Now, however, gray areas have appeared in that either/or world. Women today are much more independent than those of generations past, and many women who combine a career and motherhood do so by choice, not necessity. This metamorphosis has transpired since the 1960s and is a direct result of the women's movement. Not only have women's attitudes changed, but women have also become clearer about their personal expectations and ambitions. Nevertheless, the role of the political wife simply hasn't evolved to the same extent. Indeed, in many ways the political system continues to urge the wife of a politician to portray her role in a manner that reflects the traditional value system of years past.

Over the last 200 years, the role of the political wife has taken many forms, but traditional values have always been at the core of that role. Like most eighteenth-century women of their time, the country's first political wives had no formal schooling. Girl children were raised solely to be wife and mother, so most of them were educated at home. Their instruction consisted of the art of domesticity and social graces. By the time they married, most young girls (and yes, they were very young) were well versed in running and maintaining a household as well as presiding over social gatherings. Those who were good students of the domestic arts often married well-to-do gentlemen and spent the rest of their lives dutifully tending to their husbands' needs.

Martha Washington, or Lady Washington as she was called, set the tone for all future political wives. Martha was 58 years old when George Washington was elected president (1789–1797), and although she was not a fashion trend-setter, she brought dignity to her role as first lady and was a gracious hostess. She presided over formal gatherings once each week and responded personally to the many women who left their calling cards when she was away from home. Moreover, Mrs. Washington was instrumental in elevating the country's standing with the European heads of state.[1]

A plain woman who never wanted any part of public life, this first lady was, on occasion, even mistaken for the maid. She appears to have been the quintessential traditional wife, the supportive helpmate, following her husband wherever his work took him and continually disregarding her own needs. As she watched her husband's ascension from military officer to president, her long-held desire to live a quiet, private life was thwarted. In an effort to protect what was left of their private life, after her husband's death, the first lady destroyed all but a very few of his letters.[2]

Abigail and John Adams (1797–1801) were the first couple to reside in what was commonly termed "the Palace" (the White House), though for only the last three months of Adams's administration. As Adams had served two terms as vice president under George Washington, Abigail had the benefit of eight years of observation and experience before becoming first lady. Throughout her husband's presidency, Abigail Adams continued to entertain in the style established by the Washingtons.

Over a century later, Harry Truman remarked that Abigail was the person who should have been president. Although she had received little formal schooling, Abigail Adams was well read and knowledgeable about politics. She was her husband's trusted advisor and often influenced his policies. She was also an early advocate of women's rights.[3] Neither shy nor at a loss for words, this first lady was a prolific writer, frequently offering her view of history. One time, she wrote this message to her husband: "Whilst you are proclaiming peace and good will to men, emancipating all nations, you insist on retaining absolute power over wives. . . . Remember the ladies and be more generous and favorable to them than your ancestors. . . . Do not put such unlimited power into the hands of the husbands."[4]

As records show, Abigail dressed in fine silks and generally adhered to the protocol to which she'd been exposed when John Adams was a commissioner to France in 1778. Criticism, though, was a familiar part of the Adams administration. For example, when the President and Mrs. Adams received guests, she would sit in a "thronelike" chair, her husband stationed beside her, causing the critics' tongues to wag. People not only sneered at the affected attempt at protocol, but referred to the short, stocky, not very endearing John Adams as "His Rotundity."[5]

Dolley Madison had tremendous influence on Washington society. She was regarded as the grande dame of the nation's capitol, reigning for many years beyond James Madison's presidency (1809–1817). During the presidential tenure of widower Thomas Jefferson and while James Madison was his Secretary of State, Dolley served as official hostess at the White House. When her husband was elected president, Dolley, resplendent in yellow satin, presided over the first inaugural ball.[6]

First Lady Dolley Madison put everyone at ease with her nurturing personality and enjoyed true success as the traditional wife. More than likely, her Quaker upbringing, which emphasized the art of polite conversation, prepared her well for the role of the political wife. When she was entertaining, she offered her guests an abundance of foods, her husband's homemade wine, and snuff, and was said to be the first person to serve ice cream.[7]

Dolley Madison's influence and reputation were just as solid many years later when widowers Andrew Jackson and Martin Van Buren assumed the duties of president. On occasion she served as the president's hostess during both of these administrations. Widely respected and admired, Dolley Madison is still remembered as "the only one who exercised as much social sway in official life after her retirement from the White House as she did before."[8]

Not wanting to compete with the likes of Dolley Madison's hostessing skills, Elizabeth Monroe, wife of James Monroe (1817–1825), turned instead to improving the young nation's image abroad by setting more rigid rules of protocol and maintaining the same formalities as the Europeans when entertaining dignitaries or presiding over official dinners. In fact, she was highly admired overseas, but regarded as a snob by the people in her own country.[9] Prior to her husband's presidency, this first lady had many years of practice being a political wife. From 1794 on, Monroe was involved in politics, which included serving as the secretary of state, the governor of Virginia, and the emissary to France, England, and Spain.

It appears that Elizabeth Monroe was a bit more sophisticated and aloof than previous political wives. During her eight years as first lady, she preferred spending her time with her husband and children rather than forming new friendships. Still, the White House benefited from Mrs. Monroe's touch. French craftsmen were commissioned to embellish furniture, many new pieces of furniture were purchased, and the mansion was repainted in stark white. The choices made by this regal first lady "endured even the test of time, for today . . . [her] collection of bronze-doré, the pier table and many other pieces of furniture, clocks, and bric-a-brac survive as White House treasures."[10]

Louisa Adams was born in England and educated at boarding schools. This bright, quiet woman, who balked a bit at the notion of women subordinating themselves to their husbands' desires, was quite a match for John Quincy Adams, who served as president from 1825 to 1829. On the day of their marriage when she assumed the role of the political wife, their quarrels began. Louisa had definite opinions about the husband's role within the family: he should be at his wife's side when she is delivering their child, and he should not make strong demands upon their children or make decisions regarding his wife without consulting her. However, those opinions had absolutely no impact on her husband.[11]

After having traveled extensively for many years as a result of her husband's political appointments in Russia, England, and the United States, Louisa dreaded the thought of living in the White House. She remarked that it would be "too confining." But she was an ardent campaign worker, nonetheless, and attended untold dinners and presided over weekly receptions at their home.

After a four-year tenure that rarely went uncriticized, Adams was handily defeated by his two-time opponent, Andrew Jackson, and the Adamses moved back to Quincy, Massachusetts.[12]

For the next seventeen years, however, Adams served as a congressman, and Louisa, during this time, became a strong advocate for women's rights. Her views on women and her admiration for her mother-in-law, Abigail Adams, were revealed in an 1838 letter to one of her sons: "When I see such Women as your Grandmother go through years of exertion, of suffering, and of privation, with all the activity, judgment, skill and fortitude, which any man could display; I cannot believe there is any inferiority in the Sexes, as far as mind and intellect are concerned, and man is aware of the fact."[13]

Regardless of the early political wives' personal beliefs, up until 1845 Abigail Adams was the only political wife who refused to restrict herself to the acceptable role of hostess and helpmate. Sarah Polk, wife of James Polk (1845–1849), was the next political wife to become actively involved in politics. A rather pious, devout woman, Sarah Polk participated in few social activities. She abstained from drinking and dancing, preferring to devote her time to more serious matters. On the evening of the inaugural ball, the dancing ceased when the president and first lady arrived for the ceremonial dance, and started up again only after the first couple took their leave.[14]

Prior to becoming first lady, Sarah was James Polk's assistant and trusted confidante. During Polk's 1839 campaign for governor of Tennessee she had served as his scheduler and handled all his correspondence, a role she continued after he became president. Sarah kept her husband informed of newspaper articles and political developments when he was away, and together they discussed the current political issues. Indeed, Polk more than likely could not have remained in politics for twenty years without her diligence and hard work. After all, she was responsible for Polk's having entered politics in the first place. Sarah had agreed to his wedding proposal with the stipulation that he first run for the state legislature.[15]

Another first lady who encouraged her husband's political ambitions was Mary Todd Lincoln, who publicly predicted his presidency: "He is to be President of the United States some day; if I had not thought so, I would not have married him, for you can see he is not pretty."[16] Nevertheless, when this first lady set up residence in the White House, she was distrusted and looked down upon by Washington society. Southerners disliked her because she was in favor of abolishing slavery, and northerners disliked her because she was from a prominent southern family. To make matters worse, she was a believer in metaphysics, frequently participating in seances and entertaining psychics at the White House.[17]

The first lady was continually criticized both during and after Abraham Lincoln's presidency (1861–1865). At a time when the country was at war, Mary Todd Lincoln was castigated for overspending on her wardrobe and presiding over lavish dinner parties. In fact, when the first lady had exceeded their budget, President Lincoln opted to pay out of his own pocket for work completed at the White House.[18]

Historian and biographer Paul F. Boller, Jr. quotes social commentator Laura C. Holloway as saying that Mrs. Lincoln "found herself . . . surrounded on every side by people who were ready to exaggerate her shortcomings, find fault with her deportment on all occasions, and criticize her performance of all her official duties."[19] Indeed, First Lady Mary Todd Lincoln was the subject of discussion among the congressional committee as well. When the committee gathered in a secret meeting to investigate the accusations that Mrs. Lincoln was working on behalf of the Confederacy, President Lincoln interrupted to deny any wrongdoing on the part of the first lady.[20] Had President Lincoln not intervened and the committee's investigation continued, she may have been indicted for treason. Actually, none of Mary Todd Lincoln's efforts could overcome her poor public image, not even her charity work, which included visiting sick soldiers and contributing financially to the welfare of former slaves.

Julia Grant, wife of President Ulysses S. Grant (1869–1877), was as widely respected as Mary Lincoln was ridiculed. This first lady, who never let her crossed eyes hinder her self-confidence, reveled in the role. Moreover, she set the stage for future political wives by directing her energies toward creating a public role for the first lady.

With her own extravagance going uncriticized, Julia presided over elaborate dinners and receptions at the White House, even refurbishing the mansion by adding Grecian columns and chandeliers to the East Room. Under her direction, there were weekly public functions, and the Grants' daughter, Nellie, was married at the White House in a lavish ceremony that attracted international attention.[21]

Julia Grant, in addition to her acumen at hostessing, would often offer advice to her husband. One time, while he was still a general, Julia "tried her hand at running the war."[22] She had, Grant learned, a plan to capture Vicksburg that she wanted to share with him. General Grant, after hearing the plan, was obliged to tell his wife that her plan not only wouldn't be successful but would cause the loss of many lives. He allowed that he would take Vicksburg his own way and in his own time.[23]

When Lucy Hayes, wife of Rutherford B. Hayes (1877–1881), banned alcohol in the White House, critics labeled her "Lemonade Lucy." Lucy believed in moderation and simplicity and proved to be a successful, gracious hostess.[24] Five years later, another traditional wife, the youngest first lady in history, would become a favorite of Washington society. Twenty-one-year-old Frances Folsom had married President Grover Cleveland, a forty-eight-year-old bachelor, despite persistent gossip that he had fathered an illegitimate child.[25] She reigned successfully during her husband's two non-consecutive administrations (1885–1889, 1893–1897).

Thirty-six years after Eliza Johnson took up residence at the executive mansion as a result of Lincoln's assassination, Edith Roosevelt, second wife of Theodore Roosevelt, became first lady under the same circumstances. Within ten days after the assassination of President McKinley, the young couple arrived at the White House with their five children and the president's daughter from his first marriage. Thus began Theodore Roosevelt's administration (1901–1909).

First Lady Edith Roosevelt, who was self-disciplined, reserved, and politically astute, easily assumed her role of official hostess. Theodore's cousin, Nicholas Roosevelt, described Edith in glowing terms: "Her dignity and distinction of appearance were matched by an appropriate combination of friendliness and formality. I doubt if any First Lady since Dolley Madison better filled that exacting role."[26] The public side, however, was not all there was to know about First Lady Edith Roosevelt.

Privately, Edith was the person who held Theodore Roosevelt in check. Aware of his self-absorbed nature, she was known to refer to her husband as her oldest and worst child, and President Roosevelt often sought out Edith's views and her judgment about people. Taking her role as helpmate a little further, she was known to advise her husband on political issues as well.[27] In 1964, their daughter Ethel was quoted as saying, "We all knew that the person who had the long head in politics was Mother, and that Father depended on her advice and judgment time and again."[28]

Edith held dearly to her privacy. To that end she ordered the renovation of the White House and moved the family's quarters upstairs,[29] thereby preventing staff and official visitors from intruding upon the family. After conducting extensive research, biographer Edward Wagenknecht reported that "Roosevelt would not have been Roosevelt without Edith Carow. In intelligence and character she was her husband's equal. In tact and judgment she was his superior."[30] And after she died, at age 87, Edith Roosevelt was regarded as "one of the strongest-minded and strongest-willed presidential wives who ever lived in the White House."[31]

Another strong-willed first lady was Helen Taft, wife of William Howard Taft (1909–1913), who confessed, "It has always been my ambition to see Mr. Taft president of the United States."[32] In fact, if it hadn't been for his wife's ever-constant ambitions for him, William Taft may never have been elected president. He, it seems, aspired to a Supreme Court appointment, preferring to bypass the political field completely.[33] However, his dream wouldn't be realized until 1921, when he was appointed Chief Justice of the Supreme Court.

No matter how often Taft told his wife that "politics makes me sick," Mrs. Taft was vigilant.[34] Indeed, she had private meetings with President Roosevelt, after Taft became his secretary of war, to discuss the possibility of her husband becoming a presidential candidate.[35] After Taft's inauguration, his wife broke precedent by riding to the White House with the president in a horse-drawn carriage. And during his presidency she continued to discuss political issues with her husband, often sitting in on White House meetings and freely offering her comments afterward.[36]

Shortly after taking over the management of the White House, though, Helen Taft suffered a debilitating stroke that curtailed her involvement in political matters. Her recovery was slow, and it was several months before Mrs. Taft was able to walk and talk again. When she was well enough, she turned her energies to domestic affairs. One of her best-known projects was arranging for Japanese cherry blossom trees to be planted along the banks of the Potomac River. When she was unable to locate the type of cherry tree she had admired in Japan years before, this innovative first lady contacted the mayor of Tokyo for assistance. In short order, the mayor presented the first lady with a gift of 3,000 Japanese cherry trees.[37]

Woodrow Wilson's two wives, both first ladies during his tenure as president (1913–1921), were women with a cause. Wilson's first wife, Ellen, lobbied unceasingly and passionately for the passage of the Slum Clearance Act of 1913 and was "castigated in editorials for buttonholing members of Congress on behalf of her special project."[38] Ellen was a talented artist, and during her tenure as first lady, many of her paintings were sold, with the proceeds donated to charity.

The intelligent and strong-minded Edith Wilson, whom Woodrow met and married after Ellen died, became the subject of extreme controversy after her husband suffered a physically debilitating stroke. She served as his intermediary, keeping all cabinet members from visiting him. Publicly, Mrs. Wilson stated, "I, myself, never made a single decision regarding the disposition of public affairs. The only decision that was mine was what was important and what was not."[39] Because at that time the constitution made no provision for the transfer of executive power should an incapacitated president remain in office, Edith Wilson's actions and influence greatly alarmed those in her husband's administration. However, the passage of the

Twenty-Fifth Amendment, which defined the chain of
command, would not occur until 1967.

The three preceding first ladies, despite their valuable
contributions, seemed content to live their lives primarily
through their husbands' careers. It was no different for the
outwardly ambitious Florence Harding, wife of Warren
Harding (1921–1923). Grace Coolidge, wife of Calvin
Coolidge (1923–1929), was much more interested in family life and charitable work than in politics. And while Lou
Hoover, wife of Herbert Hoover (1929–1933), gave feminist speechees on national radio before her husband was
elected president, she, too, did not stray far from the role
of traditional first lady during her husband's tenure.

Not until 1933 did a first lady achieve such acclaim as to
be called "First Lady of the World." That title was reserved
for Eleanor Roosevelt, wife of Franklin Delano Roosevelt
(1933–1945). Like First Lady Edith Wilson, Eleanor Roosevelt was criticized for her involvement in political affairs.
Some people even suggested that it was her personal
ambitions that were behind her husband's political career.
Biographer Joseph P. Lash noted, "When she continued to
speak her mind on controversial issues, part of the press
said she was embarrassing her husband."[40]

But Eleanor Roosevelt had been a writer, teacher, and
business executive before FDR took office, and as one of
the kinder newspaper reporters wrote shortly after the
election was won, she refused "to allow the new honor
that has come to her husband to interfere with the varied
interests of her own life."[41] Indeed, Theodore Roosevelt's
niece, First Lady Eleanor Roosevelt, would be known for
her unceasing humanitarian work with the poor and mi-
norities.

As first lady, Eleanor Roosevelt was a precedent-setter,
being the first political wife ever to hold press conferences
at the White House. And these regularly held press confer-

ences were restricted to female reporters. Biographer Joseph Lash suggests Mrs. Roosevelt's intent was to "encourage the employment of newspaper women and to make it more comfortable to deal with subjects of interest primarily to women."[42] In addition to presiding over the usual official dinners, teas, and receptions, Mrs. Roosevelt continued with her writing efforts, penning a monthly column in the *Ladies Home Journal* as well as a daily syndicated newspaper column entitled "My Day." These columns provided a forum for Eleanor Roosevelt's commentary and for bringing attention to her resignation from the Daughters of the American Revolution. It seems the organization had refused to allow black opera singer Marian Anderson to sing in Constitution Hall. To demonstrate her deep belief in human equality, Mrs. Roosevelt promptly resigned and arranged for the concert to be held on the steps of the Lincoln Memorial.[43]

Even though Eleanor and Franklin provided the public with a model of outstanding leadership, their private lives were another story. Many of the details regarding FDR's long-standing affairs with Lucy Mercer and Missy LeHand were successfully kept hidden until after the death of the president. In 1918, when Eleanor learned of FDR's relationship with her social secretary, Lucy Mercer, she offered him a divorce. However, instead of breaking up the marriage, FDR and Lucy agreed to end their relationship. Twenty-five years after confronting FDR about the affair, Eleanor Roosevelt shared her feelings about it with Joseph P. Lash: "The bottom dropped out of my own particular world and I faced myself, my surroundings, my world, honestly for the first time. I really grew up that year."[44]

FDR met Missy LeHand in 1920, while she was working on his vice presidential campaign. After the loss, Missy became his secretary. Their relationship lasted more than twenty years, with Eleanor seemingly accepting their intimacy. Missy, in fact, lived with the Roosevelts both in the governor's mansion in Albany, New York, and in the White House, where she often assumed hostessing duties when the first lady was away. Biographer Lash says that although Eleanor "was hurt by Missy's role and often annoyed by the procession of young women vying for the president's favor, she blamed him more than the women. And she was sorry for Missy, for Missy, too, was a victim of this fascinating man's concentration upon himself and his objectives."[45]

There are also questions about Eleanor Roosevelt's involvement with women. According to Shelley Ross, author of *Fall From Grace,* Eleanor Roosevelt's friendship with AP reporter Lorena Hickok began in 1932 and spanned many years. The reporter, who often stayed at the White House, "officially moved in on January 2, 1941, and maintained a permanent residence there for the following four years."[46] The correspondence between the two women was donated by Ms. Hickok to the FDR library upon the condition that it not be opened until 1978, ten years after her death. According to Ross, the correspondence indicates that an intimate relationship existed between the two women, and that the contents of the 3,000 letters unlocked "many secrets of the Roosevelt era."[47]

Shortly after his fourth-term inauguration, FDR died quite unexpectedly. Although no longer the first lady, Mrs. Roosevelt was appointed delegate to the United Nations General Assembly and served in that capacity from 1945 to 1951. In 1946 she was elected chair of the United Nations Human Rights Commission, assisting in the writing of the Universal Declaration of Human Rights. Then, in 1948 Eleanor Roosevelt was asked to consider running for vice president, to which she responded, "I do not think we have yet reached a point where the electorate is ready for a woman vice-president who might possibly become president."[48]

In 1948, after completing FDR's fourth term, Harry Truman (1945–1953) hit the campaign trail. First Lady Bess Truman viewed the role of the political wife quite differently from her predecessor and rarely participated in her husband's political campaign. It was a time when most presidential candidates conducted a good portion of their campaigns from the rear platform of railroad cars, with the train making whistle-stops in as many small towns and cities as time would permit. Upon concluding his speech on one of these campaign tours, Harry Truman "pulled a cord, and a pair of blue velvet curtains parted to reveal his wife, Bess Truman, and daughter, Margaret, standing behind him. The two women waved and smiled. Neither of them uttered a single word—nor were they expected to. . . . The crowds loved the show."[49]

First Lady Bess Truman was an extremely private person who shunned publicity. As soon as she learned that Eleanor Roosevelt had been the only first lady to hold regular press conferences, she immediately discontinued the tradition. When questioned on the matter, Mrs. Truman stated simply, "I am not the one who is elected."[50] On those occasions when reporters were allowed access to the first lady, they were instructed that all comments be off the record.

In 1953 a new, more outgoing first lady took over the reins. During the traditional fifties, non-intellectual femininity was "in" and being "supportive" was where it was at. It also was a time when fairy tales could come true—a young woman from Philadelphia named Grace Kelly married the prince of Monaco and was transformed from movie star to princess. General Eisenhower was president (1953–1961). First Lady Mamie Eisenhower was the traditional wife. And all was well with the world.

In the early 1950s, politics still extended little attention, if any, to a female spouse's individuality. The political wife was hardly noticed, except perhaps to prove there was a family in the background. Neither public nor press viewed her as a separate person. Moreover, in those times a wife would never dream of campaigning on her own, without her husband at her side.

Like Harry Truman before him, "Ike" campaigned on a whistle-stop tour. On one occasion when the train arrived early, the crowds had already assembled. Not wanting to keep their supporters waiting, Ike and Mamie appeared on the rear platform dressed in their bathrobes and with Mamie's hair in curlers.[51] Yes, Mamie and Ike were real people, and Americans loved them.

Reflecting on the political wives of the sixties, Meg Greenfield, political journalist for *Newsweek,* recently remarked, "When I came to Washington in 1961, political wives were pretty much regarded as doll babies. . . . You could be a 200-pound, 78-year-old battle-ax and still qualify as one of the girls."[52] The next political wife was different, however. To Americans, the new chief executive and his wife were their first royal family.

In 1961 John F. Kennedy was elected president (1961–1963) and the White House was once more "home" to a charismatic young family. Hard-working campaigner Jacqueline Kennedy became the first lady, and in the tradition of many first ladies before her, she vowed to be "a wife and mother first."[53] Though only thirty-one years old when she moved into the White House, Jackie brought glamour, style, and culture to Washington. During Mrs. Kennedy's two-year reign as first lady, her bouffant hairstyle, pillbox hats, and tailored designer clothes became the look to strive for. Many clothing manufacturers even began replicating the "Jackie look" for middle American budgets.

After touring the White House prior to JFK's inauguration, Jackie said, "It looks like a house where nothing has ever taken place. There is no trace of the past."[54] So, resolving to do more than play the hostess, which by the way she did very well, Mrs. Kennedy set out to restore the original furnishings of the White House. To that end, she appointed an advisory committee consisting of historians, art directors, and museum curators. In addition, she sponsored a bill declaring the White House a museum.[55] In February 1962, after overseeing the restoration of the White House, Jackie took the American public, via national TV, on a personally guided tour.

As first lady, Mrs. Kennedy was an independent, private woman who shied away from publicity. Since being the first lady was her secondary role, she would pick and choose the events that she would attend in an official capacity.[56] Still, there was little she could do to discourage the many reporters who followed her in an attempt to get a story or a glimpse of the glamourous first lady. During the time that Jacqueline Kennedy was first lady, she proved to be an asset to the president both at home and abroad. In France, before a cheering crowd, the president introduced himself as "the man who accompanied Jacqueline Kennedy to Paris." As White House staffer Letitia Baldridge said, after JFK's death, "He was our President, but she was our movie star."[57] And no other "star" has emerged since the Kennedy administration.

Two years after assuming the presidency, John Kennedy was assassinated. While the country mourned, the TV cameras aboard Air Force One captured the unforgettable image of Jackie Kennedy, still in her blood-stained pink suit, standing beside Vice President Lyndon B. Johnson and his wife as he was sworn in as president (1963–1969). President Kennedy's funeral, televised for all of America to see, was attended by dignitaries from around the world. Mrs. Kennedy, who tended to all the details, proved to be a strong, unemotional heroine as she made her final public appearance as the president's first lady.

Lady Bird Johnson, the next first lady, was also a "wife and mother first." She was known for her informal get-togethers, especially the frequent barbecues at the LBJ Ranch. Her project as first lady was a "beautification" program, and she traveled the country to promote scenic beauty.

Lady Bird Johnson was, in fact, the first president's wife to campaign on her own. One of her most successful efforts was a four-day whistle-stop tour from Washington to New Orleans, which covered eight states, 47 stops, and nearly 1,700 miles. Mrs. Johnson's view on the role of women, and one she strictly adhered to was: "The great effort of women is not, I believe, to invade a man's world or to create a woman's world but to be a full partner in a warm compassionate world. . . . American women are undergoing a great revolution in our lifetime. . . . We must now try to make our laws catch up with what has happened to us as we bounce in and out of the labor market and raise a family."[58]

In the 1960s, political wives were still sharing their favorite recipes with the interested public. It was a time when men were still the responsible providers and political wives were rarely asked substantive questions by reporters. Consequently, Jane Muskie, wife of 1968 vice presidential candidate Edmund Muskie, was surprised when she was queried on her husband's "two-China" policy. At that time, our country was divided between those who would and those who would not recognize Communist China. Her response to the question was that she, too, had a two-china policy: "I like my good china better than my every-day china."[59]

Former schoolteacher Pat Nixon was also campaigning alongside her presidential candidate husband during these times. In 1969, after years of being the dutiful politician's wife who watched her husband both win and lose political elections, Pat Nixon finally became first lady. She was a woman who shunned the limelight and was very protective of her privacy. Rarely able to relax in large groups or before the media, this first lady so suppressed her own individuality that she was often referred to as "plastic Pat." Recalling the 1972 reelection campaign, writer Mary Finch Hoyt related the following incident: "Pat Nixon was in a limousine crossing a bridge over the Potomac River to Roosevelt Island. She had been on a grueling campaign schedule to help get her husband reelected. Now she slipped out of the car alone and walked briskly down a favorite secluded path in the woods—the only place, apparently, where she could find a few moments of desperately needed privacy."[60]

Most people are unaware of the projects Pat Nixon initiated as first lady, most notably her efforts to encourage people to volunteer their services to help those in need. Mrs. Nixon's remarks regarding volunteerism reflected her natural aversion to politics: "Government is impersonal, and to really get our problems solved we have to have people, too. We need the personal touch."[61]

President Richard Nixon (1969–1974) best described First Lady Pat Nixon when he commented that she was "the woman of strength and character who stands behind the President."[62] She certainly needed both strength and character when she stood by her husband on August 9, 1974 as he delivered his farewell address to his staff from the East Room of the White House. Wearing a simple pink dress, Mrs. Nixon, with a pained expression on her face, tried gallantly to hide her tears.

The 1970s became the decade of dramatic changes. Effects of the women's movement could be felt in many households. It was a confusing but exhilarating time for women as they began to question the outdated, constraining tenets of the past and to evaluate their status in society.

Many who saw the obvious inequities of their position rejected the status quo and began to examine, and oftentimes embrace, the philosophy of the women's movement. At an unprecedented rate, women were entering the workplace while maintaining a household. And it was a time when housewives who had been married for twenty years or more were getting divorced and striking out on their own, only to find themselves incapable of supporting themselves and their children.

Women in the 1970s were raising their children differently, too. Sons, in addition to thinking about future careers, were taught to operate the washing machine, and daughters were taught the importance of career planning. Boys no longer were the only young people dreaming about being president. Young girls now had the option of dreaming about political careers as well.

When Gerald Ford became president (1974–1977), Betty Ford, who moved easily with the times, became one of the most candid first ladies ever to fill that role. Indeed, she was the first lady when many women were posturing themselves as superwomen. Trying to be all things to all people, women in the seventies were wives, mothers, and professionals.

First Lady Betty Ford was another political wife who had a cause—equal rights. She gave speeches and lobbied congressmen and state legislators for the ratification of the Equal Rights Amendment.[63] Furthermore, she talked openly about her views on many issues, including extramarital affairs, drug and alcohol addiction, psychotherapy, and her mastectomy. In fact, she "did everything a political wife is *not* supposed to do—and she was smashing."[64]

But Gerald Ford lost the next presidential election, and Jimmy Carter (1977–1981) was next in line to govern the country. His wife, Rosalynn, was a very different first lady than her predecessor. Although she performed her official hostess duties, she was more often than not thought to be politically ambitious, offering her views on substantive issues and attending official committee meetings with the president. Indeed, both President and Mrs. Carter regarded themselves as "full and equal partners" in their relationship.[65]

Because of her involvement in political affairs, Rosalynn was viewed by many as a cold and calculating political wife. Indeed, reporters labeled the southern-bred Mrs. Carter the "steel magnolia." Her response to the criticism was, "I don't mind being called 'tough.' I am strong. I do have definite ideas and opinions. In the sense that 'tough' means I can take a lot, stand up to a lot, it's a fair description."[66]

With First Lady Nancy Reagan, wife of President Ronald Reagan (1981–1989), the country was back to what appeared to be both the acceptable traditional wife and glamourous designer clothes à la Jackie Kennedy. Mrs. Reagan was, as Mrs. Kennedy before her, openly criticized for her expensive wardrobe.

During the first year of her husband's administration, Mrs. Reagan became fair game for reporters and stand-up comics alike, who continually criticized her for her friendships with the wealthy and the socially prominent, her Hollywood image, her clothes, and her tastes.[67] During one interview, Mrs. Reagan added fuel to the fire when she remarked that her first priority as first lady was "to be the best wife I can."[68] Oddly enough, during that interview she gave no indication that she had a desire to become an activist for any cause—that came later, after she was publicly criticized for borrowing designer clothes and purchasing new china for the White House. Nancy's "project" was to educate young people about the consequences of drug abuse. "Just Say No" was her message. Although the project originally was perceived as an attempt to improve the first lady's declining image, it later proved to be an effective public education campaign in the war against drug use and addiction.

Behind the scenes, Nancy Reagan was an involved spouse, sharing her views on policy and personnel with her husband. She was familiar with her husband's schedule and often adjusted it whenever the pace seemed too strenuous for the president. Publicly, she was often portrayed as a manipulator, the "Dragon Lady" who convinced the president to make personnel changes in his cabinet.[69] In fairness to the former first lady, Nancy Reagan did not appear appreciably different from other first ladies who aimed to assert themselves by protecting their husbands from the perils of politics and disloyal staff. However, her wifely protectiveness was deemed inappropriate by the many women who were discovering their own power and discarding what they considered to be the unflattering "housewife" image.

Noted author Betty Friedan reminds us that throughout history few women have been independent achievers. Instead, they have used their position in the family as their power base. "Lacking male power in society, which was the only power recognized then, [a woman] got her power in the family by manipulating and denying the feelings of men and children, and her own feelings, behind that mask of superficial, sweet, steely rightness."[70]

Now, it seems, a few political wives are progressing beyond the earlier model. The younger women are moving away from being seen and not heard, and are being viewed more readily as individuals rather than extensions or appendages. Not only are most women campaigning alongside their husbands and on their own, some women are also running for political office. Gradually women are gaining personal stature, and because of that prominence they also appear to want more for themselves than being wives and mothers. Not surprisingly, these changing times have presented a dilemma for both the political system and the political wife: coming to concensus on what the role of a political wife is.

Generally, the role of the politician's wife has been restricted to wifely and motherly interests, and the first ladies' projects have been non-controversial, falling into the areas of the arts or human services. Many political wives have shunned the publicity and scrutiny inherent to their positions. Realizing that her presence at her husband's side was primarily for the sake of appearances, former First Lady Helen Taft remarked, "The same white light that beats upon a throne sheds its sometimes uncomfortable radiance upon the usually unprepared heads of America's chief executive and his family."[71] Other women have reveled in their share of the limelight and used their position as the politician's wife to their own advantage, though in many cases their ambitions have risen no higher than to live their lives through their husbands' careers. When scandal or criticism threatens the husband's political status, her position is threatened as well. Consequently, she stands staunchly by her spouse's side, defending his image and her place beside him.

Thirty years ago, little had changed for political wives. An overwhelming majority of women were still content with the limiting and erroneous message that one plus one equals one. In the 1950s, when the incoming congressional spouses attended orientation classes designed to ease the transition into public life in Washington, the women were given a book on etiquette. That book stipulated that the political wife should never chew gum and always wear gloves in public. Yes, the decade of the fifties, and to a great extent the sixties, produced women who were still clinging closely to the "woman's role." Betty Friedan suggests that in that era as well as previous ones, a woman had no life of her own. "In those days . . . a woman was defined not as a person in herself, but as someone else's wife or mother, defined by her service role in the family as less than a person, just a housewife."[72]

The traditional teachers of the fifties, be they parents or clergy, espoused that a wife should work only in the case of financial hardship. Single women were the only exception; after all, they had to go to work so they could find a husband. These women went to college to obtain what was commonly referred to as an MRS degree, and minored in teacher education, nursing, or fine arts. To go against these guidelines and unwritten rules was generally considered to be unacceptable, unladylike, and unattractive. Thus, wives were, in effect, obliged to perceive themselves as an appendage, which was and to a great degree still is viewed as a major attribute of the political wife.

In the middle seventies, it appeared that outspoken Betty Ford and politically ambitious Rosalynn Carter were forging new ground for political wives. Upon reflection, though, their behavior seems to have been a natural result of the changing times. Women were becoming more politically active and vocal, and elections were being won by younger men, whose wives were professionals with every intention of retaining their own identities and careers.

The younger political wives of the eighties have begun to impact the system, though only slightly. Now, due to the fact that 41% of married senators and 37% of married congressmen have working spouses, political wives are given the guidebook *Politicians and Their Spouses' Careers* at their orientation, which suggests that the political system has at last recognized political wives as career-oriented and independent women. The new orientation guide "examines the types of legal and ethical questions a congressional spouse must face in pursuing an independent career" and points out "acceptable" careers for the spouse as well as those that might present a conflict of interest.[73] While we can applaud the effort to accommodate political wives' personal ambitions, in reality, the political system continues to expect them to comply with the traditional rules of political wifedom. Instead of freeing them from the confines of the traditional wife's role, the "modernized" political system has simply added a new set of expectations to the old ones. Some of the additional requisites for the political wife include subordinating her career goals to those of her husband, effortlessly maintaining at least one household, campaigning with and for her husband, appearing perfectly satisfied with and fulfilled by political life, and never forgetting to smile. Consequently, most women simply have added these additional requirements to their already unmanageable list of responsibilities as wife, mother, and professional.

Perhaps Elizabeth Dole, wife of 1988 presidential candidate Senator Robert Dole, had the best opportunity to advance the cause of political wives, if only she had held her ground and her job as secretary of transportation. At the time her husband announced his candidacy, Elizabeth Dole had already established her own identity and career. In fact, she held a cabinet position in the Reagan administration. Her career, which spans more than thirty years, began in 1960 with a staff assistant position on the Lyndon B. Johnson vice presidential campaign. Forgoing marriage until she was thirty-nine, Mrs. Dole had achieved the distinction of becoming one of the select group of prominent women politicians. Indeed, in 1987 Republican pollster Linda Duvall remarked, "Until now, we've never seen a situation where the wife is just as professionally credible as the husband."[74] Duvall went on to predict that Mrs. Dole's decision about whether or not to remain in her cabinet position would "send a signal" to other working wives.

In time the Doles were billed as "Dole and Dole" and the "power couple." Queries about the possibility that she might resign her post in the Reagan administration were met with denial, accompanied by statements strongly advocating for working wives. "I love my job. It's challenging, it's tough," Dole was quoted as saying.[75] However, she did resign from her position in order to campaign with and for her husband. One possible explanation for her incongruous decision was presented in the *Economist*: "Critics say her resignation from the transport department was well timed. She had been under increasing fire for moving too slowly to solve various car-safety and airline problems."[76]

Regardless of the reasoning behind her decision, Mrs. Dole appeared to be sending mixed messages to the public. For example, as journalist Philip Weiss suggested, feminists once regarded Mrs. Dole as someone who "pushed for women's issues, and yet from the beginning of her service in the White House, her approach was remarkably conciliatory. She abandoned her commitment to the Equal Rights Amendment, explaining 'he's [Reagan's] not going to change on that.' "[77] Furthermore, when Weiss asked Dole's press secretary, Dale Petroskey, about Dole's advocacy for women's issues, he learned that Mrs. Dole's posture was actually "femin*ine* . . . appealing." Weiss goes on to say that "in a time of greater female independence, Elizabeth Dole has turned out to be just what an uneasy establishment ordered, a woman of nominal authority but old-fashioned dependence. Our ambivalence about women in power has decreed her success."[78]

The decision to resign, it seems, also conveyed the message to other working spouses that Dole was discounting herself and her years of hard work to achieve professional stature. To them, she gave in to the system that says, in effect, "we really prefer that women choose to be either political wives or career women." Author and former political wife Abigail McCarthy concluded that "in the end it never was a real option. She was a woman and a wife, and her husband wanted to run for president."[79] Mrs. Dole, however, seemed to confuse the issue even further when she suggested that her resignation was a symbol of the advancement of women. Recently, writer Katie Leishman quoted Dole as saying, "I think that is what women have been fighting for: the right to make career decisions we think are right for us."[80]

The validity of that argument, of course, depends on how the term "feminist" is defined. In the broader sense, many would consider a feminist act to be one that furthers the cause not only of the one who is making the decision but of all women who are seeking greater independence and freedom of choice. On the other hand, there are those, perhaps like Elizabeth Dole, who view their actions as being feminist solely on the basis that they themselves will benefit from those actions.

When Dole refused to advocate for women's rights once she had become a member of the cabinet and hid behind President Reagan's political position as her reason, feminists perceived it as a slap in the face. But if "feminist" is defined simply as one who makes her own decisions for her own benefit, perhaps Dole's philosophy regarding women has remained unchanged after all. If in fact she selected her course without being coerced either by her husband or by the political system, then indeed she was responding according to her definition of feminist or women's advocate. Consequently, to her mind, her decision to resign her position may have been the result not of her caving into the system's expectations but merely holding out for an opportunity to secure a better position should her husband be elected.

Be that as it may, political wives are in a unique position

to influence other women in both negative and positive ways. Their actions and attitudes hold a power not unlike that of their husbands. And, just when younger politicians were getting elected and their wives were making their independent presence known in the system, Elizabeth Dole did an about-face and scurried back to the fifties. Obviously, only Mrs. Dole knows the real reasons behind her decision to abandon her career in order to hit the campaign trail full time. A few years ago, though, Ann Taylor Fleming addressed the dilemma of the American wife, which might explain why Dole chose the course she did: "She was, finally, not that different from the rest—a 50's wife in 80's America, whereas a lot of them are 80's wives in 50's America, flip sides of the same dilemma, all laboring under the expectations and limitations of both decades, all trying to find the right balance between dependence and independence."[81]

As we examine the role of the political wife, it becomes clear that throughout history the wives of politicians have all reflected their traditional upbringing, with few straying far from their generational guidelines. It is also clear that the majority of women have chosen to follow the rules set by the political system which, by and large, has managed to keep women locked in the old traditional value system of generations past. Now, inasmuch as political wives are also traditional women, historians would have us believe that among these women there have been numerous exceptions. By their definition, an "exception" seems to be the woman who crosses over the line of acceptability for her era. And, as we all know, being a helpmate and a hostess is what the political system defines as acceptable.

Using the historians' criteria, we would acknowledge Helen Taft, who broke all the rules by riding to the White House with her husband after his inauguration, as an exception. And if an exception is one who is overtly ambitious for her husband, often advising him on policies and sitting in on official meetings, Rosalynn Carter would also qualify, as would Sarah Polk, Abigail Adams, and Edith Roosevelt. And as extravagance has never been viewed as proper for the political wife, certainly Jackie Kennedy and Nancy Reagan must be considered exceptions to the traditional role.

But are these women really exceptions? Not if we define an exception as someone who accomplishes her own goals independently of her husband and creates a role for herself based on her own personal interests. By that definition, then Eleanor Roosevelt is the one woman who stands apart from the rest. She, it seems, may be the only exception.

While society in general has advanced to the extent that women no longer must choose between being either homemakers or career women, the role of the political wife has progressed very little. That will change only when women are no longer considered "exceptions" for failing to acquiese to the political system and when, in fact, that "acceptable, traditional role" is no longer the standard.

It is only recently that women have begun to express a desire to break through to a newer and wider field of vision. More often than not, we see this striving for greater independence among the younger wives of senators, congressmen, and governors. They are the new breed of women who regard themselves as separate individuals, with their own goals and ambitions. Attorney Marilyn Quayle is an example of this more independent woman who does not feel the need to be her husband's ever-constant companion. Yet, despite the emergence of these younger political wives, the political system continues to place demands on the wife that are inconsistent with her own stage of independence.

Betty Friedan discusses this difficult transition as women

move away from their prescribed roles: "Women in the next decade have to find solutions for the practical problems, niches for themselves that feel more comfortable. We've gone through the metamorphosis. We're not worms any more, but we're not butterflies yet either."[82]

For the sake of continued progress, political wives must accept that the system is not going to change by itself. It is the woman who must break down the barriers and select her own course. She must be the one to define the role of the political wife. Otherwise, it will be "politics as usual," and the role of the political wife will remain unchanged. Only when the wife accepts the challenge of exerting her influence and her opinions will the system be inclined to respond to her.

In a January 1987 interview, I asked Wren Wirth, wife of Senator Tim Wirth, what changes had occurred over the years in the role of the political wife. She responded, "We women no longer pour tea or wear white gloves." When the same question was posed to Barbara Bush in a later interview, and I shared with her Wren Wirth's response, the first lady laughed and said, "Oh, we still pour tea. But now we do it with our bare hands."

*   *   *

The following journal entries were compiled on the road, as we rushed from one destination to another. The candidate often was asleep or reading and his political wife was talking to the driver or writing thoughts down—or both.

February 2

I was accustomed to having control of my life. Besides being a wife and the mother of three children, I've worked in the juvenile justice system teaching and counseling teenagers. I've served on boards and task forces for domestic violence prevention, senior citizens, and the county jail. I was co-founder of a nonprofit group that provides housing and services to single-parent families seeking self-sufficiency. And I designed and developed programs for juvenile probation, the District Attorney's Office, and student services at the community college. And here I am now, in the afterglow of these exciting, challenging, changing times, right back in the decade of the fifties. I'm a political wife!

April 17

When I look back at the fifties, I see a young girl who was struggling to please everyone but herself. I remember having conversations on the virtues of being a good listener. It was much more attractive and acceptable to listen to others, I was told, than to talk about oneself. Women from my generation were expected to be peacemakers, to nurture and adapt. We were raised to be available and attentive to our husbands' needs, and later, to our children's needs. Our needs simply did not exist. I remember when Steve told me he had an opportunity for career advancement but that we'd have to relocate. There was no hesitation. I packed up our belongings, and we moved 2,000 miles away from our families and friends.

May 9

We're on our way to another political event, and my mind wants to focus on another period in my life. . . . I remember having childhood fantasies about being whisked off my feet, marrying a famous celebrity (politicians were not among the famous in those days), having children, and living a carefree glamourous life, happily ever after. But in my wildest dreams, the fame was never extended to me. Like most other women of my generation, I was raised to be the supportive one, the helpmate, rather than to go out on my own and accomplish. Being successful was left to the men, the providers, and women were successful only if they married successful men.

June 20

Being a political wife is a no-win situation. . . . Today the political wife is still expected to stay home and raise her children but is also viewed as inadequate if she does not also pursue a career. If she has a career, she is viewed as inadequate if she doesn't stay at home and raise her children.

July 7

Last night I fell into bed totally exhausted again, but I couldn't sleep. My mind kept trying to make sense of the craziness of politics and our present political system. There seems to be so much confusion—the system's inconsistencies and its expectations of the political wife, and my own unclear position on my role as a political wife. I wonder how I am going to take care of myself when every event seems so critical, when the candidate is starting to believe his publicity, when the children are feeling neglected, when I have other things to do.

August 3

When the campaign began, I was confused about what my role could or should be. I expected the public or the staff, who was supposed to understand the public's mind-set, to define that role for me. But nobody seems to know what to do with the political wife; no one knows what to expect of her. What I sense is an overall confusion about the wife as traditional model and the eighties woman. It's as if they think "wife and mother" is a role determined by someone other than "woman." How absurd.

September 22

Today, we want more from our lives than to be ever-smiling, non-thinking appendages of our ambitious husbands (unless, of course, WE are the ambitious ones), but we're finding it difficult to remove the mortar from our traditional mind-set. We are in constant conflict with the voices echoing in our heads, and with the teachings of our own generation and the next. And there is little positive reinforcement from the ghostly troops of generations past.

December 9

Undoubtedly, as a young married woman I would not have questioned the political system's expectations of me or my role in the system. I would have done as I was told, regardless of whether or not I agreed. In those days, if Steve had been a politician, I would have been willing to limit myself and my horizons. Why, I can remember how difficult it was for me to have my ears pierced at that stage of life. It took me years to dismiss the thoughts that it was unladylike to have pierced ears, and that if God had wanted us to have pierced ears we'd already have holes there.

Now, after having experienced more of life and knowing myself and my capabilities a lot better, I realize how difficult political wifedom is. I know I'm not going to graciously relinquish a part of myself. It has taken me too many years to achieve and to be comfortable with some modicum of independence.

January 2

Inasmuch as I am a seeker, I'm seeking an explanation for why being a political wife feels so confining. I'm a product of the fifties, and it seems that the fifties women are affected the most. We're both traditional and feminist in our thinking. The swing generation, or so it feels. I'm moving, as if on a swing, from the fifties era of dependency to more independent times and back again, and not being wholly a part of either era.

April 27

After months of reflection, I must conclude that my upbringing has a great deal to do with my difficulties in attempting to fulfill the role of the political wife. Indeed, I think one can take the woman out of the generation, but I suspect one cannot take the generation completely out of the woman.

May 1

I picked up a book by Eleanor Roosevelt yesterday. Interestingly enough, it opened to this passage: "Women have one advantage over men. Throughout history they have been forced to make adjustments. They have adapted their own personal wishes and ambitions and hopes to those of their husbands, their children, and the requirements of their homes. In the great majority, they have arranged to fit their own interests into a pattern primarily concerned with the interests of others. This has not always been an easy process but the result is that, in most cases, it is less difficult for a woman to adjust to new situations than it is for a man."[83]

I find myself both amused and in total agreement with Mrs. Roosevelt. She's right, of course, that women are more adaptable than men. Can you picture a man portraying the political spouse as one who stands beside his wife with that adoring "I'll follow you anywhere" gaze?

July 22

Unfortunately, political wives have made very little progress since the fifties. And the system totally ignores
women's concerns. As a result, women continue to subject
themselves to a smoke-filled world that only obstructs and
distorts reality. Behind the smoke, the political system
regards women in much the same way as it always has.
Alas, time forges on and life remains the same.

NOTES

1. Paul F. Boller, Jr., *Presidential Wives: An Anecdotal History*
(New York: Oxford University Press, 1988), 3–7.
2. Arden Davis Melick, *Wives of the Presidents,* rev. ed. (Ma-
plewood, N.J.: Hammond Incorporated, 1977), 8–11.
3. Boller, *Presidential Wives,* 14–19.
4. Melick, *Wives of the Presidents,* 14.
5. Ibid., 15.
6. Ibid., 20.
7. Boller, *Presidental Wives,* 36–41.
8. Melick, *Wives of the Presidents,* 22.
9. Boller, *Presidential Wives,* 49–50.
10. Melick, *Wives of the Presidents,* 25.
11. Boller, *Presidential Wives,* 55.
12. Ibid., 53–59.
13. Ibid., 60.
14. Melick, *Wives of the Presidents,* 34.
15. Boller, *Presidential Wives,* 88–90.
16. Melick, *Wives of the Presidents,* 39.
17. Shelley Ross, *Fall From Grace: Sex, Scandal, and Corruption
in American Politics from 1702 to the Present* (New York: Ballantine
Books, 1988), 96–97.
18. Ibid., 94.
19. Boller, *Presidential Wives,* 110.
20. Ibid., 111.

21. Melick, *Wives of the Presidents*, 44–45.
22. Boller, *Presidential Wives*, 136.
23. Ibid., 137.
24. Melick, *Wives of the Presidents*, 46.
25. Ross, *Fall From Grace*, 120.
26. Nicholas Roosevelt, *Theodore Roosevelt: The Man As I Knew Him* (New York: Dodd, Mead and Company, 1967), 26.
27. Boller, *Presidential Wives*, 199.
28. Roosevelt, *Theodore Roosevelt*, 28.
29. Melick, *Wives of the Presidents*, 57.
30. Roosevelt, *Theodore Roosevelt*, 26.
31. Boller, *Presidential Wives*, 201.
32. Melick, *Wives of the Presidents*, 58.
33. Ibid., 58–59.
34. Boller, *Presidential Wives*, 211.
35. Ibid., 210.
36. Ibid., 213.
37. Melick, *Wives of the Presidents*, 59.
38. Barbara Gamarekian, "The Presidency, First Ladies Step Further Out of Shadows," New York *Times*, 10 March 1988, Washington Talk.
39. Melick, *Wives of the Presidents*, 63.
40. Joseph P. Lash, *Eleanor and Franklin* (New York: W. W. Norton, 1971), 355.
41. Ibid., 354.
42. Ibid., 361.
43. Melick, *Wives of the Presidents*, 72.
44. Lash, *Eleanor and Franklin*, 220.
45. Ibid., 510.
46. Ross, *Fall From Grace*, 177.
47. Ibid., 174.
48. Melick, *Wives of the Presidents*, 73.
49. Mary Finch Hoyt, "A Personal Look at Political Wives," *Good Housekeeping*, June 1984, 70.
50. Boller, *Presidential Wives*, 319.
51. Ibid., 342.
52. Meg Greenfield, "More Than Just a Mama Bear," *Newsweek*, 109 (23 March 1987), 88.

53. Boller, *Presidential Wives,* 362.
54. Ibid., 363.
55. Melick, *Wives of the Presidents,* 80.
56. Boller, *Presidential Wives,* 362.
57. Ibid., 377.
58. Melick, *Wives of the Presidents,* 83.
59. Hoyt, "A Personal Look at Political Wives," 72.
60. Ibid., 84.
61. Boller, *Presidential Wives,* 410.
62. Melick, *Wives of the Presidents,* 85.
63. Boller, *Presidential Wives,* 424.
64. Hoyt, "A Personal Look at Political Wives," 75.
65. Boller, *Presidential Wives,* 434.
66. Ibid., 441.
67. Ibid., 450.
68. Hoyt, "A Personal Look at Political Wives," 70.
69. Boller, *Presidential Wives,* 462–64.
70. Betty Friedan, *The Second Stage,* rev. ed. (New York: Summit Books, 1986), 56.
71. Diana Dixon Healy, *America's First Ladies: Private Lives of the Presidential Wives* (New York: Atheneum, 1988), xiv.
72. Friedan, *The Second Stage,* 45.
73. Marc E. Miller, *Politicians and Their Spouses' Careers* (Washington, D.C.: Congressional Management Foundation, 1985), 80, 82.
74. Linda Duvall, "Secretary Dole, Meet Mrs. Dole," *Time,* 130 (21 September 1987), 30.
75. Abigail McCarthy, "The Time Is Not Yet, Elizabeth Dole Steps Down," *Commonweal,* 9 October 1987, 554.
76. "Bob Dole's Better Half," *Economist,* 30 January 1988, 22.
77. Philip Weiss, "Charming Her Way to the White House," *Washington Monthly,* September 1987, 35.
78. Ibid., 43.
79. McCarthy, "The Time Is Not Yet," 555.
80. Katie Leishman, "Elizabeth Dole: A Very Private Public Person," *McCall's,* April 1988, 132.
81. Ann Taylor Fleming, "The American Wife," New York *Times* Magazine, 26 October 1986, 31.

82. Friedan, *The Second Stage*, 71.

83. Eleanor Roosevelt, *You Learn by Living* (Philadelphia: Westminster Press, 1983), 77.

SELECTED READING

1. Carole Chandler Waldrup, *Presidents' Wives: The Lives of 44 American Women of Strength* (Jefferson, N.C.: McFarland & Co., 1989).

2. Joseph Nathan Kane, *Facts About the Presidents: A Compilation of Biographical and Historical Information*, 4th ed. (New York: H. W. Wilson Company, 1981).

3. Laura C. Holloway, *The Ladies of the White House; or, In the Home of the Presidents*, 2 vols. (New York: Funk & Wagnalls, 1886).

4. Margaret Brown Klapthor, *The First Ladies*, 5th ed. (Washington, D.C.: The White House Historical Association with the cooperation of the National Geographic Society, 1987).

Chapter Five

Whose Life Is This Anyway?

> I have sacrificed everything in my life that I considered precious in order to advance the political career of my husband.
>
> —*Pat Nixon*

Making sacrifices is a reality of political life, at least for the wife of the politician. In most cases, her private life and personal priorities are relinquished in order to help get her husband elected. The irony is, should he be victorious, the cost may be even greater for the wife of the politician, who may well find herself being shuffled aside once the election has been won.

Many political wives follow a predictable, well-worn path, playing the image game to appease the expectations of the public and the press while finding themselves progressively more isolated and lonely and unsure of their position and purpose. As her identity becomes more closely linked to her husband's status, the political spouse often becomes overwhelmed by feelings of disillusionment, anger, resentment, and finally bitterness. Some women are even abandoned — either physically or emotionally — after having sacrificed all for their husbands' careers, when they are no longer useful to the cause except

for making numerous obligatory appearances as "the wife
of."

Political wives have various methods of coping with the
ruthless world of politics, which often uses them up and
then discards them. We will take a look at both the
constructive and destructive ways in which women respond to the pressures and inequities of political life. What
about those women who are unable to cope, who find
themselves helplessly trapped in a no-win situation? A
number of political spouses have come forward with con-
fessions of alcoholism, drug addiction, and serious health
problems they see as resulting from the stress of political
life. What do these women have in common? Is there a
particular "type" of individual who desperately clings to
self-destructive habits as her only way of surviving? We
will consider the experiences of a number of political wives
in an attempt to find answers to these questions.

The many challenges that face female political spouses
can be both psychologically and physically debilitating.
Maintaining the balance between being a political wife and
retaining one's individuality, critical to one's overall
health, is extremely difficult but absolutely essential. A
long list of sacrifices, ones that ultimately will take their
toll on her, is the reality of what's in store for the wife of
a politician. Very often, whether she becomes a political
wife on her wedding day or assumes that role after many
years of marriage, a good portion of her life will no longer
be her own. Thus, she needs to be aware beforehand of the
sacrifices she will be asked to make, and to be sure she is
the one who will determine the degree to which she will
be involved in her husband's career. She must count the
costs of the sacrifices before she makes them; otherwise,
they will get the better of her.

The most unassuming and yet lethal sacrifice made by a
political wife occurs during her husband's campaign.

Mary Andrews, wife of former Senator Mark Andrews, spoke from years of experience in politics when she made the comment that "in politics you don't have control of your time. In fact, your life is not your own." In a realm where politics comes first, "I was always Mark's helper, never the speech maker. And before I contracted spinal meningitis during the 1979 campaign, I was at his side at every event. For the last several years, of course, I have been forced to limit my campaign appearances."

With regard to one of her husband's political campaigns, Elizabeth Dole described one of those rare moments when the candidate's wife can escape into her private world: "When the door of your hotel room closes behind you, you kick off your shoes and savor the exquisite feeling that for the next few hours your life is your own."[1]

Indeed, once the political wife makes the commitment to help her husband win a race, an inordinate amount of her time will be devoted to both traveling and being her husband's spokesperson. And the political wife's time will steadily erode until the increasing demands of the campaign take her away from her home, career, children, and husband. And if she allows it, less and less time is going to be available for her to pursue her own personal goals and ambitions. One candid senator's wife admitted that she seemed to be "playing a tug of war" between what she wanted to do and what her husband's staff thought she should do. Congressional wife Liz McEwen commented, "It's hard to find time for myself. Actually, there isn't any time for me."

Contrary to public opinion, very few political wives lead the glamourous life of the jet set. In fact, the reality of political life is something quite different. I recall, for example, a conversation that took place during one of my telephone calls to the offices of politicians requesting interviews with their wives. The congressman's press secretary responded with "Mrs. —— is still in Paris but should be returning in a few days." The following week, when I returned the call, I was informed that the interview had been approved. On the eve of the scheduled meeting with the congressman's wife, I telephoned her to confirm our appointment. Following an extended conversation about her life in Washington, the role of political wives, and future plans, she interjected, "Joyce, I have to go to Damascus in two days. You could come with me and we'd have more time to talk. Want to go?" I must have hesitated, because she quickly added, "Sounds far, doesn't it? Well, it's in Maryland!" Instantly, I recalled hearing about her being in "Paris" for a few days. Hence this reponse: "Tell me, ——, where on earth is Paris if Damascus is in Maryland?"

The constant travel involved in both campaigning and holding political office is more grueling than glamourous. On occasion it is the politician himself who recognizes the burdens that his career places on his spouse. During an interview, former President Gerald Ford described how the wife is affected when a politician is continually on the road:

"It puts a strain on the marriage. . . . I called every night unless, through some unusual circumstance, a phone wasn't available, but I was all over the country, and sometimes overseas, and with four active children, Betty had a tough obligation. They were all doing their thing, and although they grew up to be nice kids, they had their problems, and she had to be not only mother but the father. Then, when I was home I wanted to make everything smooth and nice, which made it more difficult for her because I would never be the one to reprimand them. Even before I was Minority Leader, in election years I'd go to Michigan after Congress adjourned, be away for three weeks, come home for the weekend, go back to Michigan and my constituents for another three weeks."[2]

If they are to keep in touch with their constituents, both congressmen and senators must commute back and forth between Washington and their home state, spending week-days on "the hill" and numerous weekends at home. The obvious result is that their family life suffers. Conse-quently, many congressional wives maintain two house-holds — one in Washington and one in their home state.

Some wives, however, choose to remain in their home state. When finances are an issue, oftentimes the wives will remain at home to ease the budgetary constraints. One congressional wife stated that although it is a strain on the entire family to be separated, it also is a lot less expensive to pay for one airline ticket than five. Other political wives find it easier to remain in their home state and keep the children in familiar surroundings than to move halfway across the country. Either way, state a number of political wives, there is no such thing as a "normal family life" when you're involved in politics. The wife who stays home can campaign for her husband while he is in Washington. By contrast, the wife who moves to Washington finds herself spending uncounted weekends commuting back to her home state with the children to campaign with the candidate-husband-father — that is, of course, if they can afford the airline fares. Thus, it seems that regardless of which choice she makes, the political wife's life is difficult.

The children of politicians also have to make adjust-ments to public life. Contending with her "famous" fath-er's frequent absences, young Tricia Nixon in 1954 brought these questions to a reporter's ears: "If he's fa-mous why can't he stay home? Why is he gone all the time?"[3] To make matters worse, because they lead such mobile lives many young people miss out on some of the normal activities that others take for granted. Pamela Kostmayer, during her separation from her husband, Congressman Peter Kostmayer of Bucks County, Pennsylvania, remarked: "For two straight years after Peter and I married, [my daughters] and I drove up to the District every weekend. As a result they couldn't go to a lot of class parties or be in the school plays because the rehearsals would take place on the weekends." Kostmayer went on to say that the children would often act out their frustrations when she was not available for them. "It would take two months after an election to calm things down and get everyone back to a routine."[4]

Regardless of whether or not it is appropriate for the public to expect the politician's job to take precedence over everything else, it generally does. More often than not, if the politician goes home for dinner, meals are eaten on the run so that he can return to the House or Senate in time for evening sessions. Consequently, the wife spends much of her time without her husband. Under these circumstances, for a good portion of each week the political family resembles a single-parent household, with the wife being both mother and father to the children. Julie Nixon Eisenhower recently wrote that during Richard Nixon's tenure as a California congressman, Pat Nixon, like many of the other congressional wives, "took charge of almost all the household responsibilities, oftentimes spending time alone . . . with only the briefest glimpses of her husband."[5]

If the politician and his spouse are to spend any time together away from politics, it becomes necessary to schedule ahead. Simple outings like going to the movies or just taking a day off from the political grind now require advance planning. A congressional wife who is new to politics told me she was discovering that she and her husband could no longer meet each other for lunch on the spur of the moment or enjoy any of the recreational activities they'd participated in before his election. Another congressional wife stated that "we used to call each other on the phone during the day just to visit. Now, we rarely get to talk with each other during the day, and by the time he gets home late at night I'm asleep."

Because their private lives are at risk and less and less time is available for family activities, loneliness is common among political wives. Political life puts a strain on both the marital relationship and the entire family. It can be a time of continual frustration for the wife who is always waiting for the politician to come home. And it can be difficult for the politician because "if she's not with him, he's lonely," says Ellen Armstrong, wife of retired Senator William Armstrong. According to Christine Delay, when her husband Tom was elected to Congress, he asked other politicians whether he should move to Washington alone. He was told to "take your family with you. It's so lonely going home to an empty apartment."

Most political wives also experience feelings of isolation. Elizabeth Dole explained that fulfilling her obligation as a political wife leaves "little time to be a friend to friends."[6] As the wife's schedule expands to serve the interests of her husband's career, there is little time for casual get-togethers with old friends. In time, her friends' perception of her changes, and she is no longer viewed as just another person. In some cases, the wife's own perception of herself changes as she becomes further involved in the political world. Oftentimes she is placed on a pedestal and becomes the focus of attention. As one woman revealed, "Being the wife of a big-time politician brings you a certain 'respectability.' " A congressional spouse explained, "There's a different type of prestige when you're a congressman's wife. People's perception of you changes. I'm treated much better as a political wife than I was as a private citizen's wife. Now whenever I tell a salesperson who I am, I'm waited on immediately."

The cruel irony of political life is that the wife often sacrifices everything for a "victory" that leaves her lonely and isolated. In *Laughing All the Way,* caustic Barbara Howar calls it as she sees it: "Most of these wives spend lifetimes disguising their true feelings, nearly hiding their misery behind plucky, pleasant facades. The woman with the big-time politician is permitted no complaints. . . . They play the devoted couple for the sake of a career that inevitably takes the man away from home most of the time."[7] It's no wonder that in 1983, Lee Hart was quoted as saying: "I suppose if I had my druthers, I wouldn't have chosen this path for myself, or the family."[8] Nevertheless, she was once again campaigning at her husband's side in 1984 when he chose to toss his hat into the ring and run for the presidency. But the negative press that stalked Gary Hart's last campaign seemed to be too much for the candidate and his family, forcing his withdrawal from the race.

Above all else, a politician avoids negative press. Senator John Warner must have seen red when his wife's picture appeared on the front page of the New York *Daily News* above a caption questioning whether she had a new love interest in her life. The incident occurred just a few years after political celebrity Warner married Hollywood celebrity Elizabeth Taylor. The marriage apparently had begun to disintegrate soon after Warner's victorious campaign in 1978. Among their many differences, Taylor and Warner "operated on different time clocks, with Warner getting up at the crack of dawn and Elizabeth sleeping past noon. Sometimes he wrote a note and left it on her pillow. Usually he communicated with her through their respective secretaries. . . . The notes soon stopped. By the time Elizabeth decided to go back to work, she and John Warner were leading entirely different lives."[9]

As she witnesses the progressive disintegration of her

family life, the political wife experiences even greater stress as she attempts to hold the family, and herself, together while doing everything within her power to advance her husband's career. If one's private life becomes grist for the media's unquenchable craving for sensationalized news, the political wife experiences even greater stress. The private lives of Gary and Lee Hart, for example, have been the object of intense press scrutiny. In 1983, *Denver Post* staff writer Diane Eicher said of Mrs. Hart: "Though she knew from the outset that political life automatically puts private life on display, it has been difficult . . . to hear people 'spread rumors' about her, about him, about the two separations the Hart marriage has undergone — and survived, apparently — in the past few years."[10] Mrs. Hart has suggested that the more she tried to keep her private life out of the newspapers, the more it seemed only to incite the press to look deeper for a story. In fact, after Hart withdrew from the 1986 presidential race, a reporter from the *National Enquirer* swept past the "Private Property-No Trespassing" signs at the Hart's secluded home in Troublesome Gulch, Colorado, to inquire about interviewing Mrs. Hart. (He told her that she could decide what it would take for her to agree to do the interview.)

Beth Calloway, wife of former Georgia Congressman Howard "Bo" Calloway, makes the point that there are other ways political families can lose their privacy besides having their every move chronicled in the newspapers. During our interview, Calloway remarked that one day "they walked into our house, people we didn't know, right off the street. They would look around saying, 'how nice, how pretty,' as they admired our furnishings."

The political wife is further bewildered when she runs head-on into the harsh artificiality and deception that pervade big-time politics. She observes that no one wants to rock the boat by telling the truth, out of fear that an election may be lost; and she soon learns that if she's to survive, she must follow suit by concealing any dissatisfaction or any problems at home.

Most political wives project an image of the subordinate wife and pretend that everything is fine with their lives when it isn't. Because of the demands of the public, the political system, and the press, politicians and their spouses feel pressured to represent themselves as having both perfect marriages and children. Even when politicians or their wives are having serious problems in their private lives, a congressional spouse said, "they are inclined to conceal them." Author Marcia Chellis cites Joan Kennedy's reaction to a misleading series of photos that appeared in a Washington newspaper. At the time, the Kennedys had been living separately for quite a while though Joan had agreed to campaign with and for her estranged husband. "All those pictures of Ted and me in a haystack and I'm smiling up at him so adoringly. . . . I don't feel that way at all." Chellis goes on to say, "She was realistic enough to know that things were not going well between her and Ted, and it made her feel uncomfortable to pretend otherwise. Yet she genuinely wanted the campaign to be a success, hoping that might make a reconciliation possible. She had been trapped, it appeared, into deceiving the press and public, and perhaps even herself."[11]

During the interviews, I encountered many political wives who said they have no personal frustrations or problems with political life. Rather, I often heard, "We never have differences, not even in private." In *Pat Nixon: The Untold Story,* Julie Nixon Eisenhower cites a similar response her mother provided in an interview with *Collier's Magazine.* Pat Nixon was quoted as saying, "We've never quarreled. Dick and I are too much alike. We don't even differ in our opinions." When her daughter questioned her about the statement, Pat Nixon said, "Reporters were always asking me what Dick and I argued about. I didn't want to air differences publicly, and so in self-defense, and to turn them off quickly, I gave that answer."[12]

Some of the wives who play the image game eventually come to believe their own words and to assume that the persona they have so carefully crafted is reality — so much so that they no longer know who they are. After her husband left political office, former First Lady Betty Ford, known for her candor on many subjects, discussed her own ability to internalize her public persona: "I was so wrapped up in the image I had been presenting to the public that I didn't see anything wrong with my life. I was married to the perfect man, I had four perfect children, I had a new house. . . . As far as I was concerned, everything was going along just fine, and I didn't know why these therapists should be suggesting anything different."[13]

In my interviews, many women presented their lives in much the same light. One congressional spouse went even further, though, when she said, "Our life is so wonderful, I probably didn't give you any information you can write about, did I?" My reaction to such comments, though, was etched in disbelief and disappointment. Could political life be so wonderful? How did I miss that when I was a political wife? Indeed, I knew that denying any negativity associated with political life was one way of protecting themselves. Simply because they don't want their words to come back and somehow hurt them or their husbands, political wives become masters at playing the image game and become guarded and protective. But I wondered if that cautious exterior I continued to encounter could be a manifestation of something else. Too many women seemed particularly entrenched in denial, so much so that their words were steeped in sometimes unbelievable contradictions. "I've lost my identity, but it's okay," said one "perfectly happy" political wife.

Actually, "lying" about political life may not be the issue for a woman who is struggling with low self-esteem or who has lost her sense of self. As author Melody Beattie has written, "We are not denying whatever we are denying because we are stupid, stubborn, or deficient. We are not even consciously lying to ourselves. . . . It [denial] is an instinctive and natural reaction to pain, loss, and change. It protects us. It wards off the blows of life until we can gather our other coping resources."[14]

Denying that political life, at best, is enormously stressful can place additional pressure on the political wife. It can result in a woman having to prove to herself that she can handle even more responsibility because "stress is just between your ears anyway." With the benefit of reflection, Betty Ford had this to say about her own emotional breakdown: "Now it all seems obvious. I was resentful of Jerry's being gone so much; I was feeling terribly neglected. But I didn't let myself know these things."[15]

June Miller, wife of Washington State's Congressman John Miller, commented that "politics is difficult if a wife wants to keep her own identity." To be sure, the political wife must contend with a script that directs him to center stage and her to the wings. Inasmuch as a woman is usually referred to as "the wife of," a custom which both the system and some wives seem to prefer, it is understandable that many political wives are viewed as, and tend to think of themselves as, nonentities. For instance, Jane Sullivan, Wyoming's first lady, noted that because she "made the commitment to stay home and raise the children," she has "always battled against being viewed as an appendage." Indeed, being discounted is another source of concern for many political wives. Elizabeth Dole related an incident that occurred when she offered to speak to a group of small business owners in her husband's absence: "They wanted Bob Dole or nobody. Wives didn't count."[16]

In today's society, many women seem caught in a crossfire between the old acceptable ways and the newer, modern attitudes. And quite a few of the women who are breaking away from strict traditionalism are purposely choosing to retain their own names. "But if the wife of a politician has a different name from that of her spouse, no one knows who she is," says June Miller. Since the political wife's status is determined by that of her husband, having a separate and autonomous identity is viewed as detrimental.

Of course the political system cannot be blamed for all the challenges facing political wives, since these women do have a choice as to how much they are willing to sacrifice for their husbands' careers. Many of the wives with whom I spoke, for example, readily acknowledged that they had sacrificed their personal ambitions for the sake of their husbands. Some suggested they might be able to achieve their own goals "after he was elected," but in each case the wife was cognizant of the fact that her personal goals were indisputably secondary to those of her husband. That, after all, was the way he wanted it, the way the public and the system wanted it, and who was she to question it?

In the end, many political wives find they've sacrificed not only their family life, their privacy, and their personal aspirations and careers, but, most importantly, their own identities. And it is this final sacrifice which leads women to the point of no return. When the political wife's personal identity is at stake, seriously threatened, or sacrificed, she becomes overwhelmed by feelings of powerlessness and emptiness. Bitterness, anger, and resentment often are the manifestations, while the target for these emotions is generally some external thing or another person. She may, for example, blame the political system for encouraging political spouses to subordinate themselves. Or she may be critical of her husband for either seemingly going along with the unrealistic rules and regulations of politics or not looking out for her best interests. Indeed, the general thrust of some of the interviews was the political wife's feeling of having been greatly victimized. And while her anger in these cases may be legitimate and warranted, when all is said and done, the political wife has allowed herself to be pedestaled, discounted, used, programmed, and, on occasion, abandoned. The anger and resentment turn inward when the political wife realizes she has willingly sacrificed all to a cause in which her husband reaps the reward and she is left to live her life through him. During the interviews, the political wives often remarked, "I wonder what my life might have been," and often coupled this reflection with, "I'll never give up everything again."

Perhaps the most painful experience of the political wife is the realization that despite all her personal sacrifices, she continues to be viewed as faceless and expendable. In 1972, Abigail McCarthy suggested that "campaign aides, local chairmen, campaign correspondents — especially female correspondents — find wives something in the nature of excess baggage."[17] This expression captures the feelings of abandonment experienced by the wife who, following her husband's election, finds that her role has been greatly reduced and that her husband is no longer at her side. According to Kathy Carruthers, former first lady of New Mexico, following an election, "some women can't even get in to see their husbands."

Author Kitty Kelley related her impression of Elizabeth Taylor in 1980: "She had become just excess baggage to her husband the minute he walked into the United States Senate. Her role as celebrity campaigner was finished. She had enabled John Warner to realize his life's dream — and she expected to share it with him. After all, he had promised they would always be partners. Yet when she wanted an office near his, so they could work together, the answer was no. She was told to stay home, where she did little but eat, drink, and watch television. At night the Senator worked late while the Senator's wife waited at home, miserable and lonely."[18]

Despite having traversed the country on her own to help her husband ascend to the presidency, giving speeches and responding on national TV to interviewers' questions about Chappaquiddick and her husband's notorious philandering, Joan Kennedy was also shuffled aside after her husband's presidential campaign ended in 1980. When Senator Ted Kennedy called his estranged wife after the Democratic National Convention to set a date for lunch, Joan thought the luncheon had been arranged for the purpose of discussing the possibility of a reconciliation. After all, their public image gave every indication that the two would put their marriage back together. Joan was devastated when she realized that the luncheon was merely "another media event." Her last shred of hope for her marriage dissolved when, on their flight home from Washington after the convention, "Ted abruptly abandoned her at Montauk, leaving her to fly on to the Cape alone."[19]

When political wives are feeling used or devalued, have little or no personal identity, and are living the life of a single woman with none of the advantages, some marriages simply dissolve. Pamela Kostmayer related her frustration in trying to do too many things at one time, and doing none of them well. Divorce was her choice after trying to balance the demands of political life, two homes, a career, and marriage.

With only three years of marriage behind them, Elizabeth Taylor divorced Senator John Warner and left Washington. After her divorce, Taylor was quoted as saying, "Being a senator's wife is not easy. . . . It's very lonely. I

wouldn't wish it on anyone. . . . I wanted to help my
husband. I would have done anything — licked stamps,
typed speeches, run errands. It became very unsatisfying.
There was nothing for me to do except sit at home and
watch the boob tube. My life had no meaning, no responsibility. Don't get me wrong. John was and is a worthy
senator. But his life is his work. It's his wife, his mistress,
his family. There didn't seem to be room for anything
else."[20]

One candid congressional wife told me that she and her
husband had lived in Washington only three years but had
already seen "two couples who I thought had idyllic
marriages file for divorce." Further on in the conversation,
she added that unless the political couple is "truly in love,"
they'll probably leave Washington separately.

On two occasions during their marriage, for example,
former Senator Gary Hart and his wife Lee formally
separated. According to the *Denver Post,* the reason given
for the separations was to "deal with the problems and
stresses of public life."[21] The marital problems of Ted and
Joan Kennedy were so overwhelming that divorce was
inevitable, according to author Marcia Chellis: "While he
might have preferred to stay married for political reasons,
to spare the family the painful publicity that would inevitably surround a divorce, and even, perhaps, to retain the
personal protection that marriage afforded him, he may
also have recognized the futility of their situation."[22]

To counterbalance the tremendous pressures of political
life, many political wives become involved in some outside
activity — they may seek out a support group, a cause or
project, or some form of employment. "My closest friends
are those we came in with," says a new congressional wife,
referring to the orientation program offered to all incoming congressional spouses. Not unlike enrolling in school,
once a politician is elected, he is referred to as a member

of a certain "class," which consists of politicians from both parties. In 1986, for example, it was the "class of '86" as well as the "100th class." One wife remarked, "The orientation for new spouses was excellent. It not only helped me adapt to our new lifestyle, but provided me with a network of friends so that I didn't feel a need to join any other women's group."

Many women are invited to become members of the prestigious Congressional Club, which is bipartisan and composed of the wives of current congressman, senators, cabinet members, and Supreme Court justices. The Congressional Club offers a wide range of recreational, social, educational, and philanthropic activities. Betty Ford, who was an active participant in the club during her husband's tenure, related that "on Mondays, you could learn to play bridge, or study a foreign language. On Tuesdays, we went to Red Cross, folded bandages and listened to book reviews."[23]

For many governors' wives, the National Governors Association serves as their support group. Colorado's former first lady, Dottie Lamm, remarked that there's always an orientation offered to incoming governors and their spouses. Wives meet at least three times a year to attend meetings that are issue-oriented and bipartisan. There appears to be a consensus among governors' wives that the "pajama party for wives only" is the one can't-miss annual event. At the very private "pajama party," personal problems are aired and met with very supportive ears.

Aside from the congressional and gubernatorial women's groups, there are also a number of prayer, Bible study, and other religious meetings that politicians and their wives attend. According to Richard N. Ostling, as reported by journalist Alessandra Stanley, "Washington is known as a pinnacle of political power, a showplace of marble monuments, an enclave of high-level socializing and influence peddling. Few outsiders would think of the U.S. capital as a religious center. Yet Washington may boast more Christian prayer groups per square block than any other town outside the Bible Belt."[24] Yes, there are cabinet wives groups, congressional wives and couples groups, church prayer groups, and even by-invitation-only Bible study groups for wives.

Several of the women interviewed were members of one or another Bible study or prayer group. Some are members of a women's group as well as a couples group. All of the women who belong to such groups say their participation helps them to cope with political life. Some wives attend the congressional prayer group for Christians, which is bipartisan and intended for couples. The group meets twice each month and is open to standing members as well as past members. A few other wives said they attend a religious study group for congressional couples that is led by a rabbi.

By far, the most talked-about group is the "Friday group" that Joanne Kemp has been leading for the past seventeen years. It appears to provide a very supportive environment, where everyday problems and pressures are discussed and resolved. The group's focus is oriented toward "biblical answers" and "studying the teachings of Swiss philosopher and theologian Dr. Francis Schaeffer." Christine Delay, wife of Congressman Tom Delay, commented that most of her friends are part of the Friday group. Another member of Joanne Kemp's gathering said, "I'd give up everything else before I'd stop going to my Friday group." And still another member of the group summed up its value to her when she remarked, "There is a strong bond of trust between us."

Other wives who choose not to seek out the spiritually oriented support groups find satisfaction in their community-based charity work, by attending school, or finding part-time employment. The key to survival, according to the women who have chosen this route, is having their own interests to keep them grounded in the real world. New Mexico's former First Lady Kathy Carruthers said, "I don't need support groups because I have my friends." However, while noting that her husband will hold office for only four years because of their state's one-term rule for governors, Carruthers added, "I hope I can keep things in perspective and be able to go back to being a real person again."

A few women, whose children are grown or off at boarding school, commented that they are making time for themselves away from politics by enrolling in fine arts classes, which seem to present them with a creative outlet. The walls of one senator's home, in fact, display many of his wife's artistic creations.

Other women spend their time furthering some cause that is meaningful to them. According to Ellen Armstrong, it really isn't difficult for a woman to find a pet project because "there is every cause in the world in Washington, just waiting for someone to fall into its lap." For instance, several congressional spouses mentioned their interest in human rights issues and have traveled to Moscow to talk with high-ranking government officials about the emigration of Soviet Jews. Others have been involved in education on the local and national levels as teachers or advocates. Barbara Bush, of course, is devoting her energies to eliminating illiteracy.

There are some political wives who feel no need for a support group, or to become involved in activities outside the realm of politics. They say they are satisfied with their lifestyle and are convinced that the advantages of being a political wife outweigh the disadvantages. Being exposed to an insider's view of Washington politics rates high with some of the wives of senators and congressmen who reside at least part time in Washington. Some point to experiences they never dreamed possible, such as attending receptions and dinners at the White House. One congressional wife mentioned her pride while sitting in the gallery listening to her husband speak before the legislature. On occasion, she also receives special tickets for other sessions that are closed to the public.

An exciting new world opens up to many of the wives of freshman congressmen, and some are quick to point out the advantages of political life. Liz McEwen, wife of Ohio's Congressman Bob McEwen, recalling their early days, remarked that she felt like a college kid when they arrived in Washington. Over the years, she formed lasting friendships with a number of women and felt more sophisticated when she purchased a black suit and acquired "a sorority I never had in college." The wife of a newly elected congressman stated frankly: "Being intimately a part of government is definitely an advantage. I had a negative concept of elected officials. I thought they were out for themselves, on the take if they could get it. But now that I'm here, I see how wrong I was. They believe in what they do. They're committed to what they do."

Among veteran political wives, perhaps Barbara Bush has been the most successful at adjusting to the pressures of political life. Indeed, she has learned to roll with the punches. During our interview, for example, she stated her philosophy of political life: "You have two choices. You either like it or you don't. I choose to like it."

Barbara Bush's refreshing candor and keen sense of humor are unique among political wives. When asked to respond to a rumor that her husband was shot during a liaison on Capitol Hill, she wryly suggested that George "call a press conference, strip down, and turn slowly so everybody would know that he wasn't wounded." "He was not amused," she later reported. And when Washington journalist Sandra McElwaine asked the question, "Does Barbara Bush plan to stand by her man no matter what?" Mrs. Bush responded, "When my husband is not an elected official, we can go to parties and fight and have a lot of fun. Now, it's a united front."[25]

Few political wives, however, are as nonchalant and easygoing as Barbara Bush, who has had years to develop her style of coping with political life. And those who find no encouragement or support in groups of political wives, who fail to pursue their own interests, often are overwhelmed by their sense of uselessness and isolation. Many of these women have left behind all their old support systems to follow their husbands to Washington. And many find it difficult to form lasting friendships in the cut-throat world of politics. An often-repeated adage among politicians is, "If you want a friend in Washington, get a dog." The feelings of hopelessness and frustration experienced by the political wife caught in this trap oftentimes result in deteriorating health and devastating addictions.

I have observed women grown weary from increasing schedule demands, the negative press, and the artificiality of the political world. Some wives become so fearful about having to campaign that they need "medication" to get them through the ordeal. Others drink too much out of loneliness. With some of the women interviewed, I wondered if their greatest fear was that their husbands would lose their elections or win them. During one interview, an outspoken congressional wife even commented that if anyone tries to contend that an enormous amount of stress and strain doesn't exist in political life, as some political wives have clearly indicated, it only suggests that "the woman is lying."

While married to Senator John Warner, Elizabeth Taylor

compulsively devoured food in an attempt to ease her emotional pain. Fortunately, though, other political wives don't have as high a profile as Miss Taylor or they, too, could be besieged by comedians who find the subject of weight gain humorous. Audiences roared as stand-up comics took shots at Taylor. "Did you see the bumper sticker on Liz Taylor's car? It says 'Honk if you have groceries.' " "Liz has more chins than the Hong Kong phone book."[26] And on and on.

Taylor's fondness for fried chicken, which happens to be standard fare during all political campaigns, expanded her once lean and enviable figure up to the 175-pound mark. Her husband, who was quoted as saying, "She is prettier inside than she is outside," even went so far as to call his overweight wife "Chicken Fat" and "my little heifer." Taylor's response to it all was, "It's happy fat. I eat because I'm so happy. . . . I am content. I don't want to starve myself because my looks don't matter that much to me. John is interested in having a happy human being, not a model-type beauty."[27] Later, though, Taylor would describe her years as a political spouse as "a hot fudge hell."[28]

If the independent, free-thinking Elizabeth Taylor had problems adjusting to life as a political spouse, it stands to reason that other women have an even more difficult time of it. But rather than airing their frustrations in public, these women suffer in silence. As the women who are truthful about their eating disorders can attest, "The drive to eat compulsively is not about food. It is about hunger. The hungers of regret and sorrow, of unspoken anger, unrealized dreams; the hungers of your own potential that are waiting to be filled."[29]

Considering the pressures of political life, it isn't surprising that some political spouses turn to self-destructive habits in order to escape reality. For as long as she contin-

ues to live in politicaland, not only will the wife be alone
a lot, but she will be expected to both generate support
for her political husband and attend untold events with
and without him. At all times she must uphold the image
of the smiling, happy, carefree person we've come to know
while struggling privately with her own frustrations and
unmet needs. Trying to appeal to the public, the ultimate
god, many women are so preoccupied with nurturing
everyone else that they don't find time or sometimes don't
even know how to nurture themselves.

Consequently, when she's feeling depressed, resentful,
abandoned, or pushed to the wall because juggling all of
the responsibilities has become too much for her, one
congressional wife said, "drinking makes it easier." According to Joan Kennedy's assessment of her own situation, "Rather than get mad . . . or really stand up for
myself at all, it was easier for me to just go and have a few
drinks and calm myself down as if I weren't hurt or
angry. . . . I found out that alcohol could sedate me. So I
didn't care as much. And things didn't hurt as much."[30]

Yet like any addiction, alcoholism doesn't happen overnight. It takes time for one's self-destructive indulgences
to take control. According to Dr. LeClair Bissell, "Alcoholism is a chronic and progressive disease, one whose
causes are multiple and only gradually being understood."[31] Betty Ford recently stated, "I'm not trying to
make excuses, but I think when you are genetically predis-
posed to alcoholism, you get caught up in just the right
circumstances, your control falls away, and the progres-
sion of your disease takes over."[32]

In an effort to shed more light on the psychological state
of the female alcoholic, Dr. Jean Kirkpatrick, executive
director of Women for Sobriety, has written about the
woman who has a drinking problem. She is one who is
"unsure of herself, who doesn't know who she is, who

has little self-identity, who needs help, who is surrounded by a number of persons who ignore her for one reason or another, who leave her to struggle, and she adds to the already overflowing storehouse of negatives another one, called rejection. Thus she drinks more, gets sicker, and becomes more lost."[33]

Kitty Dukakis, wife of Massachusetts Governor and presidential candidate Michael Dukakis, is another well-known political wife who has gone public with her problems. Over the course of her husband's presidential campaign, she first admitted to a long-standing addiction to diet pills. Later in 1988, upon entering a residential treatment center, Mrs. Dukakis publicly exposed her addiction to alcohol. Writers Barbara Kantrowitz and Mark Starr reported that when commenting on the cause of his wife's alcohol problem, Governor Dukakis said it was "a combination of physical exhaustion, the stress of the campaign effort and the postelection letdown." An advisor to the governor elaborated with his own assessment of the situation: "It's no longer 18-hour days with people totally taking care of you. Suddenly you're just a governor's wife — and you're alone."[34] Regrettably, however, her problems have continued long after the election, creating even more press scrutiny and speculation.

Mamie Eisenhower, among others, has been the subject of rumors purporting her as a heavy drinker. In the case of Pat Nixon, Julie Nixon Eisenhower says that the authors of the book *The Final Days,* Carl Bernstein and Bob Woodward, among a "new breed of writers who do not hesitate to wed fact with rumor," wrote that Mrs. Nixon "was becoming more and more reclusive and drinking heavily."[35] Barrister Pamela Thomas, who occasionally saw the spouse of former Prime Minister Margaret Thatcher for tea, apparently suggested to writer Gail Sheehy that "Denis is seventy-four, and although he still appears trim and fit, he is a constant cigarette smoker and he does unquestionably drink heavily — like most political wives."[36]

As she was reflecting on her own situation, Betty Ford wrote, "Sometimes the body makes you pay for what the head is struggling with."[37] Indeed, many political wives have disclosed they believe there's a direct connection between their mental health and their physical health. Dottie Lamm, for example, talked about taking into her body everything she was feeling emotionally and then being diagnosed as having cancer. She did, though, find some humor in that difficult situation. Mrs. Lamm said she encouraged her husband to run for governor of Colorado the third time because "if I'm going to die, I might as well go in style."

Virginia Lewis, first lady of the Zunis, also experienced physical problems. Because she got sick during her husband's last campaign, she hasn't been going out anymore. "My face became paralyzed. It probably was my nerves." Another political wife's heart attack also seemed to be the result of enormous stress related to her husband's unsuccessful campaign to become senator. She was alone when it happened, and she "couldn't get to the phone to call for help." When Kathy Carruthers "fell apart" after the governor's election in New Mexico, her doctor ordered her to bed because of a "strep infection, viral infection, and exhaustion."

Certainly, Pat Nixon suffered enormous anxiety and frustration over the years as she witnessed her husband's difficult climb to the top, only to experience the disgrace of Watergate, near-impeachment, and then a final humiliating departure from the White House. Though she appeared to have survived the stress of all these events, the final devastating blow, according to her daughter Julie Nixon Eisenhower, was delivered by Woodward and Bernstein in *The Final Days*. The book "created a sensation by implying that my father had been dangerously unbalanced. . . ." But for her mother, "the most unbearable part of the book was the analysis of her marriage as loveless." Several months later, Pat Nixon suffered a massive stroke.[38]

Why do some political wives end up in such emotionally and physically debilitating states? Do they share certain characteristics? Is there a certain "type" of woman who buys into the system so completely that she ends up even sacrificing her mental and physical health? And what distinguishes those women from the ones who seem to adapt?

The few career-oriented, "modern" women who are married to politicians have no intention of subordinating their careers, or themselves for that matter, to their husbands' political ambitions. These women, it appears, have a real sense of self. They bring a clear understanding to the notion of separateness and their desire for it. Being their own person is not something they are striving for but something they're already experiencing.

The "modern" women, for example, generally are employed, travel alone on their husbands' behalf, and prefer discussing the issues with the voters. I was informed that any time taken away from their jobs must be purposeful and stimulating, and discussing political issues fits the bill. A senator's wife further remarked that some people may not regard her career as important as being a United States senator, "but it's important to me and my husband respects that." Furthermore, it appears that the politician married to a career woman takes steps to assure that his staff respects her position and defers to her on matters of scheduling.

A different set of dynamics comes into play for the women who view being a political wife as their temporary job, as opposed to those who view it as being a way of life, or their permanent role. If viewed as a role, eventually it becomes impossible to differentiate the woman from that role, as the political wife internalizes and then projects the image she has created. Thus, her role becomes a way of life. On the other hand, the "modern" political wife refuses to internalize the image that has been prescribed for her. Instead, she lives her life as a separate individual with her own aspirations and expectations, regardless of what the "job" requires of her.

For most of these career women who consider their own success a priority, their competitive nature appears to have no negative effect on their marriages. They are supportive of their husbands' political ambitions but have their own agendas. In other words, they are not playing the role of political wife as a victim. This attitude was apparent in the comments of one senator's wife about her husband's election: "It was not my victory, but I was an important part of it."

At least one woman chose to leave the political world behind in order to pursue her own interests and to resist being swallowed up by her husband's career. Former political wife Pamela Kostmayer stated that "being a political wife held me back. . . . I needed to succeed in my own right and have my own identity."[39] For her, divorce was the only option.

The political wives who continue to acquiesce to the desires of others and to conform to the edicts of the traditional role by default accept a subordinate position, losing their own identities and personalities as they become consumed by their husbands' careers. According to Luise Eichenbaum and Susie Orbach, authors, lecturers, psychotherapists, and founders of the Women's Therapy Centre Institute in New York and London, this type of woman is "easily subject to [psychological] merger within her intimate relationships. Indeed, she seeks her identity through attachment. In intimate relationships she can lose a clear sense of herself."[40]

As was the case with the political wives who spoke solely in terms of "we," I discovered that to criticize him was to criticize her. In their responses to my questions, these women seemed to be so enraptured with politics and their husbands' political campaigns that they appeared, at some inner level, to have become "one" with the candidate. Often, they had difficulty separating their husbands' views from their own, earmarking many statements with "My husband thinks." If he is a successful politician, she must be successful, too. It follows then that when their husbands are elected, these political wives say, "We were elected." As Eichenbaum and Orbach have written, "It is as though [the woman] has no boundary, no knowledge of a defined self. This is the cost [loss of a personal identity], the damage of living in the shadows of others. . . ."[41]

The authors continue: "Women today are freer to make more choices in their lives now than perhaps at any time in history. The change from a social role in which the mandate was connection to others, availability to others, self-deference and support for others, to a role that includes self-actualization, self-interest, entitlement, and desire for a place in the world as well as in the family, requires differentiation. And differentiation defies the very essence of feminine psychology."[42]

To be sure, the challenge for political wives is to achieve a balance between the seemingly opposing notions of separateness and union. I purposely use the word "seemingly" because being a separate person does not preclude one from having some connectedness to another person. For separateness and oneness are not opposites, but the sum and unity of personal wholeness. Yet many political wives tend to live their lives in a state of perpetual connectedness, never having learned the importance of integrating that connectedness with separateness and finding the balance that allows them to be both.

When a woman elects entirely for the oneness of the political wife persona, which is founded on female subordination and a symbiotic attachment to others, she ultimately forfeits her identity, power, and self. For when she chooses to live her life as just a part of the whole, she inevitably experiences tremendous conflict and inner turmoil.

The wife of a politician, however, may feel that it's safer to live her life through her husband, because hiding behind an image presents little or no challenge to be separate. She and he, in essence, can merge on a psychological level and become one. However, as she gets caught up in portraying the image, sometimes even convincing herself that she has actually become that "created" self, she perpetuates those illusions that presented the problem in the first place. Because, at this point, the political wife has no idea who she really is, she has to look to others for her definition and becomes the epitome of the dependent personality.

In politics, many role models have reinforced the notion of psychological enmeshment. Actually, marriage has been held up to women as an incentive for attaining a merged identity. Indeed, a merged identity was the goal. Betty Ford, for example, remembers the Eisenhowers as having great affection for each other and in a 1977 commencement speech repeated Mamie's comments on Ike's "wonderful hands": "Every knuckle was broken from football or whatever, but I always felt in all the years we were married that I could grab onto them when I felt sick or worried, and nothing was ever going to happen to me."[43]

Colette Dowling, who spent years researching women's

fear of independence, states that "togetherness was the fifties term for describing the ideal marriage — a cozy, intimate relationship in which wives and husbands shared everything: ideas, opinions, dreams, epiphanies."[44] As any woman from the fifties can attest, that was the model by which most women structured and organized their lives. Dowling goes on to note that "it seems that marriage still offers, for many women, an escape hatch — a retreat from autonomy that's stamped with society's approval."[45] Despite outward appearances of independence, many political wives still hold fast to the notion of oneness with their spouses.

Dowling further identifies the problem: "Personal, psychological dependency — the deep wish to be taken care of by others — is the chief force holding women down today. . . . Like Cinderella, women today are still waiting for something external to transform their lives."[46] However, unlike the fairy tales we used to love to listen to as children, a politician is not necessarily Prince Charming and marriage to him doesn't necessarily include living happily ever after, although that image continues to be displayed by political couples.

Thus, if the political wife is to survive, she must create and maintain the delicate balance between being a separate person and being a wife. And she must deal with the totality of the problem, which includes accepting or rejecting her traditional upbringing, and the illusions, images, and duplicity that are a part of the political system, as well as her own expectations and ambitions for herself. Granted, that is no easy task, yet it's one that will eliminate a great deal of psychological and physical debilitation for political wives.

The personal conflicts caused by the narrowness of the political wife's role will be resolved only when a few courageous women break away from that prescribed role and set the pace and tone for the others. That is not to say that these women will be redefining the role of the political wife. Rather, they will be expanding the possibilities for other women so that they may define the role for themselves. In order for women to achieve personal identity and control of their own lives, they must begin the process by taking responsibility for themselves and embracing a new mind-set created to fit their own particular situation. To that end, Betty Friedan notes in *The Second Stage:* "What we are facing now is not an absolute division between women, but an evolving continuum — an evolution from those age-old roots of female identity in the family . . . to the new necessities of selfhood, personhood, economically rewarding work and the new possibilities of choice, personal control, personal growth. The either/or swings of the pendulum, the excesses of reaction on either side of this critical leap in women's identity, can be seen as a stage in that evolution."[47]

*   *   *

My understanding of the emotional and physical hardships that are unique to political wives was slow in developing. It grew from my stubborn attempts after the campaign to reduce my journal to some common denominator. It took me almost one year to realize that the energies I was devoting to this book and to the complete restructuring of my journal were merely disguising a more pressing need to come to terms with the reality of what I had just experienced.

The emotional aspects of campaigning were the hardest on me. After every event, every speech, I was left with either a triumphant or defeated feeling. And as I became more physically tired, my emotions had a tendency to swing with public opinion. I found it difficult to always live my husband's challenge and to feel his excitement. The following journal entries offer additional insight into the issues that confront political wives and the effects that the demands of political life have on the family.

January 6

A new year. A new beginning. What was the significance of that black cat? She just appeared from out of the darkness after we arrived. She came and made the connection. Those were the biggest, roundest, and saddest eyes I've ever seen. She ate and slept for four days and nights, never leaving the house or my side. As we were leaving our vacation home, I put some food out for her on the deck. While she was eating, she stared at me and then at the others as they carried suitcases out to the car. When I looked away, for just an instant, and then turned back to say goodbye, she had disappeared as mysteriously as she'd arrived. It made me think that we must make the most of each experience, enjoying it to the fullest, for the moment is really all we have.

February 2

Funny how time has helped me get over both my initial panic about the political campaign and my concerns about sacrificing too much of myself in the process.

March 5

Well, here we go again. I've had plans to take this afternoon off for three weeks now. Somehow the word did not make it to the person or persons who scheduled me to campaign with Steve. So, what do you think happened? After I fussed and fumed at everyone for having scheduled me, I put on my best smile and went campaigning with Steve. Terrific! All bark and no bite. . . .

March 25

I've finally done something that seems to be working for me. I've set some limits on when I can and cannot be scheduled. In fact, I told the scheduler not to test me, because if there's a conflict I don't think they'd like having to make excuses for an absent political wife. If all goes well, I suspect it won't be due to their respect for my wishes but to save themselves from appearing incompetent. But as the saying goes — I'll take it any way I can.

April 6

I've just resigned from the boards I sit on, after years of service. In time I'm going to have to stop working, too. That's going to be hard, psychologically. It's like giving up my independence, identity, reality, and satisfaction. I'm not the candidate's wife when I'm working. I'm Joyce, and I must say I like it that way. Hopefully, my "appendage" status will end when the campaign is over — win or lose.

August 20

Feel like I've come full circle on so many things, but have landed on a higher plane this time. I've become much more self-aware. I know what I need to do for myself, and I know what makes me most content. So I've decided to go back to hands-on work, but to do it as a volunteer. Will go to the Marian House (soup kitchen and dorm for the homeless) tomorrow. Also, I've decided to look into taking a course at night. Will call Father Angelo tomorrow to see if there's room in his class on dream analysis. I've decided that the best way of handling the role of the candidate's wife is to be supportive while pursuing my own interests. My strength is in meeting people one-on-

one. That, and keeping up-to-date on the issues, is what I'm willing to commit to this campaign.

September 5

I've just signed up to take a class that requires me to be in school certain nights of the month for nine months. No, I'm not pregnant. I'm going to study Jungian psychology and dream analysis. The required reading is intriguing, and I'm eager to continue my quest for understanding and knowledge.

September 9

Now that school is a reality, I'll have to stop volunteering at the homeless center. There doesn't seem to be enough time for family, volunteer work, campaigning, and maintaining a household, let alone adding extra time for me to attend school. I have to admit my days of juggling that many responsibilities have come to a screeching halt. So, I guess it's goodbye to superwoman, hello ordinary person, with many limitations. Who, me?

September 11

I have been home all day and haven't gotten anything done. I've been answering phone calls and preparing for a dinner for the campaign workers this evening while Steve is up in Denver doing his part. What annoys me more than anything else is that no one ever asks if they're interrupting anything I am doing, or questions whether I'm available. They just assume that I'm waiting here for them to tell me what to do and to solve their problems.

September 28

"Put a heater in the garage so the snow will melt when we park the cars overnight.

"Paint the pantry so the canned goods look appetizing all winter long.

"Package corn and salsa for a welcome change in January and February.

"Harvest the apples and zucchini for sauce, pies, and breads. . . ."

I can't believe I've been taking time to make lists of things to do when I don't know how or when I'll ever get to them. Even more interesting is that I haven't done any canning in over ten years! I must be cracking up. . . .

October 4

My dreams are indicating a major transition. . . . I wonder where I'm going.

December 15

Just when I think I've finally gotten a handle on this campaigning business, the roof caves in. It would help if someone from the staff were here to assist me. Steve always has someone to take him around on campaign stops and to introduce him at events. I'm left to fend for myself. Most of the time I drive myself to the events and confront the sea of unfamiliar faces alone.

The side effects of this is a feeling of uselessness. All my energy is being spent on helping the candidate get elected. I'm tired of hearing that I'm such an asset to Steve only to discover that that's what people think is required of them — that is, give her a compliment and hope she'll go away.

I suppose the smartest thing a political wife could do for herself is to take advantage of a support system. But if such exists, I haven't discovered it yet. Right now, I could use one. My friend Patty just called to see how I'm doing. Ah, how curious to have that happen right now.

February 21

Whenever I'm feeling unsettled or confused about something that's going on in my life, I have to ask myself what I'm supposed to be learning from the experience. Today I'm wondering how my loss of identity, to whatever extent it is, has affected the way I relate to both myself and the world. . . .

I can almost *feel* my personal identity slipping away. The biggest problem for me has been trying to remain separate but at the same time connected in my relationship with Steve. I'm experiencing feelings of low self-worth, powerlessness, and helplessness, as well as resentment and anger. At times like this, I must remember that power comes from within, and if I am in tune with my own power I can make some changes. I can rid myself of the negative forces around me, or at least refuse to be affected by them. Too, I must remember that when I'm feeling powerless my perceptions of the world and of situations reflect that feeling.

Campaigning puts me to the test each and every day — sink or swim. I absolutely have to set boundaries and limits or I'll end up completely merged with Steve on a psychological level and lose me in the process.

Now, oh great thinker, all you have to do is do it! Whose life is this, anyway?

*   *   *

My illness occurred about six months before the campaign was over. It lasted three weeks and was a most unpleasant experience.

March 1

What's happening here? My feelings about the campaign must be triggering all this stuff. Yesterday I was fine and today my body aches so much I can hardly move. I think I'll take a nap this afternoon.

March 25

It's been 25 days since I decided to take that nap. I never got the nap but managed to contract two strains of the flu as well as a strange intestinal disorder called giardia. I feel like I've had a systems breakdown. I have to recognize the danger signs sooner and take better care of myself. I must not be dealing with the stress as well as I thought I was. The one positive thing I can think of right now is that all my needs can be met in the confines of the master bath, which by the way needs new paint. There are moments when I'm afraid I'm going to die, then wish I would.

Mindy wants to start scheduling me again. Told her right now walking to the mailbox and back is all I can handle.

April 2

My illness has gone on too long. I'm back to full-time work on the campaign, but my energy is sapped so much earlier in the day than it used to be. Talked to a group of women yesterday, and fortunately there was a table in front of me to lean on. It was all I could do to get through the afternoon without keeling over.

NOTES

1. Bob and Elizabeth Dole with Richard Norton Smith, *The Doles: Unlimited Partners* (New York: Simon & Schuster, 1988), 172.

2. Betty Ford with Chris Chase, *The Times of My Life* (New York: Ballantine Books, 1978), 139.

3. Julie Nixon Eisenhower, *Pat Nixon: The Untold Story* (New York: Simon & Schuster, 1986), 146.

4. Pamela Kostmayer, "Fed Up with the Demands of Her Husband's Career, a Congressman's Wife Drops Out of the Race," *People,* 12 October 1987, 74.

5. Eisenhower, *Pat Nixon,* 97.

6. Dole and Dole, *The Doles,* 215.

7. Barbara Howar, *Laughing All the Way* (New York: Stein & Day, 1973), 358.

8. Diane Eicher, "Adjustment a Way of Life for Candidate's Wife," *Denver Post,* 28 June 1983, 4C.

9. Kitty Kelley, *Elizabeth Taylor: The Last Star* (New York: Dell, 1982), 405.

10. Eicher, "Adjustment a Way of Life for Candidate's Wife," 4C.

11. Marcia Chellis, *Living with the Kennedys: The Joan Kennedy Story* (New York: Simon & Schuster, 1985), 135.

12. Eisenhower, *Pat Nixon,* 145.

13. Betty Ford with Chris Chase, *Betty: A Glad Awakening* (New York: Doubleday, 1987), xiii.

14. Melody Beattie, *Codependent No More* (New York: Harper & Row, 1987), 123.

15. Ford, *The Times of My Life,* 135.

16. Dole and Dole, *The Doles,* 187.

17. Abigail McCarthy, *Private Faces/Public Places* (Garden City, New York: Doubleday, 1972), 315.

18. Kelley, *Elizabeth Taylor,* 404.

19. Chellis, *Living with the Kennedys,* 206.

20. Kelley, *Elizabeth Taylor,* 412–13.

21. Eicher, "Adjustment a Way of Life for Candidate's Wife," 4C.

22. Chellis, *Living with the Kennedys,* 215.

23. Ford, *The Times of My Life,* 70.

24. Richard N. Ostling, reported by Alessandra Stanley/Washington, "Inside the Bible Beltway," *Time,* 6 February 1989, 56.

25. Sandra McElwaine, "This is Your Wife, Barbara Bush: Guardian of Her Husband's Ego, Even If Not Paid for It," *Lear's,* November/December 1988, 135 and 218.

26. Kelley, *Elizabeth Taylor,* 356.

27. Ibid., 357.

28. Margaret Carlson, "I'm Nobody, Who Are You?" *Time,* 8 May 1989, 29.

29. Geneen Roth, *Feeding the Hungry Heart* (New York: New American Library, 1982), 100.

30. Chellis, *Living with the Kennedys,* 43.

31. Rachel V, intro by Dr. LeClair Bissell, *A Woman Like You* (San Francisco: Harper & Row, 1985), xvii.

32. Ford, *Betty: A Glad Awakening,* 40.

33. Jean Kirkpatrick, *Goodbye Hangovers, Hello Life* (New York: Atheneum, 1986), 105.

34. Barbara Kantrowitz and Mark Starr, "She Clearly Recognizes She Has a Sickness," *Newsweek,* 20 February 1989, 54.

35. Eisenhower, *Pat Nixon,* 446.

36. Gail Sheehy, "The Blooming of Margaret Thatcher," *Vanity Fair,* June 1989, 170.

37. Ford, *The Times of My Life,* 137.

38. Eisenhower, *Pat Nixon,* 446.

39. Kostmayer, "Fed Up with the Demands of Her Husband's Career, a Congressman's Wife Drops Out of the Race," 72.

40. Luise Eichenbaum and Susie Orbach, *Between Women* (New York: Viking Penguin, 1988), 180.

41. Ibid., 66.

42. Ibid., 50.

43. Ford, *The Times of My Life,* 104.

44. Colette Dowling, *The Cinderella Complex* (New York: Summit Books, 1981), 143.

45. Ibid., 143.

46. Ibid., 31.

47. Betty Friedan, *The Second Stage,* rev. ed. (New York: Summit Books, 1986), 233.

Chapter Six

No More Pizza at Midnight

> Political wives, like sea captains, are required to go down with the ship — or the 'slip,' as the case may be. These women remain in the national memory bank as shadowy figures, glimpsed ducking into taxis or standing tight-lipped behind their men at final press conferences. We remember their last poignant backward glance as they disappear into the limbo of the runalongs, the Lees and the Jills and the Joans and the names we can't quite remember.
>
> —*Nicols Fox*

Twenty years ago, syndicated columnist Ruth Montgomery began her column with these words: "Once upon a time a presidential candidate could climb aboard a whistle-stop special, ease off his shoes, pour himself a short-snort and prepare to enjoy the comforts of home. The train might rock and roll a bit, but if the candidate was hungry he could eat. If he felt the need of a shave or a shower, his private bathroom was rolling along with him. But what goes today? . . . Nowadays the plane swoops in, taxies up the runway, and the door flies open. The candidate steps out, and may heaven help him from then on."[1] To be sure, after completing many months and sometimes years of this rigorous ordeal — 18-hour days, no family life, non-

stop travel from one political event to another, while
always upholding the public image — in each election
there is only one candidate who will prevail. Like world-
class skiers who train their whole lives for that one moment of glory but miss a gate, fall, and get disqualified,
politicians are involved in a win–or–lose proposition.

Yet win or lose, most of the candidates who enter the
political realm enter it equipped with spouses who seemingly agree with all their views and stances. Of course,
some spouses embrace politics more than others. A case
in point is Eleanor Roosevelt, who was not at all happy
with her husband's decision to enter the 1932 race for the
Democratic presidential nomination. An enormously frustrated Eleanor wrote a note to a friend saying she had no
intention of living in the White House should FDR become
president. A short time later, however, during the general
elections, Eleanor was quoted as saying to AP reporter
Lorena Hickok, "It's good to be middle-aged. Things
don't matter so much. You don't take it so hard when
things happen to you that you don't like."[2]

Throughout history most political wives have had to
make some critical decisions along the way — decisions
that are difficult to change once the die has been cast.
Some of them have learned to accept the many unpleasant
situations that are an integral part of political life, subsequently finding their way clear to being gracious about
them. Others have accepted, even fostered, their prescribed
role of being a submissive partner, and still others have
been able to turn what had appeared to be a negative into
a positive by creating a life for themselves that met not
only their own needs but many of their husbands' needs as
well.

According to columnist Ruth Montgomery, Nancy Kefauver was an avid campaigner in 1952, the first time her
husband, Senator Estes Kefauver, sought the Democratic

nomination for president. But in 1956, because Kefauver felt that President Eisenhower was unbeatable, she was opposed to her husband entering the presidential race again and she refused to go on the campaign trail. The senator subsequently withdrew from the race just a few weeks prior to the national convention, when it became clear to him that he wouldn't receive enough votes to win the nomination. At the national convention, though, Kefauver was selected as Adlai Stevenson's running mate, and Mrs. Kefauver was quoted as saying that she planned to "keep right on teaching art classes" instead of campaigning with her husband.[3]

Since my interviews with the wives of politicians were conducted after the long 1986 political campaigns, many of the women with whom I spoke already had taken some time to reflect on the election results. How and where they perceived themselves fitting into the political equation was the primary focus of our conversations. And their responses regarding winning or losing an election provided additional insight into the women and their role in the political process.

The reactions of women whose husbands had won their elections ran all the way from elation to disappointment. A newly elected senator's wife, for example, was delighted that she would be living in the Washington area for "at least six years," instead of spending most of her time commuting and campaigning as a congressman's wife. I heard, "The first win is the most exciting" and "A win opens doors for the children" from two veteran political wives.

On the down side of winning, a political wife must continue to deal with unfair criticism and personal attacks, just as she did during the campaign. For example, June Miller, wife of Congressman John Miller, expressed her distaste for the negative campaign tactics employed by various candidates in 1986: "Once in a while I see the insensitivity in campaigns and the covert use of religion." Miller went on to add that "We'll reevaluate life after four years and then make a decision about staying in politics after that." Yet another political wife, who noted the down side after her husband had won his election, insightfully offered this candid statement: "In business there is always next year. Not so in politics. It's unsettling. I'm not sure I'd do it again. I haven't reconciled yet that I've given up everything."

Two weeks before the 1988 election, Barbara Bush commented to Susan Watters, an interviewer for the newspaper *W*, that there are disadvantages to being first lady. Bush is quoted as saying, "I have all these people with me. They are wonderful, fabulous people — the staff, the Secret Service. I wish I didn't have them. You have to rev everyone up to go with you, plan ahead. I don't get to run to the drugstore, pop in to see anyone. The spontaneity isn't there anymore."[4]

So if winning an election is not necessarily euphoric, then how does it feel to lose a political race after sacrificing yourself so completely? From all indications, losing a political race seems an awful lot to handle. "Heartbreaking is more like it," said a Native American woman whose husband was defeated in his bid for political office in New Mexico. During our conversation, she went on at great length about how excited and enthusiastic she had been in the beginning, only to run up against the harsh reality of losing.

Conversely, after her husband Mark's 1986 senatorial loss in North Dakota, Mary Andrews commented that "defeat is not shattering. It's a clean break with politics." She added, with obvious relief, "Now with the loss we'll be entering a new phase in our lives where we can all be together for birthdays, anniversaries, even doing things spontaneously for a change." And it was no different one hundred years ago, either. For example, when Winfield Scott Hancock was awakened by his wife with the news that he had lost the 1880 presidential race to James Garfield, he responded with, "That is all right. I can stand it," and with that, he turned over and went back to sleep.[5]

As Mr. Hancock's reaction indicates, whether or not the politician is an incumbent, his life generally changes very little if he's defeated at the election polls. After all, he still has a profession to return to, if he so chooses. A case in point is that despite Millard Fillmore's defeat in 1856 for reelection to the presidency, for which he expressed being a "little mortified" for "being so unanimously rejected," he did lead a "full life devoted to civic and philanthropic activities in the Buffalo community."[6]

In the case of John Quincy Adams's political defeat in 1828 for a second term as president, his despair was revealed in one of his diary entries: "The sun of my political life is in deepest gloom." According to the authors of the book *If Elected,* Adams obviously was unaware at the time that "the most fruitful portion of his long career lay ahead. Elected to the House of Representatives from Massachusetts in 1830, he served there until his death in 1848, championing the causes of science and education, and tirelessly leading the resistance to the slave powers."[7]

If holding political office becomes one's ultimate goal, there undoubtedly will be other attempts. Many defeated candidates and deposed politicians throughout history have been known to set the wheels in motion again and again, doing whatever is necessary to enter the next election. When one former congressional wife told me about her husband's long-standing dedication to public service, she suggested that he was considering running for governor in their state since he'd lost his bid for the senatorial seat. And when queried by columnist Ruth Montgomery prior to the 1960 presidential election, Jackie Kennedy was quoted as saying, "I married into a whirlwind. Jack has been running for Vice President or President ever since our marriage seven years ago, and I have learned to adjust."[8]

Another aspiring presidential hopeful was William Jennings Bryan, who ran unsuccessfully three consecutive times for the office of president. His final deed, however, as prosecutor in the famous Scopes trial of 1925, "overshadowed the very substantial accomplishments of his career."[9] But the office of president has been one position many a politician would do almost anything to achieve. As Daniel Webster said of the chief executive office in 1852, after being beaten by Winfield Scott for the presidential nomination, "I am but a man, sir. I want it. I want it."[10]

One glaring exception to the rule that life doesn't change much for the politician after a loss is Horace Greeley, founder of the New York *Tribune*. He chose to oppose the nationally revered hero and incumbent President Ulysses S. Grant in 1872. After losing the election, Greeley was "wounded deeply by campaign attacks; there seemed nothing left for which to live. His wife's death during the campaign increased his depression. Still a further source of demoralization was the fact that in returning to the *Tribune* in November . . . he found his influence had been pretty much displaced by his younger co-worker. . . . By the middle of November, Greeley had given up on life and within a few weeks was dead."[11]

More often than not, it's the wife's life that undergoes tremendous change, not only when her husband makes the decision to run for political office but after the election, whether or not he is elected. In an unsuccessful effort, she is usually the one left to cope with the immediate and subsequent void produced by her husband's political defeat. Many wives must suddenly adjust, after having been "on call" 24 hours a day, to not being called at all, which can have a devastating effect. For example, in a December 1987 *Newsweek* article, writer Garry Wills wrote that after Jimmy Carter was defeated in the 1980 general elections, "we are told by the Carters themselves that Rosalynn Carter could only bear life for a while by nursing the hope that her husband would return to the White House."[12]

Unlike Rosalynn Carter, who was privy to and even influenced many of her husband's decisions, sometimes a political wife will learn secondhand that her husband has entered or withdrawn from a race. Muriel Humphrey, for example, learned of her husband's decision to enter the 1960 presidential race from the morning newspaper. Drawing her sense of humor to the forefront, she sent Hubert Humphrey a telegram that read: "Congratulations. Let me know if I can help."[13]

According to author Marcia Chellis, Senator Ted Kennedy neglected to inform his wife of his decision to admit defeat and withdraw from the 1980 race for the Democratic presidential nomination. Abruptly left "with no appointments to keep, no interviews to give, and few of the domestic chores that attach many women to their homes and children, [Joan] was floating free, once again alone and unneeded." In a phone call to Chellis from Cape Cod, Joan shared her sense of loss and her confusion: "I feel so lost. I get up and go for walks, trying to sort things out. I really wanted to just go away for a while."[14]

Sometimes the politician is the "carrier of her ambition" while the wife is the "carrier of the dream," as Michael and Kitty Dukakis were described by Gail Sheehy in a recent issue of *Vanity Fair*. But after her hopes and dreams have become dependent upon her husband being the successful one, if the politician loses, as Dukakis did in 1978 in his bid for reelection as governor of Massachusetts, the wife, much more than the politician, has a difficult time handling the defeat. "According to close friends, Kitty felt equal measures of annoyance at Michael for losing, a protective affection toward him for his deep pain, and a yearning to retreat from it all."[15]

Governor Dukakis's last defeat, in the 1988 presidential general elections, was the most difficult for Mrs. Dukakis to endure. Still despondent one year after the loss, she experienced a setback in her alcohol recovery by ingesting unknown quantities of rubbing alcohol. Her fight to overcome severe depression, drug dependency, and alcohol addiction yet again became national headline news, eliminating the possibility of maintaining any privacy while regaining her strength and attempting to work through her problems.

In losing campaigns, it is often the political wife who lets loose with words etched in bitterness. One congressional wife who was bemoaning her husband's loss disclosed that "people know who you are, when you win." Winning often is viewed as unqualified acceptance, while defeat is frequently interpreted as personal rejection. And defeat is particularly painful for those who have been in the spotlight a number of years, as those individuals' primary fear is that their once bright light will dim to obscurity. To suddenly lose the attention and status accorded the high-level politician can be a devastating and overpowering experience, one that can generate a great deal of resentment.

Soon after President Jimmy Carter was defeated at the polls in 1980 and was commended for setting a good example in defeat, Rosalynn Carter cast all pretenses aside. "I'm bitter enough for both of us," she said. Later, she elaborated on the causes: "I was bitter at what I had seen on television for weeks that I thought was unfair to Jimmy; bitter about the hostage capture; bitter at the opposition for deliberately misleading the American people; bitter that they blamed Jimmy for the hostage crisis when they should have praised him for his sound judgment and patience. Jimmy could have blown up Tehran and been reelected. Yes, I was bitter. And so was everyone else in the room. But I was the only one who admitted it."[16]

A former congressman's wife spoke of her pain in a contrasting manner, though, by saying, "When you don't know what you should have done differently, it's frustrating, and very disappointing." To be sure, all political wives feel that their husbands should be the victor. And most feel that they have done as much as, if not more than, was necessary to ensure a win. After a loss, some wives begin to wonder if the election could have been won had they done just a little more campaigning or attended just one more event. And when the candidate has lost an election by a very small margin, it's not uncommon for there to be feelings of guilt, as well as frustration and disappointment, for all involved.

After his second defeat as a presidential candidate, Thomas Dewey discovered something that he might have done differently in his campaign to turn the election around. Dewey's insight occurred during a brief vacation after the election, when he decided to go outside to join his two sons in a game of pitching pennies. When he removed his jacket and began rolling up his sleeves, his wife quickly reminded him that the press might be nearby, waiting for a photo opportunity. And according to biographer Richard Norton Smith, "Dewey straightened himself, stared off blankly into space for a moment, then said in an even voice, 'Maybe if I had done this during the campaign, I would have won.' "[17] Although he was never successful in his bid for the presidency, the 1948 presidential election was a hard-fought battle, and so close that the morning edition of the Chicago *Daily Tribune* incorrectly proclaimed Dewey the victor over incumbent President Harry S Truman.

Political wife Betty Ford certainly knows how disappointing it is to observe one's husband lose a presidential
race — in Gerald Ford's case, by a mere two percent of the
vote. Reflecting on the late hours of that election night
when it became clear that President Ford had lost the race
to the relatively unknown Jimmy Carter, Mrs. Ford
wrote, "You don't go through a fight like that without
wanting to win, and you can't help but have a feeling of
regret that you haven't accomplished what you set out to
do. It's a disappointment with yourself; you feel if you'd
only gone to such and such a place, given such and such a
speech, made such and such a point. You think you've
done as much as possible, but when the election is so close
. . . you're sure that with a little more push your man
could have taken it."[18]

Because her husband was suffering from laryngitis and
couldn't read his concession speech, the difficult task fell
to Betty Ford. She remarked later that as she read the
prepared speech, "My whole family was standing behind
me, looking very sad, but so far as I was concerned, it was
a matter of facing the facts. I'd been through many elections with Jerry, I knew someone had to win, and someone
had to lose, and we lost. . . . You can see that I was
conflicted. My conviction that my husband was the better
man, my dissatisfaction that we hadn't been able to win
with him, these were real. But so was my vision of a soon-
to-be-restored private life, and my relief that our ordeal
was over."[19]

While it may sound like a contradiction in terms, the
losing candidate and his family usually experience a very
real sense of relief when their campaign is terminated. No
longer do they have to contend with the media's scrutiny
of their every word and move or keep up the pretenses
every moment they're in public. When Harry S Truman
learned that FDR had died, he asked Eleanor Roosevelt,

"Is there anything I can do for you?" Mrs. Roosevelt responded with, "Is there anything we can do for *you*? For you are the one in trouble now."[20] Calvin Coolidge summed it up best when he remitted his annual dues to the National Press Club. On the card, "he filled in his name and address and then, on the line provided for 'Occupation,' he wrote 'Retired.' After a moment's thought, he wrote on the line labeled 'Remarks': 'Glad of it.' "[21]

Even incumbent Benjamin Harrison's reaction to his defeat in the 1892 presidential elections was one of relief: "For me there is no sting in [defeat]. Indeed after the heavy blow the death of my wife dealt me, I do not think I could have stood the strain a reelection would have brought."[22]

One political wife who talked about feeling greatly relieved following her husband's loss was Lady Bird Johnson, who was quoted as saying that after Lyndon lost the presidential nomination to John Kennedy in 1960, "I had the best night's sleep I'd had in some time."[23] Another wife who experienced some relief when her husband lost at the polls was Peggy Goldwater. According to Ruth Montgomery, Mrs. Goldwater was not at all enthusiastic about the prospect of becoming first lady or moving into the White House. In fact, during an interview with Montgomery during John Kennedy's presidency, Mrs. Goldwater commented, "If you want to know the truth, I told Barry that if he won the nomination and election, I thought he should make a contract with Jackie to stay on at the White House, because she was doing a fine job."

Senator Goldwater, on the other hand, was philosophical about the outcome of the 1964 presidential race. On the evening before the election, Montgomery asked him what he thought his chances were of winning, to which Goldwater responded, "I believe that I have a chance, but not an overwhelming chance. I'm a fatalist, and I think if I'm meant to win, I will. Otherwise, I won't."[24]

Another philosophical response came from a Native American political wife. As we talked about her husband's loss, she remarked that what had sustained her through the aftermath of his defeat was reminding herself that "maybe it wasn't your time. You have to stop, listen, and ask. All the answers are there." Over forty years ago, Clementine Churchill offered a similar view when she referred to Winston Churchill's defeat in the general elections in 1945 as a "blessing in disguise." Winston, however, saw things otherwise. He responded with, "If it is a blessing, it is certainly very well disguised."[25] No sooner had incumbent President Harry S Truman been proclaimed the victor in 1948 than Winston Churchill took it upon himself to write a note to Thomas E. Dewey. Churchill hailed "the dignity and poise with which you received the heavy political reverse. . . . Such experiences are not agreeable, as I know only too well myself."[26]

Perhaps the only person in Thomas Dewey's camp who expressed no remorse over the presidential hopeful's defeat was Dewey's wife, for Frances Dewey was not a fan of politics. She, it seems, was ailing a great deal of the time that her husband held political office, suffering from a multitude of minor illnesses and allergies. A friend of Mrs. Dewey's was quoted as saying, "Frances thought she was allergic to everything in the book," to which a Reverend Ralph Lankler responded, "The only thing she was really allergic to was politics."[27] Based on the experience of another political wife, it may be fair to say that Frances Dewey's aversion to politics was understandable.

In the 1960 presidential race, Vice President Richard Nixon was defeated by Senator John F. Kennedy in one of the most controversial elections in history. In *Pat Nixon: The Untold Story,* Julie Nixon Eisenhower writes that her father was defeated by "two-tenths of 1 percent out of a total vote of nearly 69 million, and he had lost in the face of unmistakable evidence of vote fraud." Explaining why her father chose not to initiate a vote recount, she adds: "It would take up to a year in Cook County to examine the balloting; and in Texas, since there was no provision for a defeated candidate to obtain a recount, he would have to undergo months of partisan wrangling in the Democratic-controlled state legislature before the process even could begin."[28] Shortly after the campaign was declared unsuccessful, Richard Nixon's long-standing secret service agent, Jack Sherwood, shared his views on the loss, and on the toll taken on all those who are involved in a losing presidential campaign: "A campaign takes everything out of you and the loss is the final drain of energy, both mentally and physically. You're just empty, almost devoid of feeling, zombie-like. . . ."[29] But there had been other political losses in the past for Pat Nixon to observe and endure, and there would be more in the future.

She apparently became disillusioned with politics after her husband's bitter defeat in 1960. In 1962, after having served as an elected official since 1947 and as a private citizen for the previous two years, Richard Nixon entered and was defeated in the California gubernatorial race. And in 1974, during her husband's second term as president, Mrs. Nixon suffered the ultimate humiliation of standing by him as he delivered his resignation speech amidst threats of impeachment. She had courageously endured brutal criticism and heart-wrenching losses during her husband's nearly thirty years in politics, but the final disaster for the politician and his wife appeared to have been too much for her. Recalling her final farewell to the first lady, a close friend of Pat Nixon's stated, "For a moment, she looked more worn and fragile than I had ever seen her, as if a little puff of wind could have blown her away. And she looked forlorn. She had always been a doer and now there was nothing she could do."[30]

While President Gerald Ford officially pardoned Nixon, which may have contributed to Ford's defeat in the next election, fifty years earlier Florence Harding was accused of more drastic measures in sparing a president public humiliation. According to biographer Richard Norton Smith, when President Warren Harding died in August 1923, "detractors hinted of foul-play — poison was the favorite culprit, allegedly administered by Florence Harding, who preferred for her husband an early grave to sitting in a docket at impeachment proceedings. The scandal called Teapot Dome enveloped the dead man's memory in unpleasant odor."[31]

As disillusioning and distasteful as politics is, and always has been, for many politicians' wives, some would jump at the chance to enter the fray once again. Rosalynn Carter concluded her 1984 memoirs by stating her passion for a return to the political limelight: "I would be out there campaigning right now if Jimmy would run again. I miss the world of politics. Nothing is more thrilling than the urgency of a campaign . . . and the tremendous energy it takes that makes a victory ever so sweet and a loss so devastating."[32]

It's amazing that there are so many political hopefuls ready and willing to put themselves through the ordeal over and over again. More amazing is the high price the political wife seems willing to pay to help her husband realize his dream. Many of the wives believe that the woman's role should be subordinate; others emotionally fight the supposition but do nothing to challenge it. Regardless of their views on this subject, most women inevitably put their needs on hold to help their husbands get elected, often becoming a major force in the campaign and assuming more and more responsibilities so that the politician will be free to concentrate on winning votes.

Most political wives share a common, naive belief that

their husbands will surely be elected if only they give it their best effort. A case in point is Pat Nixon, who, when queried on what she thought her husband's chances were of winning the 1960 election, was quoted as saying, "I have a philosophy that if you are doing the very best you can, and working hard to do the things you should, everything will work out."[33] Needless to say, such an attitude can run up against a generous dose of reality when a hard-fought battle ends in bitter defeat.

When a campaign comes to a screeching halt, the road to recovery for all involved is long and difficult, one that leaves the politician's wife especially vulnerable. It takes a great deal of time and effort to adjust to a normal lifestyle and to work through the myriad of emotions that go along with a loss. Though the wife cannot always significantly affect the outcome of her husband's political ambitions, she *can* change herself. She can alter her attitudes so that they reflect a more rational belief system; she can take responsibility for her own actions so that she no longer lives her life as a victim; and she can learn to take her own needs and ambitions into consideration in order to live a fuller and more productive life. But to accomplish all this takes time, energy, desire, dedication, and a good sense of humor. More than anything else, a sense of humor can put an election defeat in the proper perspective, bringing a ray of hope that there is life after politics, that the world will not come to an end after all.

Some people are more innovative than others when it comes to calling upon their sense of humor to overcome the pain of an unsuccessful political effort. For example, in response to my query on how she dealt with her disappointment, anger, frustration, and bitterness after her husband's defeat at the polls, a candid veteran political wife gave a matter-of-fact response. With a twinkle in her eye and a broad smile, she said: "For one week, I used a magic marker to blacken the newspaper pictures of my husband's opponent. That made me feel so good."

* * *

Frankly, I didn't expect our move into politics to be anything more than hard work for him and for me. It was his campaign, I believed, his dream to realize, and I had no intention of becoming consumed with the prospects of his electability. As his wife, I wanted and agreed to campaign with and for him, to support him and his dream, but vowed also to maintain my own individuality, regardless of the campaign's demands.

When the campaign ended, though, my reaction to the abrupt, unexpected break with politics surprised me. I felt enormous pain, not unlike that associated with mourning the death of a close friend. But I suppose none of us are ever entirely ready for the onslaught of conflicting emotions that accompany any major defeat, no matter how prepared we think we are.

Based on the polls conducted just a few days before the election, Steve's standing appeared positive. On primary night, however, I watched my husband's appearance mirror his confidence and later his defeat as the votes were tallied, learning the hard way that the good guys don't always win.

My journal entry dated two days after the primary election recounts the election results.

August 14

Well, it's all over. Steve lost by 2,000 votes. Less than one vote per precinct. Seems unreal. Now unless something unforeseen happens or a miracle occurs, Colorado will have another Democrat for governor. Tuesday was such a difficult day. We voted at 10 a.m., and then spent the rest of the day at home waiting for the results to come in. Others joined us during the day to discuss the general election strategy. How curious.

We went to the Antlers Hotel at 7 p.m. for what was supposed to be a "victory party," then drove up to the Marriott in Denver for the longest night of our lives. The cameras and microphones were in front of us constantly, with reporters wanting comments from the candidate. I felt as though we were in a movie, and it was just a matter of suspense and time before Steve would be declared the winner. First Steve was ahead, then not, then Steve again, and finally the people's choice by 1,000 votes. Then the computers broke down in Jefferson County, and Arapahoe County had problems, too. We waited. At 3 a.m. Steve sent everyone home. At 7 a.m. we learned the results.

While I firmly believe that everything happens for a reason, knowing what that reason is would be so consoling now. Today feels like the third day post-op. Steve does not articulate his feelings, but there's an ache in the pit of my stomach and nothing seems to help.

My conflict continues. I don't want to be in the limelight, yet I don't like to lose; and in politics the limelight shines on the winners.

Now how do I thank all the wonderful people who have worked so hard, and given so much of themselves to help Steve? How do you thank people for believing in you? "Thank you" is simply not enough.

*   *   *

Within a matter of hours, the campaign was over. Finished. History. No more 18-hour days. No more telephone calls from Tony at 5 a.m. urging Steve to read the morning headlines or editorials. And no more pizza at midnight. I was exhausted and somewhat disillusioned, needing to rid myself of that bitter aftertaste.

The next set of journal entries addresses some of the emotions I grappled with after the defeat.

August 15

Whereas I firmly believe Steve entered politics for the right reasons, sometimes I can't help but wonder if his outspokenness and candor didn't contribute to his loss. He always told people the facts, his views on the issues. He stubbornly refused to buy into the shallow, show-biz side of campaigning. There is no question in my mind that his motivations for aspiring to political office were beyond reproach; he wanted to devote his energies and himself to improving the quality of life for all Coloradans by simply using common sense. He had outlined concrete, innovative ways in which government could accomplish more with less money and no new taxes, the depressed economy could be given new life, and the criminal justice and education systems could be reformed. Yet despite his vision for the state being clear, for whatever reason his message did not reach enough people.

I don't like to think being forthright about the issues will be counted as a strike against you, but rarely did I see the seasoned veteran confront the issues candidly. So many candidates were so careful to voice only what they thought the voters wanted to hear, and they busied themselves with life's superficialities while damaging the reputations of their opponents. As I look back, political campaigns seem more like a beauty contest than anything else. The added attraction, of course, is the mud-slinging competition. And I think I must be at a very low emotional point to believe that this is our current state of politics. I remember hearing a politician say, "You do what you have to do." How sad.

August 16

For days now I've been walking around the house not wanting to see or talk with anyone. I've been swimming, taking long walks, and getting reacquainted with myself. Friends have called, even flowers arrived, only intensifying the ache in the pit of my stomach. Regardless of whether I chose this path or liked it, it feels like I've lost a very close friend.

August 18

Rarely do I allow my pain to surface publicly. Instead, I am trying to console others as we tear down headquarters, folder by folder, room by room. Decisions have to be made about storage for all the computer printouts, voter registration lists, polling data, stationery, equipment, furnishings, and even signs on the outside of the buildings. And this has to be done in each of the headquarters throughout the state.

August 21

I thought working at headquarters, overseeing the breakdown, would be one way of achieving closure. What I didn't anticipate was my reaction to the final moments at Denver headquarters. I never would have guessed that anger would be a manifestation of my sorrow. I truly expected to feel great relief that there was an end to this period of my life.

But before driving those 70 familiar miles home, I took a few moments by myself. As I looked around, I stared in disbelief at the bare walls and worn carpet. Suddenly the campaign had been reduced to nothing more than several enormous piles of rubbish uncompromisingly deposited on the basement floor.

October 22

I still feel great sadness for Steve. He placed all his energy and time into the campaign, but his dreams would

not be realized. Not in the conventional way, that is. An
alternate plan, one outside the system, would need developing for his dream's continuance. And while Steve lost
the election, our political life, the life that I thought had
ended, has a curious way of resurfacing. In fact, sometimes
I think I am the only one who believes the campaign is
over.

One year after the loss

We have just attended a reunion that was planned by and
for the campaign staff and workers. People are still calling
to advise Steve about his abilities on handling the media,
and invitations to political events from around the state
still fill our mail box.

Late one night, several months after the defeat, I asked
Steve, "Can't we talk about anything else besides politics?
After all, the campaign is over, the general elections are
over, and we should be moving forward with our lives."
Looking directly into my eyes, he whispered as he turned
out the light, "Joyce, it's just beginning."

NOTES

1. Ruth Montgomery, *Hail to the Chiefs; My Life and Times
with Six Presidents* (New York: Coward-McCann, 1970), 160.

2. Joseph P. Lash, *Life Was Meant To Be Lived: A Centenary
Portrait of Eleanor Roosevelt* (New York: W. W. Norton, 1984), 55.

3. Montgomery, *Hail to the Chiefs,* 157.

4. Susan Watters, "Feisty Lady: *W* Hits the Campaign Trail
with Barbara Bush," *W,* October 31–November 7, 1988, 16.

5. Lillian B. Miller et al., *'If Elected . . .' Unsuccessful Candidates for the Presidency 1796–1968* (Washington, D.C.: Smithson-
ian Institution Press, 1972), 237.

6. Ibid., 170.

7. Ibid., 97.

8. Montgomery, *Hail to the Chiefs,* 224.

9. Miller, *'If Elected . . . ,'* 307.

10. Ibid., 107.

11. Ibid., 206.

12. Garry Wills, "Hart's Guilt Trick," *Newsweek* 110 (28 December 1987), 18.

13. Mary Finch Hoyt, "A Personal Look at Political Wives," *Good Housekeeping,* June 1984, 74.

14. Marcia Chellis, *Living with the Kennedys: The Joan Kennedy Story* (New York: Simon & Schuster, 1985), 207.

15. William A. Henry, III, "This is Your Wife, Kitty Dukakis: Keeper of Her Husband's Humility, and Expecting To Get Paid for It," *Lears,* November/December 1988, 221.

16. Rosalynn Carter, *First Lady from Plains* (New York: Fawcett Gold Medal, 1984), 323.

17. Richard Norton Smith, *Thomas E. Dewey and His Times* (New York: Simon & Schuster, 1982), 545.

18. Betty Ford with Chris Chase, *The Times of My Life* (New York: Ballantine Books, 1979), 294.

19. Ibid., 295, 296.

20. Paul F. Boller, Jr., *Presidential Anecdotes* (New York: Oxford University Press, 1981), 278.

21. Ibid., 249.

22. Miller, *'If Elected . . . ,"* 271.

23. Montgomery, *Hail to the Chiefs,* 220.

24. Ibid., 290.

25. John Daintith et al, *The Macmillan Dictionary of Quotations* (New York: Macmillan Publishing Co., 1989), 434.

26. Smith, *Thomas E. Dewey and His Times,* 543.

27. Ibid., 227.

28. Julie Nixon Eisenhower, *Pat Nixon: The Untold Story* (New York: Simon & Schuster, 1986), 200.

29. Ibid., 198.

30. Ibid., 417.

31. Smith, *Thomas E. Dewey and His Times,* 80.

32. Carter, *First Lady from Plains,* 338.

33. Montgomery, *Hail to the Chiefs,* 157.

Afterword

> It occurred to me when I was thirteen and wearing
> white gloves and Mary Janes and going to dancing
> school, that no one should have to dance backward
> all their lives.
>
> —*Jill Ruckelshaus*

While I can't say that I relished every moment of campaigning, I did truly enjoy traveling the state and meeting people who had the courage to speak their minds. For all the work, excitement, pain, and frustration, politics afforded me the opportunity to share ideas, to meet intelligent women, and to do all this in an expanded environment. For that I am grateful.

My experience in the political world, however, left me with this arsenal of unanswered questions, neglected emotions, a burning curiosity, and the time to devote to gaining a better understanding of the ways in which political life influences the wives of politicians. At present, my life seems to be going in a different direction and probably won't resume as it was before the campaign. Too much has happened. My needs are different. Still, I feel fortunate because my questions may not have surfaced had Steve won the election.

Today, writing a book about political wives feels appropriate. I'm no longer under those pressures and have an unrelenting need to contribute to a better understanding of the political wife. My eighteen months on the campaign trail indicated that very little progress has been made from the days when political wives were regarded merely as helpmates and that the political system reflects that lack of progress. My intention has been to present a clear picture of the political wife and where she fits in the political equation. The next step is determining what can be done to improve the situation.

If changes are to occur within the political system, the political spouses will be the ones to initiate those modifications. Certainly, there's little chance that the public will budge from its celebrity-obsessed priorities, the candidate will relinquish his star status, or the press will decrease its scrutiny or investigative work. To complicate the matter, the political system enforces one set of expectations for the political wife; the public another; and the modern women still another. And most women are put to the test each day in the political world. Thus, it appears that the only way of impacting the political system is for the political wife to take control of herself and her life. And while she cannot be responsible for transforming others, she *can* change herself. That alone will bring a new set of dynamics into play.

Because traditional values have been the cornerstone of their value system, many women stay locked in this mode of operation and limit their horizons. But if the political wife is open to making changes in her life and wants more for herself than to be wife and mother, she must be forthright about her needs and ambitions and resist the temptation to buckle under when the inevitable conflicts arising from traditional expectations occur. Rather than complaining about the inequities of political life or suppressing her anger and frustrations, she must be willing and fully prepared to go her own way and according to her own terms.

The issue is clear — the woman must maintain her balance, power, and identity; that is, knowing herself as a powerful, unique, and separate individual with her own needs and striking the balance within herself to be both political spouse and separate individual. The question still remaining is whether or not the political wife is courageous enough to take control of herself and her life to effect these changes.

On a more practical and concrete level, while I am uneasy about offering advice to others when I'm still angry and conflicted about the entire political process and the well-defined, restrictive, and totally unrealistic expectations that have been forced upon the political wife, if I were asked to advise other women on the art of political survival, I would first compile a checklist for them to keep handy for those moments when they need an unpoetic blueprint. To ensure surviving the ordeal of a political campaign, the list would contain an ample supply of suggestions flavored with some humor, philosophy, and common sense.

NOW THAT I'M HERE, WHAT DO I DO?

• Pack a small overnight case, no matter where you're going, and have it with you always. You never know when you may be stranded overnight in a remote area. And the benefit of having a fresh change of clothes along with your own toothbrush is greater than simply feeling sorry for yourself.

• Carry an extra pair of panty hose in your purse. It's easier to change your hose than it is to fabricate an excuse for wearing a pair with a run in them. No woman will ever believe your excuse anyway.

• Have something of your own to do, be it work, school, a project, or just an hour set aside each week. It may be the only thing that saves your sanity.

• Eat light—fruits and vegetables—when attending events with your favorite politician. Big meals tend to make one tired, and you certainly don't want to fall asleep during your husband's speech. It doesn't do much for his or your image.

• Record your dreams in a diary. You may not completely understand them, but it definitely will give you something to ponder when you're searching for some answers.

• You don't need a flamboyant wardrobe. In fact, you don't want to wear anything people will remember. All that's needed are some simple, tailored clothes you can wash and wear over and over and over again.

• Let go of blame and worry. You can't control the outcome anyway.

• Guilt is a useless emotion. Do as little or as much work on the campaign as you want to do. Everyone, including you, will like you better for it.

• Take ownership of your personal power. Power from any other source is merely an illusion.

• When you're nervous, say so. People like to know you're not any different than they are—and you're not.

• Keep a journal. You'll be astounded by some of your words. You probably will have some food for thought, too, if you take the time to read it.

• Don't try to portray an image. Nothing is more ridiculous than opting for a poor imitation when the real thing is readily available. And it costs less emotionally, too. After all, who can portray you better than you?

• At all times, wear flat shoes or shoes with very low heels. You deal with the limelight better when you have both feet planted firmly on the ground.

• Buy presents for all occasions and all members of your family long before the dates or events arise. No one enjoys being forgotten, and you'll have more than enough to do just to remember your name.

• Don't drink, swear, yawn, swallow a pill, smoke, or chew gum in public. There's only one guarantee in politics — someone will surely notice if you do.

• Remember that no matter what you do or where you go, you're bound to find both good and bad people there. It's the terrain that changes.

• When you become tired of being thought of as excess baggage, do something outrageous. Take a suitcase with you to the next event. When the time seems appropriate, with suitcase in hand, break into your own soft-shoe rendition of "Shuffle Off to Buffalo." Of course, it doesn't resolve the issue, but think how much fun you can have acting out your frustration. Who knows, when the campaign is over perhaps you'll be asked to audition for an upcoming Broadway play.

• Be genuine. Imitations are just that, and they belong in your jewelry box, unless, of course, you're Barbara Bush, in which case you wear them around your neck.

• Never before have you been in this place with these thoughts — and you never will again. You're here for a reason — learn from it.

• If you're at an event and don't remember someone's name, ask them to refresh your memory. Better yet, insist on name tags with everyone's name written in big bold letters. If your depth perception is good and/or the letters are large enough, you can still read the name while looking at the person's face. If you're still experiencing difficulty, it may be time to see your friendly ophthomologist.

• Always bring some little covered dish to a potluck party, even if you have to buy the food and transfer it into a dish of your own. At these events it's the action that counts — thoughts don't have a place at political potluck suppers.

• Remember your manners and "don't talk with your mouth full." Relax. This is a sure-fire way to lose some weight and to avoid putting your foot in your mouth.

• After each event, write a thank-you note to the host and/or hostess. Even if it was inconvenient to have to drive a great distance to get there, be mindful that your hosts weren't forced to open their home to you and your favorite politician. They believe in you.

• It helps to regard politics as an adventure. When viewed this way, you can withstand most absurdities, and the unknown is just a part of it all.

• If your energy is continually being sapped, it's time to take a look at why that's happening and what you're going to do about it.

• Don't be too hard on yourself — understanding the "politics" in politics is less difficult than coming to terms with it. Others have a difficult time adjusting, too.

• Politics is no place for a timid spouse — you must develop a keen sense of humor and some callouses in order to endure public exposure.

• Be true to yourself or you just may wake up at the end of someone else's life.

• Bear in mind that when the media criticize your favorite politician, that's exactly who they're criticizing—you are not your husband. If you want to be the politician, you'll have to generate your own criticism.

• Stay in close contact with the people who know you best. It will help to keep you grounded in reality.

• Recognize that you're going to have to fight daily to retain your personal identity and power and to maintain balance in your hectic life. Unless you acknowledge your emotional need for separateness and set clear boundaries, you will be viewed as simply an extension of your husband.

• Being a political spouse doesn't have to be experienced as a state of dependency. Psychological dependency is a condition, and loss of one's identity is a result. Political wives can change their image if they choose to.

• Come to terms with the fact that we create our own world and therefore are responsible for everything that happens to us.

• Look at your situation as if no choice you make or road you take is ever wrong. You just learn a different lesson with each choice you make or road you take.

• If your favorite politician's campaign ends in defeat, don't fret too long — there really is life after politics. And, you'll get your privacy and your husband back, unless, of course, he decides to run again in the next election. If that occurs, start reading this list again.

• Difficult as it may be, get off the pity potty and be thankful for the opportunity to be directly involved in a political campaign. Most people never get a chance to witness firsthand the inner workings of the political process and to gain the insights attainable only through the unique perspective that that experience allows.

• If your husband enlists the services of an image-maker, tell the consultant that you already know who you are.

• Let's face it — every campaign has at least one female who lusts for the candidate's body. And this is one of those times when you may be feeling a multitude of emotions. If the candidate is more than flattered by the attention, remember that there's no such person as a home-wrecker — the home was already wrecked before she arrived on the scene. If, however, your husband asks you to help him out with the problem and you're feeling charitable, invite her to your home for a nice evening with the family. Then rent a video to watch after dinner — something like *Fatal Attraction*.

• Have someone from the staff assigned to escort you to events, parties, or any public gathering. It certainly makes things easier than being left hanging by your fingernails as you attempt to accomplish on your own what the candidate accomplishes with the benefit of a host of facilitators.

• If all else fails, follow Yogi Berra's advice and, "When you come to the fork in the road — take it."

Index

Adams, Abigail, 111, 114, 137
Adams, John, 111
Adams, John Quincy, 113–14, 191
Adams, Louisa, 113–14
Ailes, Roger, 48, 85
Alsop, Stewart, 72
Amole, Gene, 47
Anderson, Marian, 121
Andrews, Mary, 9, 47, 149, 190–91
Armstrong, Bill, 54, 61
Armstrong, Ellen, 12, 54, 153, 165

Babbit, Hattie, 12
Baldridge, Letitia, 125
Beattie, Melody, 158
Beatty, Warren, 36
Bernstein, Carl, 170, 171–72
Biden, Jill, 12
Biden, Joe, 45
Bissell, LeClair, 169
Bono, Sonny, 40
Breslin, Jimmy, 57
Brokaw, Tom, 51
Bush, Barbara, xvii–xviii, 58, 165; humorous quotes, 166–67;

on the news media, 52; on political life, 78, 166, 190; on role of political wife, 138; refusal to play image game, 5
Bush, George, 7, 48, 58, 85

Calloway, Beth, 155
Campaign ads, 84–86
Campaign managers, 80, 81
Campaign schedulers, 82–83
Campaigning. See Political campaigns
Campbell, Linda, 5
"Candidate's Wife," 2–3, 12
Carruthers, Kathy, xiv, 13, 53, 160, 165, 171
Carter, Jimmy, 128, 129, 193, 194–95, 196
Carter, Rosalynn, 132; and the news media, 48; political involvement, 128–29, 137; response to husband's election loss, 193, 194–95; on returning to politics, 200
Cavanaugh, John, 15
Chellis, Marcia, 156, 162, 193
Chung, Connie, 51
Churchill, Clementine, 198

Churchill, Winston, 198
Congressional Club, 163
Coolidge, Calvin, 197
Coolidge, Grace, 120

Darden, Claibourne, 7
Delay, Christine, 4, 153, 164
Dewey, Frances, 198
Dewey, Thomas E., 195, 198
Dickinson, Angie, 92
Dole, Elizabeth: career, 133; and
    feminism, women's issues,
    134–35; on political wives' loss
    of privacy and friendships, 149,
    153; on political wives' low
    status, 158; resignation from
    cabinet position, 10, 44, 134–
    35
Dole, Robert, 44
Dowling, Colette, 175–76
Drucker, Peter F., 49–50
Dukakis, Kitty, 170, 193–94
Dukakis, Michael, 85, 170, 193–
    94
Duvall, Linda, 133

Eastwood, Clint, 40
Eichenbaum, Luise, 173, 174
Eicher, Diane, 155
Eisenhower, Dwight, 50, 92, 123,
    124, 175, 189
Eisenhower, Julie Nixon, 152,
    156–57, 170, 171–72, 198–99
Eisenhower, Mamie, 123, 124,
    170, 175
Election losses, 188, 190–99, 201

Fall from Grace (Shelley Ross), 94,
    122
Fillmore, Millard, 191

Final Days (Carl Bernstein and
    Bob Woodward), 170, 172
First ladies: Native American, xii,
    xvi, xvii; U.S., 110–30
Fisher, Carol, 11–12
Fleming, Ann Taylor, 136
Folsom, Frances, 117
Ford, Betty, 132, 163, 175; on
    alcoholism and emotional
    breakdown, 158, 169, 171; and
    Equal Rights Amendment,
    128; on husband's loss of presi-
    dential election, 196; on public
    image, 157
Ford, Gerald, 150, 196, 200
Foxe, Fanne, 40
Friedan, Betty, 130, 131, 137, 177

Galbraith, John Kenneth, 53
Garfield, James, 191
Goldwater, 37
Goldwater, Barry, 37, 38, 85–86,
    197
Goldwater, Peggy, 197
Grant, Julia, 116
Grant, Ulysses S., 116, 192
Greeley, Horace, 192
Greenfield, Jeff, 42
Greenfield, Meg, 124

Hancock, Winfield Scott, 191
Harding, Florence, 120, 200
Harding, Warren, 200
Harrison, Benjamin, 197
Hart, Gary, 39, 56; and Donna
    Rice, 41, 44, 92–93; and Lee
    Hart, 162; and the news media,
    44, 45, 47, 155
Hart, Lee, xvi, 3, 154, 155, 162
Hawn, Goldie, 36
Hayes, Lucy, 116

Index

Index   221

Hays, Wayne, 41
Herger, Pam, 54
Hickok, Lorena, 122, 188
Hoover, Lou, 120
Howar, Barbara, 93, 154
Hoyt, Mary Finch, 127
Humphrey, Hubert, 193
Humphrey, Muriel, 193

If Elected (Lillian B. Miller et al.), 191

Jackson, Andrew, 112, 114
Jackson, Jackie, 48
Jefferson, Thomas, 112
Jennings, Peter, 44
Jennings Bryan, William, 192
Johnson, Eliza, 117
Johnson, Lady Bird, 126, 197
Johnson, Lyndon B., 92, 125
Journalists (Code of Ethics), 42. *See also* News media

Kantrowitz, Barbara, 170
Kefauver, Nancy 188–89
Kellerman, Sally, 36
Kelley, Kitty, 160
Kemp, Joanne, 8, 49, 164
Kennedy, Edward M. (Ted): and Chappaquiddick, 41, 45, 93; and Joan Kennedy, 161, 162; loss of presidential nomination, 161, 193; and news media, 45, 156
Kennedy (Onassis), Jacqueline, 38, 124–25, 137, 192
Kennedy, Joan: on alcoholism, 169; on campaign trail in 1980, 16; and news media, 156; reaction to Ted Kennedy's loss of

presidential nomination, 193; and Ted Kennedy, 161, 162
Kennedy, John F., 53, 56, 72–73, 92, 124, 125, 197, 198
Kirkpatrick, Jean, 169
Kolbe, John, 51
Kostmayer, Pamela, 151–52, 161, 173

Lamm, Dick, 67
Lamm, Dottie, 8, 11, 12, 13, 163, 171
Lancaster, Burt, 36
Lash, Joseph P., 120, 121, 122
Laughing All the Way (Barbara Howar), 93, 154
LeHand, Missy, 121–22
Leishman, Katie, 135
Lewis, Virginia, 55–56, 171
Lincoln, Abraham, 115, 116
Lincoln, Mary Todd, 115–16
Long, Russell, 93

Madison, Dolley, 111–12, 117
Madison, James, 112
Malino, Emily, 82–83
McCarthy, Abigail, 135, 160
McCarthy, Larry, 85
McElwaine, Sandra, 167
McEwen, Liz, 149, 166
McGovern, George, 36
McMillan, Caroline, 13, 49
Mecham, Evan, 51, 84
Mecham, Florence, xvi
Mercer, Lucy, 121
Miller, June, 158, 159, 189–90
Miller, Marc E., 42
Mills, Wilbur, 40
Monroe, Elizabeth, 112–13
Monroe, Marilyn, 92

Montgomery, Ruth, 187, 188, 191, 197
Moore, Carolyn, 9
Moyers, Bill, 85
Mudd, Roger, 45
Muskie, Jane, 126

National Governors Association, 163
Native American political wives, xii, xvi, xvii, 55–56, 57–58, 198
News media: increasing power, 50–52; Journalists Code of Ethics, 42; and political wives, 43, 46, 47, 48–49, 50, 51–52, 155; and politicians, 41–52, 92–93, 154; questionable tactics, 42–49, 50–51
Nichols, Mike, 51
Nicholson, Jack, 36
Nixon, Pat, x, 37, 126–27, 201; health problems, 172; and husband's election losses, 199; and news media, 156–57, 170, 171–72; on relationship with Richard Nixon, 156
Nixon, Richard M., 200; and Pat Nixon, 127, 156–57; political defeats, x, 198–99
Nixon, Tricia, 151
Nixon Eisenhower, Julie. *See* Eisenhower, Julie Nixon
Norton Smith, Richard, 195, 200

O'Neill, Tip, 57
Orbach, Susie, 173, 174
Ostling, Richard N., 163

Pat Nixon: The Untold Story: (Julie Nixon Eisenhower), 156, 198

Patten, Lavender, 11
Petroskey, Dale, 134
Political campaigns: affect on marriages and families, 10–11, 14, 15, 77–78, 79; appeal, 16; designing women, 90–91; family's participation, 13, 14; pace, 11, 15, 16, 150; political wives' participation, 4–7, 8, 10–11, 12, 13, 15; scheduling of candidate and wife, 6–7, 82–83; staff and workers, 77, 79, 80–84, 87
Political consultants, 39, 59, 83–84
Political life: affect on marriage and family, 150–56, 159–62, 173; superficiality, 35–41
Political wives: on advantages of political lifestyle, 165–66; affect of campaigns, 10–11, 14, 15, 48–49; affect on campaigns, 4–5; affects of election loss, 192–95, 196, 197, 199, 201; alcoholism, 169–71; changing role, 130–33, 136, 137–38, 172–77; emotional and physical impact of political life, 147–48, 153–60, 161, 171; false image projected, 155–58, 169, 175; loneliness and isolation, 10, 77–78, 79, 152–54, 161–62, 167; Native American, xii, xvi, xvii, 55–56, 57–58, 198; and the news media, 43, 46, 47, 48–49, 50, 51–52, 155; of 1988 presidential election, x; orientation classes, 131, 132–33, 162–63; outside activities, 162–65; participation in campaigns, 4–7, 10–11, 12, 13, 15; percentage in

workforce, 132; political system's expectations, ix–x, xi, xvii, 136; on power, 52–56, 57–58; public's perceptions, x, xvii, 12, 133; reactions to election losses, 189, 190, 191, 192, 193–95, 196, 197, 198, 199, 201–2; reaction to election victories, 189–90; sacrifices, 147–49, 151–54, 159–60; scheduling in campaigns, 6–7; self-destructive habits, 167–70; speechmaking and debating, 6, 8, 11; survival guide, 211–17. *See also* names of individual women

Politicians: avoidance of issues by, 37, 38; as actors, celebrities, 35–41, 51, 59; marital infidelity, 91–94; and the news media, 41–52, 92–93, 154; public's expectations, 3–4. *See also* under names of individual politicians

Politicians and Their Spouses' Careers (Marc E. Miller), 42, 132

Polk, James, 114–15

Polk, Sarah, 114–15, 137

Press secretaries, 81–82

Quayle, Marilyn, 7, 49, 137

Rae, Elizabeth, 41

Reagan, Nancy, 48, 129–30, 137

Reagan, Ronald, 40, 54, 56

Rice, Donna, xvi, 3, 41, 44

Romer, Roy, 59

Roosevelt, Edith, 117–18, 137

Roosevelt, Eleanor, 120–22, 123, 137, 142, 188, 196–97

Roosevelt, Franklin D., 92, 121–22, 196

Roosevelt, Nicholas, 117

Roosevelt, Theodore, 117–118

Ross, Shelley, 94, 122

Sawyer, Diane, 51

Schuck, Ann. *See* Journal entries

Schuck, Bill. *See* Journal entries

Schuck, Joyce (Journal entries): campaign staff, 94–98, 102–4; campaigning, 1, 17–32, 100–101, 106–7, 178–79, 180, 181; changing role of political wives, 138–43; designing women, 105; election loss, xi–xii, 202–6; emotional and physical impact of political life on political wives, 179–83; news media, 62–70; political ads, 100, 101; political power, 70–73; speechmaking, 20–23; superficiality of politics, 58–62; survival guide for political wives, 211–17

Schuck, Steve. *See* Journal entries

Schuck, Tom. *See* Journal entries

Scott, Winfield, 192

Second Stage (Betty Friedan), 177

Seighart, Mary Ann, 11

Sheehy, Gail, 170, 193

Sherwood, Jack, 199

Solarz, Nina, 9–10

Stanley, Alessandra, 163

Starr, Mark, 170

Stevenson, Adlai, 189

Streisand, Barbra, 36

Sullivan, Jane, 13, 158

Taft, Helen, 118–19, 131, 136

Taft, William Howard, 118

Taylor, Elizabeth, ix, 154, 160–62, 168
Thatcher, Denis, 170–71
Thomas, Pamela, 170
Truman, Bess, 123
Truman, Harry S, 50, 111, 123, 195, 196, 198
Truman, Margaret, 123

Van Buren, Martin, 112
Voight, Jon, 36

Wagenknecht, Edward, 118
Waihee, Lynn, 13, 53

Wallace, Mike, 48
Walters, Barbara, 51
Warner, John, ix, 154, 160–62
Washington, Martha, 110
Watters, Susan, 190
Webster, Daniel, 192
Weiss, Philip, 134
Wills, Garry, 193
Wilson, Edith, 119
Wilson, Ellen, 119
Wilson, Woodrow, 119
Wirth, Wren, 15, 138
Woodward, Bob, 170, 171